In the Shadow of Catastrophe

Weimar and Now: German Cultural Criticism

Martin Jay and Anton Kaes, General Editors

In the Shadow
of Catastrophe

German Intellectuals between
Apocalypse and Enlightenment

Anson Rabinbach

UNIVERSITY OF CALIFORNIA PRESS

Berkeley • *Los Angeles* • *London*

University of California Press
Berkeley and Los Angeles, California

University of California Press
London, England

Copyright © 1997 by The Regents of the
University of California

Library of Congress Cataloging-in-Publication
Data

Rabinbach, Anson.
    In the shadow of catastrophe : German intel-
lectuals between apocalypse and enlightenment /
Anson Rabinbach.
        p.   cm. — (Weimar and now ; 14)
    Includes bibliographical references and index.
    ISBN 0-520-20744-0 (alk. paper)
        1. Germany—Intellectual life—20th cen-
tury.   2. Germany—Politics and government—
1918–1933.   3. Arts and society—Germany—
History—20th century.   4. Enlightenment—
Germany.   5. Jews—Germany—Intellectual
life. I. Title. II. Series.
DD239.R3   1997
943.085′086′31—dc21   96-39459
                                                            CIP

Printed in the United States of America

1 2 3 4 5 6 7 8 9

Contents

Acknowledgments

I am grateful to the friends, colleagues, and students who heard and discussed these chapters at conferences and colloquia in Europe and America for their critical engagement and encouragement. In Frankfurt, Gunzelin Schmid Noerr permitted me to work among the treasures of the Horkheimer Archiv of the Johann Wolfgang Goethe Universitätsbibliothek, which he oversees with passion and archival skill. K. D. Wolff and Florence Springer kept me apprised of the latest German controversies while Cilly Kugelmann provided more than just her considerable translating skills in preparing chapter 4 for the memorable Arnoldshain colloquium "Erinnerung: Zur Gegenwart des Holocaust in Deutschland—West und Deutschland—Ost" in 1992. I also am indebted to the editors of *Radical Philosophy* for publishing an earlier version of the same chapter. David Roberts of Monash University in Australia was kind enough to organize a superb symposium on *Dialectic of Enlightenment* with his colleagues at *Thesis Eleven*. The Princeton University Committee on Research in the Humanities and Social Sciences generously assisted in preparing the manuscript. At the University of California Press, Ed Dimendberg's sage advice as a colleague and editor has been indispensable throughout.

Two of these chapters originally appeared in *New German Critique,* a uniquely collective enterprise that after more than twenty years remains my most important source of intellectual sustenance, scholarly standards, and personal support. I owe far more to those friends who helped launch and maintain the journal than a mere acknowledgment—David Bathrick, Miriam Hansen, and Jack Zipes. And my special gratitude to Andreas Huyssen and Martin Jay for their critical and scrupulous comments on the manuscript in its penultimate version, and for their help in providing a glimpse of totality, even if that word has lately come into disrepute. Finally to Jake, Jonah, and Jessica, for tearing me away from this project often enough to remind me why it was worthwhile.

Introduction

Apocalypse and Its Shadows

After the end of the catastrophic century we look backwards, not from the plateau of the end of history, but from
the flatland of the absolutely historical present. We could
enter this absolute present with the empty consciousness of
forgetting. Or we could instead practice a kind of remembering, which Hegel first called "Andenken" (reflective remembrance). Remembrance is respect, the respect of thinking. If
there is to be mourning, then the respect of thinking is a
requiem. I am speaking of a requiem for a century.
                                    —*Agnes Heller (1995)*

In his masterful history, *The Age of Extremes,* Eric Hobsbawm reminds
us that "the decades from the outbreak of the First World War to the
aftermath of the Second, was an Age of Catastrophe for this society. For
forty years it stumbled from one calamity to another. There were times
when even intelligent conservatives would not take bets on its survival."[1] As the end of the century approaches there have been no dearth
of triumphalist visions of the end of history, or of sincere resolutions to
undertake the work of mourning necessary to overcome the long-term
effects of trauma and disaster. As intellectual historians reflect on the
ways in which ideas have been complicit in the making of that catastrophe, we would do well to heed the Hungarian-American philosopher
Agnes Heller's caution that in this domain neither exultation nor lamentation is appropriate, that mourning should be reserved only for murdered human beings, not for "guilty ideas and expectations."[2] Those
expectations require something else: perhaps regret, but more certainly
deep reflection (*Andenken*) on how their philosophical underpinnings
are burdened with responsibility for what Heller refers to as the "phan-
tomachieia" of the twentieth century, its belief in the redemptive power
of violence.

Heller's eloquent "Requiem" makes us aware that the twentieth century's man-made catastrophes were to no small extent bound up with a deep propensity to apocalyptic thinking. Conceived in Heller's spirit of reflection, as opposed to lamentation or nostalgia, this study attempts to consider some of the ways that apocalyptic thought and apocalyptic events were deeply entwined. The five essays that follow address aspects of German thought in the shadow of the two world wars. What unites them is their proximity to catastrophe, both in their choice of themes and in the dates of origin of the texts I will examine. All of the thinkers with whom I am concerned experienced at first hand the apocalyptic events of this century, and I am most interested in those of their writings that were composed in their direct aftermath. Date of composition and publication may not always be the most felicitous principle of selection, one that at times can set certain statements above more substantial works that preceded or followed those composed in close propinquity to the event. Nor is the choice of a few well-known texts by major thinkers intended to be in any way comprehensive. Many equally important texts symptomatic of the post–World War II era, for example, Friedrich Meinecke's *The German Catastrophe* (1946), might have been considered. Yet it is my contention that precisely because they were written in the direct aftershock of the event, and despite their often allusive, metaphorical, and highly esoteric character, those texts are among their authors' most powerful philosophical attempts to translate that experience into a philosophical language whose legacy still exerts a powerful intellectual and sometimes even political influence today.

The two essays in the first section deal primarily with the thought of Walter Benjamin, Ernst Bloch, and Hugo Ball, three intellectuals (and close friends) who contributed to the mood of messianic expectation and world repudiation that gripped like-minded communities of Central European intellectuals during and after World War I. Like many Central European intellectuals they were convinced that World War I was the product of the alliance of a military-aristocratic bureaucracy and large-scale capitalism. For them that bourgeois order had collapsed in the apocalypse of war, and they dedicated their considerable intellectual talents to imagining a redemption commensurate with the conflagration. If Benjamin and Bloch were pivotal figures in the renewal of Jewish messianic thinking after 1914, Ball was their Catholic counterpart, the founder of Berlin Dada and a passionate admirer of the Russian anarchist Mikhail Bakunin. His 1919 *Critique of the German Intelligentsia* along with Benjamin's 1916 essay, "On Language as Such and on the Language of Man," and Bloch's 1918 *Spirit of Utopia* demonstrate what Michael Löwy calls a remarkable "elective affinity" between messianism and anarchist utopianism, though not, as he claims, one limited to the Jewish intellectual milieu.[3]

Benjamin and Bloch first experienced the pre-1914 revival of Jewish intellectual life in the person of Martin Buber. Attracted to his spiritual approach to Zionism but repelled by his emphasis on the emotional core of Jewish mysticism, neither adopted political Zionism or Buber's call for a Jewish culture of "inner experience." Only an authentic and deeply esoteric intellectual response seemed to them appropriate to express what they both regarded as the intellectual mission of the messianic idea, to overcome, through programmatic antipolitical reflection, the "hollow space" at the core of the modern conception of reason in its moment of crisis. Yet whereas both Bloch and Ball, whose remarkable *Critique of the German Intelligentsia* is the subject of chapter 2, regarded the destructiveness of revolutionary violence as an essentially theological act of creative genesis, ushering in a new evangelium—Jewish and Catholic, respectively—Benjamin's embrace of violence is far more equivocal, recognizing that in contrast to law and revolution there remains a "sphere of human agreement," of language, that could never be entirely encompassed by profane politics.[4]

After 1918, German writers on the left and on the right shared a belief in the transfiguring power of the war and revolution and considered the modern world, to borrow the conservative jurist Carl Schmitt's words, as always hovering on the brink of the "state of emergency." Both Ball and Schmitt shared the opinion that Bakunin was the near-perfect embodiment of an "apocalyptic hatred of Europe," though they were separated by Ball's embrace of Bakuninist theology and Schmitt's championing of authority against the anarchy of Europe he foresaw coming "sous l'oeil des Russes."[5] Despite Ball's admiration for Schmitt, his Catholic romanticism and anti-Semitism might have placed him much closer to the thinkers of the German right, had he not utterly despised them for their nationalism and prowar propaganda. Benjamin, Bloch, and Ball were all linked by their passionate opposition to the war, and all three, along with the historian of Jewish messianism Gershom Scholem, spent time during the war in Bern, the center of the German exile community in Switzerland. All expectantly anticipated the military defeat of Germany, the real apocalypse that would bring about the redemption of culture, liberating language from platitude and instrumentalization.

   The three essays that follow are concerned with texts that appeared
between 1946 and 1947: Karl Jaspers's *The Question of German Guilt*
(1946), Theodor Adorno and Max Horkheimer's *Dialectic of Enlightenment* (1944, 1947), and Martin Heidegger's "Letter on Humanism"
(1946-1947). These authors suffered wholly different personal fates
during those years, each emblematic of the choices faced by German intellectuals during the Nazi era: inner exile, emigration, and, in Heidegger's notorious case, complicity with the Nazi revolution. Jaspers confronts the collapse of German liberal Great Power politics in the Weberian
mode; Adorno and Horkheimer cast doubt on the capacity of liberalism
and Marxism to account for the suffering and unreason unleashed by a
surfeit of enlightenment and the technical domination of nature; Heidegger's text goes still further, calling into question the trajectory of
Western thought since Plato.
   To be sure, these thinkers are diametrically opposed in their political
evaluations and judgments. Jaspers's *The Question of German Guilt*
called on Germans to break with the tradition of power politics and the
nation-state—to assume collective responsibility and self-consciously
acknowledge that they must become a pariah people until they demonstrate the moral capacity to reenter political life.[6] Adorno and Horkheimer's *Dialectic of Enlightenment* concludes with a meditation on the
dark side of Reason whose relentless homogenization of difference ultimately elicits anti-Semitism, the projection of evil onto the Jews as the
initiators and carriers of the taboo on mimesis. In the false anti-Semitic
"overcoming" of the prohibition and in the return of the archaic impulse to mimesis, the Jew becomes the victim of a radical compulsion
to liquidate those who retain the semblance of distinctiveness. Heidegger's "Letter on Humanism" is notoriously silent on the murder of the
Jews yet has achieved canonical status both as a founding document of
deconstruction and as an extraordinary discourse on the apocalyptic
collapse of Western metaphysics into nihilism and a plea to return to
the shelter of Being.
   Though none of these works broke new philosophical ground for
their authors, each is far more than a *piece d'occasion*. Because of the
immediacy of the events they attempted to register and because of their
sometimes astonishing philosophical compression, they are all reflections on the limits of what might be called the burdened traditions of
modernity. Certainly Jaspers and Adorno/Horkheimer were insistent
that in its blindness and nihilism, German philosophy had contributed
its portion to the catastrophe. As witnesses, each of them tried, not to

achieve a kind of "mastery" over a traumatic occurrence, but to write from the point of its historical caesura. Here we should perhaps question, as does Saul Friedländer, the fit between historical events and the psychoanalytic premise that understanding is temporally delayed by the trauma, requiring a "period of latency" before the "return" of the experience (and its "working through") allows an elaboration of historical meaning. It may instead be true that as far as historical occurrences are concerned, time intensifies rather than diminishes the opacity and irresoluteness of the event.[7] At the same time, however, Dominick LaCapra has suggested that the very construction of modern history as trauma, which is abundantly evident in many of the texts discussed here, may, by demanding "full closure" or "redemptive totalization," in fact "aggravate trauma in a largely symptomatic fashion."[8] A historical approach to "traumatic" events demands a more rigorous and specific approach, attentive to the profoundly distinct ways in which the apocalyptic event is deployed and configured.

What all the authors I have chosen have in common is their shared acknowledgment that the catastrophic event was a *caesura* in a philosophical as well as a political sense. The apocalyptic "event" becomes a kind of negative ground for philosophical reflection, or a "groundless" ground, to use Heidegger's term (in German, *Abgrund,* or abyss, is also the un-ground), from which historical progress, the autonomy of the self-reflecting ego, and even language itself are deprived of a secure foundation. As Philippe Lacoue-Labarthe put it, the "caesura of the speculative" is a space or temple "where death in general, decline, and disappearance, is able to contemplate 'itself.' "[9]

This book is an intellectual historian's meditation on that apocalyptic divide as it emerges in the works of some of the major thinkers and texts of the two postwar eras. It examines how the foundational philosophical texts that appeared in the immediate aftermath of World Wars I and II attempted to negotiate that divide and how, from the perspective of the abyss, they reconceptualized the relationship between epistemology and event.

Manichaean scenarios of world destruction and world redemption, images and symbols of the corrupt, unfulfilled earthly world of pain and death, and prophecies of fulfillment and perfection in the redeemed world to follow are familiar tropes in the political ideologies, modernist art movements, and philosophies that emerged during and after World War I. As Jay Winter has admirably shown, the war provided ample opportunity for artists already so inclined to explore their preoccupations with the apocalypse. He also convincingly documents how the apocalyptic image straddled the divide between modernity and tradition, avant-garde and rear guard, exposing the "messiness" of a cultural history excessively focused on the war as a modernist trope. Artists and poets like Ludwig Meidner and Georg Heym saw the violence and destruction of the war as "a necessary and cathartic evil" while Max Beckmann painted the madness of war in his apocalyptic vision, *Resurrection*.[10] In Germany protagonists of the earthly kingdom and prophets of the divine, enthusiasts of the war and its most pacifistic opponents, left-wing revolutionaries and fascists *avant la lettre,* all shared a similar vocabulary of decline and destitution, and many competed to portray themselves as avatars of the "new man."[11] The vision of a present that is so completely pathological, so utterly destitute that its very fallenness signals the inevitability of revolutionary change or transformation, can be observed in thinkers as distinct as Oswald Spengler, Georg Lukács, and Walter Benjamin.[12] Many of the same rhetorical and symbolic motifs were employed, for example, by expressionist revolutionaries as well as by nationalist ideologues for whom the cataclysmic disappearance of the existing world is only a passage from the order of decline, destitution, and depravity to a new order of fulfillment.[13] As the Protestant theologian Friedrich Gogarten reproached an earlier generation, "You cannot require us to stem the tide of this decline; for you have taught us to understand it. And now we are glad for the decline since no one enjoys living among corpses."[14]

Carl Schmitt's famous 1922 assertion that "all significant concepts of the modern theory of the state are secularized theological concepts" sums up the widely shared view that the rationalism of the Enlightenment was no less metaphysical for its rejection of religious concepts.[15] In 1918 Max Weber spoke of "something that is pulsating that corresponds to the prophetic *pneuma* that in former times swept through the great communities like a firebrand, welding them together."[16] An enthusiastic reviewer greeted Bloch's 1921 paean to the sixteenth-century peasant leader and theological adversary of Luther, Thomas Münzer (who was also Ball's great hero), as a "communist-apocalyptical manifesto," a document of the religious-social radicalism and expressionist mood of the postrevolutionary years.[17] Gershom Scholem, too, commented on this aspect when he referred to Benjamin as a "theologian marooned in the realm of the profane."[18] The redemptive politics of a fallen world preferred the charismatic leader or dynamic movement to the soulless bureaucrat, prophetic speech to the "chatter" of the parliament, and the authenticity of "experience" to the rationality of historical progress. There can be no doubt that the poetic and artistic disruption of modernity preceded the Great War, yet so intense was the postwar radicalization and politicization of its aesthetic and theological impulses that it is justified to speak of "the caesura of 1918."[19]

Many commentators have reflected on the reasons for the ubiquity of the apocalyptic imagination in the disenchanted heart of twentieth-century avant-garde movements, with their prophetic tone, pessimistic mood, fascination with violence, and hope of artistic and political deliverance. The critic Frank Kermode has described the "apocalyptic set" that predisposes individuals and mass movements to imagine that they are only suffering the ravages of war and terror in the anticipation of a new and more perfect age.[20] The canonical apocalyptic texts of the Hebrew and Christian tradition, such as the Book of Daniel and the Revelation of John, drew their strength from the correlation between a reading of historical events as signs of future occurrences and the template of an apocalyptic vision that permits unique access to the meaning of those events. He points out that both Hebrew and Christian commentators treated these texts as "something of a powder keg in the basement" of their religious traditions, and preferred to keep them at a safe distance from the more accepted and normative tradition. Kermode suggests that the history of apocalyptic thought is to be found in the interaction among the sociological predisposition, canonical text, and more worldly "interpretive material."[21] Perhaps for that reason the apocalypse's reinscription in modern ideological forms still retains something of their primordial canonical force.

Mapping a plenitude of modern German apocalyptic visions, political programs, and philosophical motifs onto the "canonical" Christian apocalypse, Klaus Vondung has further distinguished between an apocalyptic interpretation of history that, because it finds no meaning in all previous history, anticipates the "breakthrough of perfectibility" and the eschatological interpretation that sees the events of providential history as signs of a steady progress toward that goal.[22] Vondung draws on Hans Blumenberg's useful distinction between a heterogenous "event breaking into history" and the progressist notion of a secure historical future—even one that is profoundly millenarian—"that is immanent to it."[23] Clearly, Benjamin's famous angel of history in his last work, the "Theses on the Philosophy of History," is emblematic of the former approach, a figure who by turning away from the future, faces

backward to gaze on "one single catastrophe that keeps piling wreckage upon wreckage."[24] For Benjamin, whose catastrophic antihistori-
cism explicitly challenged the nineteenth century's triumphalist philosophy of progress, redemption lay far more in fragments of remembrance
than in any future utopia, a stance that Scholem once called a "theolo-
gia negativa."[25] Scholem also identified the salient characteristic of all
such expectation: if history has only an anticipatory, provisional, and
ultimately unreal character, if hope is temporally relocated as it were,
in the epoch of fulfillment, until then, there is only "a *life lived in deferment.*"[26]

Whether modern apocalyptic movements and ideas can be completely and squarely mapped onto the canonical template is open to
question, but there is little dispute that apocalyptic fantasies, as Martin
Jay points out, have "continued to thrive even in the ostensibly postre-
ligious imaginaries we have called scientific and postmodernist."[27] Following Julia Kristeva, Jay suggests that there may be a close connection
between the persistence of the apocalyptic imaginary and the return, in
the form of a melancholic identification, of the lost, unmourned, sym-
bolically integrated, maternal image. That this "unworked through"
loss is constantly reinvigorated by being cathected to real-world objects,
like the earth or historical catastrophe, makes mourning more difficult,
while, at another level, the figure of apocalyptic fire and redemption
still harbors the "utopian myth" of the "complete working through" of
which postmodern thought has taught us to be wary.[28]

Neither the meticulous mapping of the literary apocalypse of the
twentieth century onto the canonical Christian texts accomplished by
Vondung (though with far too little attention to the Jewish Bible and
the Qumran sects) nor the suggestive psychoanalytic explorations of
Kristeva and Jay is sufficient to account for the profound differences
that mark the styles of thinking about the apocalypse that followed
each of this century's cataclysmic world wars. Indeed, it is not theology
per se but the historicity of both modernist and postmodernist visions
of the apocalypse that continue to fuel the current debate on the "project of modernity." If the First World War produced images of universal
destruction and messianic redemption, of a corrupt world transfigured
by death and sacrifice, reflections on the catastrophe of midcentury
tended to be more austere and, like Benjamin's angel of history, capable
only of a Saturnian backward glance at the wreckage.

Ernst Jünger, who once called himself a "seismograph" of the epoch,
entered the following note in his diary of August 1943: "Letters assume

an apocalyptic character, which has not been the case since the Thirty Years War. It is as if in such situations the shocked reason of human beings loses all sense of earthly reality; it becomes caught up in the cosmic confusion, and is thereby open to a new world of visions of world destruction, prophecies, and spectral appearances."[29] Yet even Jünger's own reflections decisively refuse to participate in such appearances, and are in marked contrast with the canonically theological apocalypse that always brings forth redemption in the fires of destruction. Rather, as Elliot Neaman has suggested, at the end of the Second World War Jünger and other German conservative intellectuals abandoned their revolutionary stance for a more muted critique of Americanism and the "West" as the purveyors of a globally technological nihilism.[30] Such abstract thinking about the apocalypse might be characterized as both "pre-postmodern" and antiredemptive. To put it in a convenient formula, World War I gave rise to reflections on death and transfiguration, World War II to reflections on evil, or on how the logic of modernity since the Enlightenment, with its legacy of progress, secularism, and rationalism, could not be exculpated from events that seemed to violate its ideals. Hannah Arendt registered the distinctive moods of the two postwar eras: "The reality is that 'the Nazis are men like ourselves'; the nightmare is that they have shown, have proven beyond doubt what man is capable of. In other words, the problem of evil will be the fundamental question of postwar intellectual life in Europe—as death became the fundamental problem after the last war."[31]

In their bleak and dispirited mood, in their profound distrust of all liberatory schemes—nationalist, metaphysical, and revolutionary—the texts written after World War II call to mind the first photographs documenting the vastness of ruin visited on the European cities in the final months of the war. To document the extent of the devastation, a certain artificial distance, a wide-angle vision, is required. In their backward glance at the ruined traditions of Central European thought, these texts are the philosophical analogy to the panoramas of cataclysm.[32] These texts also bring to mind Benjamin's angel and Kafka's depiction of a world devoid of all trace of a positive message, the negative theology in which the apocalypse is not an event in the past or future but a constant presence where redemption is no longer manifested in the world of human affairs.[33]

The first two essays in this book treat texts that have recourse to the traditions of Jewish and Christian messianism, respectively, and that, not unlike other political and artistic renderings of political catastrophe, recapitulate the canonical redemptive gesture. The three essays that follow demonstrate how the antiredemptive tone was echoed in markedly different ways by postwar thinkers. Perhaps the aspect of the "man-made apocalypse" that most sharply separates the messianic and apocalyptic texts that Benjamin, Bloch, and Ball composed during and after the First World War from those that appeared in the aftermath of World War II is the absence of any figure of redemption. At that later juncture Thomas Mann, whose own writings also exemplify the distinction, recalled that "just after the First World War the Germans, unlike the French, had little better to do than to dream of apocalypses."[34]

In his allegory of the angel of history, Benjamin conceived of modernity as an apocalyptic tempest roaring toward the present. Where we perceive only continuity or a causal chain of events, Benjamin's angel envisages a "storm blowing from paradise."[35] The wreckage, as Benjamin foresaw, required more than a mop-up operation. The fragmentation of historical consciousness reflects a fracturing of experience, and even if the angel "would like to stay, awaken the dead, and make whole what has been smashed," the pile of debris mounts. Many years later, Adorno compared the impact of Auschwitz on philosophy in the twentieth century to that of the Lisbon earthquake two hundred years earlier. The first catastrophe of nature called into question the theodicy of G. W. Leibniz; the second, the catastrophe of history, the theodicy of G. W. F. Hegel. It rendered the very idea of progress in history suspect and made "a mockery of the construction of immanence as endowed with a meaning."[36] For the first time perhaps, the catastrophic historical event becomes the insurmountable horizon of philosophical reflection against which any account of Western thought would have to be measured. As Dan Diner has written, the "rupture with civilization which is Auschwitz" robbed secular humanity of that optimism and secure perspective on the future that persisted despite all skepticism.[37]

To think and write philosophically and historically about the twentieth-century apocalypse has always been fraught with difficulty, a realization evident even in the earliest written reflections on the catastrophe. World War I was fought between traditional European nation-states on conventional battlefields; World War II, by totalitarian empires, nation-states, and democracies on a global scale. In both conflagrations "total war" unleashed an unprecedented destructive force. Casualties in World War I were still largely limited to combatants, while World War II all but erased the distinction between combatants and noncombatants: civilian populations, captive peoples, and arbitrarily designated internal enemies accounted for more than half of the total dead. But once the murder of the Jews was discovered, the image of the war was altered by the "moral enormity" of the crime.[38] As one of the first journalists to witness the liberation of the Majdanak extermination camp wrote in the summer of 1944, he was now "prepared to believe any story of German atrocities, no matter how savage, cruel or depraved."[39] It should be recalled that in 1945 there was as yet no distinct name for, or any distinct history of, the Holocaust, but the acknowledgment of the destruction of the Jews was already one of the key reasons for the insistence of the allies on the Nuremberg trials. This sober discovery may also account for the fact that, unlike after World War I, neither intellectuals nor politicians were inclined to adopt a redemptive vision, and why World War II might therefore be called "the nonredemptive apocalypse."

Arendt was perhaps the first philosopher to recognize the *Shoah* as a rupture with civilization, as an event that was catastrophic and apocalyptic without being in any sense redemptive. As early as 1943 she became aware that the Nazi murder of the Jews was an event that signaled the destruction of the common bond of European civilization, the notion of a common humanity held together by respect for human life and for a minimum of legal and political culture. Whether one adopts the definition of civilization characteristic of the later seventeenth century, when *civility* meant a "sincere, gentle, and polite way of conducting oneself towards others and conversing with others," or the more restrictive Enlightenment notion of civilization as progress in moral instruction (considered, of course, an exclusive property of the European world), the idea of civilization was demarcated from a degree of violence and barbarism that remained outside its precincts.[40] With the destruction of the Jews, Arendt maintained, this simple demarcation, this boundary, no longer stood, and for that reason the murder of the Jews was neither an incident of local significance nor an event affecting Jewish history alone but one that implicated European humanity: "The comity of European peoples went to pieces when, and because, it allowed its weakest member to be excluded and persecuted."[41]

Historians are aware that sometimes their own sincere attempts to bring the catastrophic events of this century under the scrutiny of historical understanding, to make explicit the chains of causation and logic that led to the escalation of horror, bespeak understatement. It was this awareness, this need to introduce a sense of "rupture" into the lines of causation that had already prompted some of Benjamin's most hostile barbs directed at "historicism." At the same time, however, the persistent rhetorical amplification that has made "Auschwitz" or "Hiroshima" signifiers for all genocide or mass technological destruction does not justify removing those events from historical debate. Rather, the difficulty today is that when Auschwitz has become intellectual shorthand for all politically motivated and efficiently executed evil, its eventness no longer represents a rupture but is assimilated to the telos of modernity. This banality of catastrophe is often what is at stake in the postmodern view of the "darker, savage, unspeakable side of a modernity that culminated in the genocidal policies of Stalin or Hitler."[42]

In his pathbreaking essay, "Dramatization and De-dramatization of 'the End,' " Klaus Scherpe has perceptively observed that " 'playing with the apocalypse' is an integral part of postmodern social philosophy."[43] Paradoxically, he argues, the destructive and apocalyptic impulses of modernity are "de-dramatized" in the critique of modernity's redemptive programs and grand narratives but are simultaneously "redramatized" in the characterization of a permanent apocalyptic caesura that brings about modernity's end.[44] Scherpe points out there was no lack of an "apocalyptically charged situation" in 1945. Evocations of catastrophe appear in Mann's *Doktor Faustus,* in visions of German rebirth in the ashes of destruction, and in the moral presumptions of a "Stunde Null" (zero hour). However, in the apocalyptic consciousness that emerges in Ernst Jünger's postwar reflections, or in those that we will examine in regard to Heidegger's "Letter on Humanism," "the pure and self-sufficient logic of catastrophe" is permanentized, so that it "frees itself from the necessity of expecting an event that will alter or end history."[45] Consequently, postmodernity inherits from modernity the dramatic "faith in the expressive and explosive movement of 'breaking out' and 'breaking through,' " while the dedramatized apocalypse is transformed into "an aesthetic consciousness of 'indifference.' "[46] Seen from this perspective, the abyss of catastrophe appears as the only plausible groundless "ground" from which to retrospectively render judgment on the history of Western humanism. In a dramatic inversion of the idea of progress, the apocalyptic event transfigures eschatology, reversing what Michael Ignatieff refers to as "the heavy burden of Jewish Messianic history."[47]

The drama of the apocalypse is no longer reenacted but short-circuited, subordinated to a critique that underscores the paradoxical character of modernism for giving expression to and ultimately sanctioning violence and excess while simultaneously canonizing that transgression in an "aesthetic of the sublime." In *The Postmodern Condition,* for example, Jean-François Lyotard regards terror as the consequence of indulging in the ultimately nostalgic attempt, characteristic of all political and aesthetic modernism from Hegel to Proust, to render the unpresentable presentable. From this perspective, even in its most antitotalizing, nonidentical, and radical expression, Adorno's later aesthetics, modernist art's refusal of any reconciliation with its object remains parasitically fixated on the "ruin of totality." Jacques Derrida has also argued that by its very insistence on terms like explosion, ruin, collapse, or dissolution, the rhetoric of modernism is fetishistically attached to a nostalgic figure of totality. He finds, in Benjamin, for example, the "longing for an architecture, a construction, that is irretrievably destroyed, but one in which the phantom of totality still haunts the ruins."[48] For Lyotard, such thinking is ultimately "future anterior" to a world that has already ended in terror and cataclysm: "The nineteenth and twentieth centuries have given us as much terror as we can take. We have paid a high enough price for the nostalgia of the whole and the one, for the reconciliation of the concept and the sensible, of the transparent and the communicable experience."[49]

With these closing remarks of his essay "Answering the Question: What Is Postmodernism?" Lyotard sets forth the dictum that the essential divide between modern and postmodern is indistinguishable from the caesura brought on by apocalyptic violence. If degrees of apocalypse are even possible, Maurice Blanchot's *The Writing of the Disaster* is an even more extreme example of what Derrida has referred to as the "apocalyptic tone" in philosophy, reflecting circuitously, darkly, and opaquely on the impossibility of writing the experience of the catastrophe. A series of paradoxical equivocations encircle the event: "Inasmuch as the disaster is thought, it is nondisastrous thought, thought of the outside. We have no access to the outside, but the outside has always already touched us in the head, for it is precipitous." The very thought of the event is synonymous with an endless cycle of forgetting and remembering culminating in equanimity, in the conclusion that "we are passive with respect to the disaster, but the disaster is perhaps passivity."[50]

Since for postapocalyptic thinking "Auschwitz" now signifies the point at which the project of modernity reveals itself as fated to culminate in barbarism, contemporary postmodernist thinkers unquestioningly regard it as legitimate to collapse the logic of modernity with the most extreme manifestation of politically organized terror. The event thus condemns not merely the bureaucratic and administrative procedures of the man-made apocalypse, but the ethical, technological, and political structures of the modern world. As Zygmunt Bauman has argued, "modernity" harbored two hopes: a single, anthropologically invariant self-identical subject capable of fulfillment and the utopian aim of transforming society in the image of perfection. When a uniform ideal of existence was imposed on any community, the willful surrender of traditional moral conscience was sanctioned. In this view, totalitarianism was made morally and politically feasible by the various "projects" of social homogeneity and social identity endemic to the Western ideal of a rational society.[51] By contrast, Bauman argues that postmodernity is the capacity to live with ambivalence and contingency whereas modernity aims at their eradication: "The battle of order against chaos in worldly affairs was replicated by the war of truth against error on the plane of consciousness. The order bound to be installed and made universal was a *rational* order; the truth bound to be made triumphant was the *universal* (hence apodictic and obligatory truth). Together, political order and the true knowledge blended into a design for *certainty*. The rational-universal world of order and truth would know of no contingency and no ambivalence."[52]

Whereas the initial response to the catastrophic events of midcentury often involved both a sense of shock and disorientation in the face of a profound collapse and disintegration of intellectual and cultural traditions, texts like Blanchot's, Lyotard's, and Bauman's all but require that the apocalyptic outcome is prefigured in the very structure of modernist language and discourse in order to make plausible their claims. In so doing, they have prompted Eric Santner to ask whether "the postmodern critical agendas that direct themselves against the nostalgic dreams of Western man [are] also to be considered adequate modes of assuming the moral and psychological burdens of the post-Holocaust."[53] They also lend credibility to LaCapra's observation that "much recent debate in critical theory and historiography is recast if the Holocaust is perceived as at least one more or less repressed divider or traumatic point of rupture between modernism and postmodernism."[54] Despite the positive emphasis given to words like "ambivalence" and "contingency" in these accounts, it is precisely these antitotalitarian dimensions of the modernist tradition that ultimately disappear in the rhetorically inflated and apocalyptic image of a totalitarian modernity.

Was the dark side of modernity ultimately created by the Enlightenment dream of a "world without shadow, of everything bathed in the light of reason"?[55] There is no doubt that the postmodernist's unequivocal answer to this question is no longer convincing. One reason for skepticism is that this question also lurked behind the "Heidegger Affair" of 1987, provoked by Victor Farias's none too subtle account of the philosopher's active participation in the Nazi revolution. The facts of Heidegger's Nazism could hardly be disputed. The debate on Heidegger's complicity in Nazism was far more important for its confrontation with the philosophical and political legacy of Heidegger's own confrontation with his Nazi past. Farias's often clumsy revelations caused a profound crisis for those French intellectuals who had, by the 1980s, become "more Heideggerian than Heidegger himself" because of their attraction to Heidegger's postwar thinking. French thinkers frequently drew on his pivotal text of 1946–1947, the "Letter on Humanism" (the subject of chapter 3), which subjects all "humanisms" to the merciless scrutiny of a thinking that stands in lonely opposition to "man," the purveyor of metaphysical and scientific projects. This subject, whose relentless drive to mastery and transcendence obliterates the essential "difference" (between the being of man and Being) is the hallmark of Western Reason. Writing during the deliberations of the academic tribunal that accused him of playing a major role in the Nazification of Freiburg University, the question, as he himself posed it, was never of the philosopher's own commitment to Nazism, but of the authority that could be wrested from his involvement. Indeed, Heidegger's interest was in whether a purified Heideggerianism could rescue philosophy from *all* politics of the "will," of subjectivity, humanism, and metaphysics.

At once compelling and apologetic, Heidegger's 1946 essay admitted only to betraying his greatest philosophical achievement by a temporary descent into the arena of contending nihilisms, of succumbing to a Nietzschean politics of the will that led inexorably to Germany's defeat and disaster. According to this reasoning, all of the catastrophic events of the first half of this century are implicated in, and predicated on, the West's "translation" of ontology into a metaphysics of the human subject. The history of that metaphysics, which encompasses all "philosophy" and culminates with Friedrich Nietzsche's doctrine of truth, is equally responsible for the Nazi biological myth, fascist ethnocen-

trism, proletarian vanguardism, capitalist productivism, and technology. Heidegger's infamous embrace of National Socialism could then,
as Lacoue-Labarthe wrote, be interpreted as "one of the last possible
grand philosophic-political gestures."[56] His "metaphysical" commitment to transcendence "ends in politics" because it is this same commitment of which all of Western metaphysics has been guilty: the Western ideal of overcoming the constraints of Being in a political mission.
All that the Nazis undertook, except perhaps that they and they alone
accomplished it, belong, in some way, to the metaphysical traditions
originating in and characteristic of modernity: "In the apocalypse at
Auschwitz, it is no more or less than the essence of the West that is
revealed—and that has not ceased since that time to reveal itself."[57]
During the first half of the twentieth century, similar ways of thinking,
powerful ideological mechanisms made the projection of a particular
enemy indispensable: the Jew as embodiment of the heterodox, the
anomalous, and the aberrant; the bourgeois or "social fascist" as the
subversive agent of counterrevolution. In these totalitarian logics the
heart of political rationality is inflated into a will to unanimity, an
absolutism of truth, and the extermination of difference. "Nazism,"
Lacoue-Labarthe could conclude, "is a humanism."[58]

Despite the apparent perversity of the assertion, the seduction of this
stance for a generation of French intellectuals has been amply documented.[59] If, according to Heidegger, the entire tradition of Western
metaphysics was implicated in the forgetting of Being, Enlightenment's
most strongly held values—subjectivity, science, humanism—were made
suspect by their emplotment in an intellectual trajectory that seemed to
lead inexorably to a catastrophe that philosophy confronts as its own
ruin. Ironically, postmodern defenders of this radical standpoint, and
their most liberal critics, share the presupposition that "that generation
of German anti-democratic thinkers who intellectually prepared the
way for German fascism are all inseparable from the phenomenon of
'European nihilism.' "[60] Both sides in the debate are invested in returning to the trope of a relatively homogenous "German ideology," which
can be characterized either in terms of a radical "Kulturkritik" or a
"sweeping negation of the principles of democratic humanism."[61] If a
decade ago it seemed more suitable to separate left-wing from right-
wing critics of technology, mass society, and consumerism, today the
pendulum has shifted toward emphasizing their common elements and
their illiberal presuppositions. But it is no longer sufficient to caricature
German thinking as "irrationalist," "antimodernist," and "romantic,"

or to regard its repudiation of the West as the chief symptom of a fundamentally flawed intellectual tradition. Instead it is important to distinguish among the different ways of questioning the culture of the Occident, as to some degree all of the texts discussed in Part II seek to accomplish.

My approach seeks instead to restore the necessary "history-mindedness" that would distinguish adequately between different weaves of the argument and emphasizes that there was not a singular or univocal repudiation of the West that can be apportioned among the thinkers I consider. Rather, the intellectual implications that each drew from their confrontation with the events were often radically different, sometimes irreconcilably so. For Heidegger, the caesura was the consequence of the collapse of an abortive effort to recapitulate the *arché*, the primordial "Greek" beginning of the West that had reached its denouement, and that he had hoped would be repeated in the German "advent"—a project that for him was, at least during the mid-1930s, identical with the National Socialist revolution.[62]

Even before the end of the war Heidegger began to regard the catastrophic events of the first half of this century as the consequence of the West's own "flattening" of Being into the anthropological worldview of "humanism"—in which the realization of an unfulfilled identity of "human nature," social class, or race promised to redeem "humanity." Adorno and Horkheimer shared the view that Western metaphysics had led inexorably to the catastrophic attempt to enforce, by political means, the "identity" of the totalizing logic of the concept, a project they claimed had deep roots in the culture of the Enlightenment, and which they saw as originating in a more anthropologically primitive fear and need to control rebellious nature. They too believed that a monolithic Reason exerted a powerful drive and will to unity, to an absolutist ideal of scientific truth, and to the extermination of difference. But, unlike Heidegger, they regarded the Jews as the chief victims of the Nazi effort to restore a world of primordial images. Nazi anti-Semitism, they claimed, tried to extinguish the distinction between image and Being by literally doing away with the carriers of that distinction, the people whom Freud credited with the "invention" of abstract thought. They drew an opposing conclusion to Heidegger, that the Enlightenment ideal of autonomous, critical reason could only be sustained by an ever-intensifying capacity for self-reflection, rather than abandoned for the murky mists of Being.

Karl Jaspers, by contrast, conceived of his own reconsideration of the ethical tradition of Western humanism as a direct response to what he called "the evasion of his [Heidegger's] philosophy from the responsibility of life-practice and politics."[63] After 1933, Jaspers broke off his friendship with Heidegger, with whom he had established a deep personal and philosophical bond in the 1920s and with whom he was constantly paired in popular discussions of "existentialism." But Jaspers's thoughts, as his literary remains prove, were often preoccupied with his former ally. Although he maintained a stoic public silence in regard to his philosophical "adversary," Jaspers's postwar path was in many ways influenced by Heidegger's negative example. After the war, Jaspers chose to affirm neither the formal universalism of Kant nor his own prewar conservative antimodernism but an ethics of communication and public discourse in postwar Germany, in the permanent awareness of the real possibility of shipwreck for his enterprise.

My discussion of Horkheimer, Adorno, Jaspers, and Heidegger is concerned also with how their arguments and controversies contributed to and structured the political culture of postwar Germany for more than forty years. Their most influential texts have themselves become "events" in a different sense. More important, the discussions they generated reach beyond the German context and have long since become part of the larger dispute over the ground on which much of twentieth-century European philosophy has staked its epistemological and ethical claims. Can, as Heidegger claimed, the catastrophe be identified as the beginning, unfolding, and end of Western metaphysics as such, or does, as Jaspers believed, the very rejection and repudiation of the West implicit in Heideggerian antihumanism—and German thought in general—require a decisive break with that tradition?

As Arendt observed of Heidegger and Jaspers some years later, "the sheer horror of contemporary political events, together with the even more horrible eventualities of the future are behind all the philosophies we have alluded to. It seems to me characteristic that not one of the philosophers has mentioned or analyzed in philosophical terms this background in experience."[64] Though this assertion is somewhat overstated, and far less true for Horkheimer and Adorno, it is essential for the intellectual historian to demonstrate in what ways events were indeed central to the texts that these philosophers produced in their direct aftermath. This is not to "efface" the distinction between text and context but to reaffirm it in a different way, to treat the "external" historical event not as "background" or a social fact but rather as the organizing moment in how a specific text is constructed and how it operates. In this sense a text is more than a document, but it is also not entirely open to "dialogic" exchange.[65] The event structures the response, even if the response "supplements" it by redeploying or repositioning the event in a new constellation. At the same time, as Hans-Georg Gadamer has argued, each text becomes an event to the extent that it is effective and assumes its own history of interpretations.[66] If there was no agreement whatsoever between Jaspers, Heidegger, and Horkheimer and Adorno on the nature of the catastrophe, I will argue that each of these thinkers nonetheless attempted to narrate the event as the apotheosis of a Western tradition and simultaneously to regard it as a deep rupture in that tradition. Reflection on the intellectual significance of the event and on the responsibility of intellectual traditions for it, rather than its reconciliation into a grand scheme of history, is of primary concern to each of these thinkers. In writing about catastrophe there are numerous strategies and voices that might be adopted—prophetic, transfigurative, prosaic—in which the event functions as the "groundless ground" from which and through which history is considered. The event becomes at once the end point of a long historical trajectory and a "rupture with civilization." The attempt to "master" the event, like the attempt to master trauma and acquire a perspective on the extent of the ruins, requires an artificial distance, in order for reflection—in different ways—to bring the caesura to consciousness.[67]

It may appear paradoxical, but since World War II, historians have been more profoundly skeptical of the "eventness" of the past than their nineteenth-century predecessors, preferring instead to focus on long-term social and cultural transformations rather than on superficial and ephemeral political occurrences. They generally justify this shift in focus by arguing that the long perspectives of economic and social history necessarily require a longer time span and that even in periods of convulsive revolutionary change, the "fixity" of mental frameworks is as significant as that of geographic settings. Still, the magnitude of the twentieth-century catastrophe cannot be entirely discounted in accounting for the apparent discrediting of historiographical perspectives established in the nineteenth century. The Hegelian monumentalization of events as part of an upwardly spiraling dialectic of Reason and Law, or Jacob Burckhardt's recourse to the more prosaic distinction between those occurrences that could be judged as "fortunate" and those that were more "unfortunate," could hardly be appropriate to events portending global destruction, Hegel's notorious remark about the "slaughter bench" of history notwithstanding.

One of the enduring ironies of the approach to history pioneered by the prestigious French *Annales* School is that its chief protagonists despaired of writing the history of events under the circumstances of political events that all but dictated their collective and individual destinies. The murder of the *Annales*' founder, Marc Bloch, in 1944 and the internment of Fernand Braudel, Bloch's heir and the historian who contributed most to its worldwide acceptance, in a German prison camp where he wrote his great history of the Mediterranean eloquently testify to the close proximity of the central figures of French historiography to the cataclysmic events of the 1940s.

Braudel was certainly aware of the events that shaped his preference for a history that was far less subject to exigency, contingency, and emergency than his own. "Down with occurrences," he once wrote, "especially the vexing ones! I had to believe that history, destiny, was written at a much more profound level."[68] On reflection, is it so surprising that under those conditions Braudel would draw so sharp a contrast between the "sensational events and dramatic reversals" that characterize the surface of what he called "event-based history" and the slow, rhythmic changes that occur over centuries in the deep sediments of a collective, anonymous past? Did the need to escape the traumatic occurrences that he had to face each day lead Braudel to adopt a philosophy of history that constantly reproached, disparaged, and even ceased to wholly admit to the significance of the "mere events" of storytelling historians? "Rejecting events and the time in which events take place was a way of placing oneself to one side, sheltered, so as to get some sort of perspective, to be able to evaluate them better, and not wholly to believe in them. To go from the short time span, to one less short, and then to the long view (which, if it exists, must surely be the wise man's time span); and having got there, to think about everything afresh and to reconstruct everything around one: a historian could not but be tempted by such a prospect."[69]

Suspicion of events is understandable in a century that on balance has been far richer in cataclysms than in occurrences that inspire faith in progress and collective purpose. Yet after the program of the *Annales* School has become synonymous with modern historiography, its criticism of event-based history has reached an impasse. One reason, perhaps, is that recent struggles over memory—involving historians, museums, public programs—have exhibited not the disappearance of "events"—as the *Annales* School once anticipated—but what Pierre Nora has announced as "the return of the event."[70] Andreas Huyssen has noted the paradox that despite the waning of interest in historical consciousness and the widespread proliferation of discourses on "post-histoire," there has been a massive outpouring of public interest in memory and in memorialization.[71] Historians too have begun to confront the dilemma of how to write the "history of history," at the end of a century that has produced multiple claims to an increasingly ambiguous past. This does not mean a return to the conventional narrative approach to political or social history, but rather to a more sophisticated understanding of the impact of events on the ways that traditional narratives are composed and, perhaps more important, also rendered incoherent. For example, all three of the chapters in Part II are concerned with the ways that the same event is understood as a marker in a tradition that simultaneously made that tradition implausible.

In his provocative book *Foregone Conclusions: Against Apocalyptic History,* Michael André Bernstein suggests that there might be a third way between a modernity cast in terms of the singular historical logic of totality and wholeness and the explicitly antiapocalyptic postmodern, between "the antithetical but twin reductionisms of teleological determinism and radical undecidability."[72] Bernstein's argument is useful because it demonstrates that apocalyptic metanarratives often engage in a "foreshadowing" that endows reflection on the signal event with the Olympian power of retrospective necessity or even inevitability. Nor does his approach succumb to the reverse gesture, as does, for example, Blanchot's, foreclosing reflection on the historicity of what did occur. For Bernstein, both stratagems overburden the event with "foreshadowing" that either requires its "global and monolithic" inevitability or, conversely, its radical indeterminacy. His alternative term, "side-shadowing," does not deny the overwhelming significance of the event, nor does it bracket out our knowledge of the "end," while it pays "attention to the unfulfilled or unrealized possibilities of the past" in ways that are disruptive of "the affirmations of a triumphalist, unidirectional view of history." Bernstein does not obscure or cast doubt on the events that did take place, but he draws our attention to the important ways that a catastrophic historical event, in the specific case of the Holocaust, narrows the range of freedom when it is subsequently recast "as the climax of a bitter trajectory whose inevitable outcome it must be."[73]

Though Bernstein argues largely through the examples of recent lit-

erary renderings of the Shoah, his emphasis on retaining the "eventness," or full texture of historical events, strikingly parallels some of
the important issues raised at the margins of the Historian's Controversy of 1986–1987.[74] Though at that time the lion's share of attention
was paid to the cruder and more obviously nationalistic stratagems of
German historians interested in relativizing the significance of the murder of the Jews for German politics, Martin Broszat raised a concern that was of far more universal interest for historical scholarship:
whether the history of National Socialism might ever overcome what he
called the "blockade" imposed by exclusive focus on its singular crimes
in favor of "a new, long-term view of the arena of modern German history in which National Socialism played itself out."[75] Broszat's most
controversial argument was that the imperative to retrospectively evaluate National Socialism through its apotheosis in the crime of the murder of the Jews might block understanding of the ways that the regime
garnished, secured, and mobilized mass support. A more nuanced and
textured approach to the history of National Socialism, the distance
suggested by the term "historicization," permitted scholarly investigation of all aspects of the regime. There was, he implied, a heavy price
to be paid for reading German history and the history of the Nazi era
solely as what Peter Gay once referred to as "clues of crimes to come."[76]

To be sure, as Saul Friedländer replied in a series of lengthy exchanges, and as the subsequent polemics over the "history of everyday
life" elaborated, the issue is surely not simply the degree of "distancing" or whether "normal" developments should or should not be included in the investigation of German society during the Nazi era but
the relative weight given to these noncriminal elements "in a system
whose very core is criminal from the very beginning."[77] Broszat's "plea
for the historicization of National Socialism" was vulnerable on several
counts: it established a set of dubious antitheses between the "moral"
and the "historical," between the "pathological" and the "modernizing
tendencies" of Nazism, and, most prominently, between "normaliza-
tion" and moral sensitivity. If for Bernstein an excess of "foreshadowing" "overshadows" the contingent and alternative possibilities of
events by obliterating their "eventness," too excessive a focus on the
plethora of events that did not directly participate in the annihilation
of the Jews dilutes the fact that the Nazi regime was not ordinary and
that it did "something no other regime, whatever its criminality, has
attempted to do."[78] Here again we find that neither the rhetorical
inflation of events to the status of metahistorical tropes nor their

deflation to contingent occurrences is entirely adequate. These essays argue that the antiredemptive stance of the post–World War II theorists often replicates the "foreshadowing" described by Bernstein by regarding all of history as the anticipation of trauma, as already occurring in the shadow of catastrophe. It is perhaps useful, then, to remember that though this century's beginning was, as Hobsbawm writes, "the Age of Catastrophe," the shadow of those events has been elongated, not merely by the events themselves, but by their intellectual consequences. This is the theme of the essays that follow.

Chapters 1 and 3 appeared in *New German Critique* 34 (Winter 1985) and 62 (Fall 1994). Chapter 2 appeared as the introduction to Hugo Ball, *Critique of the German Intelligentsia* (New York: Columbia University Press, 1993); copyright © 1993 by Columbia University Press; reprinted with permission of the publisher. An earlier version of chapter 4 appeared in *Radical Philosophy* 75 (January–February 1996).

PART ONE

World War I

CHAPTER I

Between Apocalypse and Enlightenment

Benjamin, Bloch, and Modern German-Jewish Messianism

I.

In the years approaching the First World War, the self-confidence and security of German Jewry were challenged by a new Jewish sensibility that can be described as at once radical, secular, and messianic in both tone and content. What this new Jewish ethos refused to accept was above all the optimism of an older generation of German Jews nurtured on the concept of Bildung as the German-Jewish mystique.[1] The equally new political anti-Semitism and antiliberal spirit of the German upper classes made many of them call into question the political and cultural assumptions of the postemancipation epoch. Especially irksome was the belief that for German Jewry there was no contradiction between *Deutschtum* and *Judentum;* that secularization and liberalism would permit the cultural integration of Jews (as Jews) into the national community.[2] For German Jews of that earlier generation, the *Bildungsideal* of Kant, Goethe, and Schiller assured them of an indissoluble bond between Enlightenment, universal ethics, autonomous art, and monotheism (stripped of any particularist "Jewish" characteristics). The mission of the Jews could be interpreted, as did Leo Baeck in his 1905 *Essence of Judaism,* as the exemplary embodiment of the religion of morality for all humanity.[3]

The unproblematic understanding of Judaism as "the religion of Reason," as Hermann Cohen called it, was equally characteristic of secular nineteenth-century Jewish Socialist intellectuals like Rosa Luxemburg, whose universalism permitted no special pleading for Jewish suffering, and Eduard Bernstein, who took Marx and Kant as the gospel of a self-assured Socialist future.[4] Not only the intellectual elite but other less well known writers on "the Jewish Question" echoed this overconfident appraisal. The words of the German-Jewish Socialist Ludwig Quessel, a pro-Zionist, in the *Sozialistische Monatshefte* of June 1914 provide a not atypical example: "With the beginning of the twentieth century organized political anti-Semitism in Germany has gradually died out, and I do not believe that it can be brought back to life."[5] Even political Zionism was not immune from this late Wilhelmine Jewish attitude that only in retrospect appears to us as a fatal blindness. Zion, too, we must recall, was a distant political ideal, while German Zionists remained faithful to the values of the transitory national community until the utopia could be realized.[6]

It is not surprising, then, that for the young German-Jewish "generation of 1914" it is this modern Jewish type that emerges as the negative image of the assimilated German Jews.[7] As Béla Balázs observed of Georg Lukács in a diary entry written in that crucial year: "Gyuri has discovered in himself the Jew! The search for ancestors. The Chassidic Baal Shem. Now he too has found his ancestors and his race. Only I am alone and forlorn." Lukács, he noted, believed that "there is emerging or re-emerging a Jewish type, the anti-rationalist or Jewish skeptic, one who is the antithesis of all that is commonly described as Jewish."[8] This new Jewish spirit, a product of the "post-assimilatory Renaissance," can be described as a modern Jewish messianism: radical, uncompromising, and comprised of an esoteric intellectualism that is as uncomfortable with the Enlightenment as it is enamored of apocalyptic visions — whether revolutionary or purely redemptive in the spiritual sense.[9]

One could of course also point to many parallels with the non-Jewish "generation of 1914" that Robert Wohl and others have written about, with its revolt against rationality and authority. We can also see the connection to the entire tradition of what Lukács referred to as pre-1914 European "romantic anti-capitalism," which ranged across such a wide "political" spectrum, providing the impetus for such diverse figures as Lukács, Georg Simmel, Max Weber, Paul Ernst, Hermann Hesse, Paul de Lagarde, and Möller van den Brück.[10]

The crucial component of the new Jewish sensibility, however, is a commitment to a different kind of modern Jewishness that stood under the sign of messianism. The messianic stance rejected traditional religiosity, the rational and secular Judaism of the German middle classes, and the personal Judaism of "renewal" represented by Martin Buber and the Bar Kochba circle. Nor did it participate in either the renaissance of Jewish orthodoxy during Weimar or the repudiation of assimilation characteristic of secular radicalism. Messianism demanded a complete repudiation of the world as it is, placing its hope in a future whose realization can only be brought about by the destruction of the old order. Apocalyptic, catastrophic, utopian, and pessimistic, messianism captured a generation of Jewish intellectuals before the First World War. The messianic impulse appears in many forms in the Jewish generation of 1914, and this chapter is an attempt to characterize it as a modern form of Jewish thought—secular *and* theological—as a tradition that stands opposed to both secular rationalism and what has been called "normative Judaism."[11]

Lukács, who embodied the new Jewish "type" far more than he would ever later admit, clearly understood that messianism was a prepolitical vision of the world made whole. He was also attuned to an element that constantly surfaces in messianic visions of the apocalypse: death and destruction as the harbinger of that integral world. In the same diary entry Balázs recorded "Gyuri's great new philosophy, messianism. The homogenous world as the goal of salvation. Art is Lucifer's 'making things better.' Seeing the world as homogenous before the process of becoming so."[12] This study focuses on the early writings of Ernst Bloch and Walter Benjamin because they represent a particularly "pure type" of this thinking.[13] There were others, of course, who embodied the new Jewish spirit, but only Bloch and Benjamin—initially without any mutual influence—brought, in varying degrees, a self-consciously Jewish and radical messianism to their political and intellectual concerns.

The messianic idea implied the radical rejection of any sort of quotidian politics combined with a characteristically apocalyptic attitude, which often incorporated an antipolitics in extremis. The new messianism turned on the double problem of redefining the "crisis of European culture" through a specific kind of Jewish radicalism and at the same time of redefining Jewish intellectual politics through a new attitude toward European culture. Yet, as a result of the abandonment of the Enlightenment, messianism was implicated in the subsequent political fate of its adherents, particularly after the First World War. How, to what extent, and with what consequences did messianism influence their political decisions and choices, especially in regard to the era of war and revolution that followed their first brush with Jewish messianism in the years around 1912, is the question posed by this chapter.

II.

Modern Jewish messianism, encompassing a broad political and cultural spectrum, can be found among many Jewish thinkers before and after World War I. It was not identical with but part of a far more general trend toward redefining Jewishness without Judaism. The goal of messianic Judaism was not, however, simply a redefinition of Jewish culture. It also emphasized a certain kind of intellectuality as politics, a spiritual radicalism that aimed at nothing less than "total transformation" of the individual and society, sometimes coupled with activism, sometimes wholly without any concrete political touchstone. Whether theoretical or actual, the politics of Jewish messianism is in the final analysis apocalyptic. Even when it assumes a political guise it is most allergic to institutional politics and to political evolutionism, which it avoids in any form: Social Democracy, Zionism, and liberalism. As Scholem remarked about the appeal of Zionism for his generation, "We did not come to Zionism in search of politics."[14]

Michael Löwy has suggested that modern Jewish messianism was the product of an important intellectual convergence that took place between 1900 and 1933, the fusion of libertarian anarchism with hermeneutical Jewish motifs organized around the common purpose of romantic anticapitalism in a situation of general European crisis. He places great emphasis on two mutually reinforcing currents, "religious Jews with anarchist tendencies" (e.g., Martin Buber, Franz Rosenzweig, Hans Kohn, and Gershom Scholem) and the "anarchist, anarcho-bolsheviks, and antiauthoritarian Marxists" (Gustav Landauer, Ernst Bloch, Erich Fromm, Ernst Toller, Georg Lukács). This distinction somewhat exaggerates the significance of the utopian libertarian tradition of the left, whereas the messianic element was central to a wider variety of currents, including important strands of Catholicism and Protestantism, whatever political consequences might have emerged from it. Nonetheless, Löwy is right to suggest that the messianic impulse appears *within* different Jewish-secular frameworks, from Kafka's images of exile in the alien landscape of the body to the political Zionism of Scholem in the Blau-Weiss epoch.[15] Max Brod once wrote to a friend that "Jewish nationalism must not create a new chauvinist nation, but . . . must create a real foundation in the messianic direction."[16] If we see Jewish messianism as an ethos in the Greek sense of a characteristic spirit or attitude (*Haltung*), it appears as a significant moment among a variety of Jewish radical sensibilities of the fin de siècle rather than in any *pure* form.

Indeed, if we cast the net widely enough we can include many Jewish types that bear the marks of this messianic ethos. Lukács, for example, whose radical messianism is as evident in his non-Marxist *Soul and Form* and *Theory of the Novel* as it is in his self-avowedly "sectarian-messianic" *History and Class Consciousness* never chose (apart from the brief episode recorded by Balázs) to make explicit the Jewish aspect, and Gershom Scholem brought a similar radical ideal into his Zionism, while rejecting—at least from the Jewish standpoint—the arena of European politics *tout court*.[17] Rosenzweig's *Stern der Erlösung* (1916) belongs to the messianic tradition in its emphasis on redemptive radicalized Jewish religiosity, while remaining estranged from any sort of political radicalism.[18] The Jewish Nietzscheans, most notably Kurt Hiller, Theodor Lessing, Salomo Friedländer, and Martin Buber, and the "linguistic" mystics, from Gustav Landauer and Benjamin to the Oskar Goldberg circle, would certainly also have to be included.[19] Or we can restructure the axis along other lines: for example, Benjamin and Bloch as "theological Messianists," Landauer/Buber/Scholem as "radical Zionist Messianists," Rosenzweig and Lukács along a critical Hegelian axis; perhaps with Kafka, Brod, and the Prague Bar Kochba circle as the antithesis of that constellation.[20]

My point is that whether one chooses politics, theology, philosophy, or aesthetics as the starting point, the messianic tradition appears in different guises. There are at least four different dimensions to Jewish messianism, and it is useful to consider them separately for a moment. First, there is a restorative aspect that opposes the idea of *restitutio* to reform or any kind of gradual change. As Scholem notes, the messianic idea restores "the ideal content of the past and at the same time delivers the basis for an image of the future."[21] The utopian content of the past becomes the material basis for a vision of the future of mankind, the dim recollection of the golden age before the Fall. The messianic concept is thus intimately connected to the idea of a return to an original state that lies in *both* the past and the future. Karl Kraus's motto Origin Is the Goal, cited by Benjamin among others, captures this idea most succinctly.[22] This gives the messianic idea a special mission that accords a central place to language as the medium of redemption. Thought focuses on the *restoration* of lost meanings, suppressed connections, which is often linked to a sense of redemption through language and through the reading of texts that reveal the hidden presence or traces of a messianic epoch. Whereas the prophetic tradition involved public testimony, the messianic tradition involves an esoteric or even secret form of knowledge. Certain images or words, combinations of letters, or even entire works evoke the lost utopian content of the past. But these works demand a special allegorical reading to disclose their message. The restorative element therefore involves "revelations or disclosures of God's hidden knowledge of the End."[23] This notion of the esoteric function of the intellectual, which is strongest in Benjamin, is also present in Bloch's gnostic notion of utopia as a *restoration* of the lost truth of the world: "The world is not true, but it will successfully return home through human beings and through truth."[24] Knowledge is thus linked, not to power, but to the triumph of translucent redemption—it takes on an esoteric cast.

Second, there is a *redemptive* utopian aspect that conceives of utopia in terms of a new unity and transparency that is absent in all previous ages which is its central ideal. The utopian vision is that of a future that is the fulfillment of all that which can be hoped for in the condition of exile but cannot be realized within it. Redemption appears either as the *end of history* or as an event *within* history, never as an event produced by history. In every case it is experienced as a decisive and total break with the past and the restoration of an esoteric truth. Lukács's extraordinary thesis in *History and Class Consciousness* that the proletarian revolution will necessarily restore the identity of subject and object in philosophy, overcoming the "antinomies of bourgeois thought," and end the "prehistory" of mankind depends on the proletariat having access to a secret truth by virtue of its privileged historical position, the "standpoint of totality."[25]

Third, there is a strong *apocalyptic* element that opposes salvation to historical immanence (evolution, progress, reform, even some forms of revolution) and conceives of the coming of the messianic age as an event that occurs publicly, either historically or suprahistorically.[26] The apocalyptic event disrupts and intrudes into the historical unfolding of events from outside, with the emphasis on the caesura that separates the messianic age from the past. In one of his earliest essays, Benjamin notes that "there is a conception of history which, in its faith in the endlessness of time, distinguishes only between the differences in tempo of human beings and epochs rolling with more or less speed toward the future along the tracks of progress. . . . The elements of the ultimate state of affairs are not manifest as formless tendencies of progress, but rather are embedded in *every* present as the most endangered, discredited and ridiculed creations and thoughts."[27] The apocalyptic element involves a quantum leap from present to future, from exile to freedom. This leap necessarily brings with it the complete destruction and negation of the old order.

Scholem has emphasized the tension between "the destructive nature of the redemption on the one hand and the utopianism of the content on the other."[28] This tension, which the Marxian idea of revolutionary "transition" only weakly captures, is the essence of the apocalyptic vision of catastrophic upheaval as the handmaiden of redemption. This image constantly recurs in history, appearing in the Muenster Anabaptists destroying the records of the old church, in the creation of the revolutionary calendar of 1793, in the Komsomol youth disinterring the bones of the saints in the Russian revolution, or in the specter of the Maoist Red Guards demolishing the ancient artworks of Confucian China—each symbolizes a *total* destruction of the prior age as the precondition for the full restitution of the messianic period.

In Jewish messianism, however, the cataclysmic element remains otherworldly and consequently makes redemption independent of either immanent historical "forces" or personal experience of liberation. It differs from all of the aforementioned secular manifestations of messianism as historical eschatology since "redemption is not the product of immanent developments such as we find it in modern Western (or Eastern) reinterpretations of messianism since the Enlightenment."[29] As Blumenberg has shown, the Jewish apocalyptic tradition involved a radical devaluation of the world, and accorded preeminence to a fulfillment that occurs "beyond history."[30] Freedom may occur in history, but it is not brought about by historical forces or individual acts. Messianism therefore cancels out the possibility of an optimistic and evolutionary conception of history, of progress, without of course foreclosing the possibility of freedom.

Fourth, the chasm that separates the historical quotidian from redemption is too wide to be bridged by determined action or profane events. This creates a dilemma for the ethics of messianism between the idea of liberation and the absolute superfluity of any action that is often difficult to sustain. This dilemma also gives messianism its characteristically pessimistic cast of mind, "contempt for the day and a mockery of the hour because of a belief in the future."[31] The optimism of the messianists "is not directed to what history will bring forth, but that which will arise in its ruin, free at last and undisguised."[32] Since messianism is nurtured by its vision of the total negation of the existing order of things, there is always a desire to break out of its contemplative and pessimistic constraints in the present in order to hasten the end.[33]

This dilemma accounts for a profound *ethical ambivalence* in the messianic idea. In his *Ancient Judaism,* a work that bears more than an accidental relationship to the problems of pre–World War I German Jewry, Max Weber recognized that Jewish messianism, faced with the strong element of *expectation* coupled with a profound pessimism about "this-worldly" salvation, vacillates wildly between its fixation on the liberatory potential of eschatology and an ethical attitude toward the present that is one of humility, patience, and passivity.[34] The pendulum swings constantly between doom and hope, and the result is that the messianic tradition is caught between the poles of contemplative inaction and action. In Weberian terms its "this-worldly" ethos is in permanent conflict with its "otherworldly" image of redemption. Ethically speaking, passivity and amoral violence are often coupled in the messianic tradition. On the one hand, "the unreal alone imparted the hope that made life bearable."[35] On the other hand, the concrete actions of individuals in the pivotal moment of apocalyptic catastrophe could not be measured by normal human standards. Esoteric knowledge and political extremism are the two poles of the political ethics of messianism. In its modern form (as opposed to its prophetic incarnation) this particular tension between esoteric intellectualism and politically transcendental morality (amorality) is especially strong. The idea of revolutionary nihilism as the counterpoint to esoteric intellectualism—often embodied in the same figure, for example, Auguste Blanqui, Bakunin, or again Lukács—is the fundamental aporia of this aspect of messianism.

A great deal has been said about the revolutionary, redemptive, and restorative aspects of the modern messianic idea. Far less attention has been paid to the context in which it emerged, and still less to the notion that esoteric intellectualism was seen as a specific Jewish cultural alternative prior to World War I. This chapter then focuses on three specific questions. First, how did the radical messianic idea emerge in the Central European Jewish community in the prewar years, specifically in regard to Martin Buber's influence on the Jewish revival of the fin de siècle? Second, how did the specific type of radical messianism that Bloch and Benjamin personified reflect both Jewish concerns and the experiences of the Great War? Third, how did Bloch and Benjamin come to their respective political choices (Marxism and Benjamin's "theoretical anarchism") in the early 1920s?

III.

Both Bloch and Benjamin had their first contact with specifically Jewish concerns in the atmosphere of the Jewish revival of 1909–1913, which coincided with Buber's enormous influence among young German-Jewish intellectuals. We cannot underestimate the tremendous impact of Buber's *Three Speeches to the Jews* (1909, 1911), with its conception of Judaism as a living teaching and as a personal and inner experience.[36] Buber's early philosophy embraced, in stark Nietzschean language, a central core of existential and mystical Jewish experience as that which is "primordially Jewish" against its rationalist absorption into secularized neo-Kantianism.[37] For Buber, Zionism was not simply a political movement but a "Lebensphilosophie." In the face of anti-Semitism and the vicissitudes of assimilation, his romantic recasting of Hasidism provided a road to Judaism that embraced the "East" without the "Ostjuden"—adopting only its religiosity and traditionalism—Hasidic mysticism without the Hasidim.

Buber's *Speeches* and the influential collection of essays published by his devotees and followers of the Prague Bar Kochba Union, *Vom Judentum* (1913), carried a clear message: modern Jewry had to undergo a "decisive transformation," a "transvaluation of values."[38] As opposed to the assimilated Jew of the Wilhelmine epoch, who was "the idolater of his own ego," the new Jew had to affirm his ties to history and return to an essential and personal Judaism. Though Buber always maintained that Palestine was the Jewish homeland, political Zionism with its emphasis on emigration was secondary to this goal: "Before there can be external emancipation there must be liberation from the inner *Galuth* (diaspora), from inward slavery, a purification of the heart and a growth of the people beyond itself." Zionism, in short, was "not knowledge but life."[39]

For both Bloch and Benjamin the year 1912 marked, as it did for so many others, a first confrontation with the challenge of Buber's call for self-definition. "Finally the pride of being Jewish has woken," Bloch announced in his essay "Symbol: The Jews," written in that year.[40] "It stirs within us restlessly, yet these people remain mixed and ambiguous."[41] "Among younger Jews," Bloch noted, "there is a new pride, and the social manifestations of submissiveness and self-deprecation have disappeared."[42] Scholem, too, recalled the profound impact of Buber's addresses on him when they appeared.[43] At that time Benjamin wrote to his Gymnasium friend Herbert Belmore that he experienced Zionism and its influence for "the first time" and that these were to him "a possibility and a duty," though he intended to remain firmly within the secular youth movement of his teacher Gustav Wyneken.[44] Wyneken's Free School Community (Freie Schulgemeinde) represented an elite, aristocratic, and fiercely intellectualist wing of the German youth movement that was opposed to populist *volkisch* myth and stressed the formation of the individual as an ethical being. Wyneken's ideal of a dedicated, studious, and highly ethical *männerbund* (male cult) devoted to the timeless truths of Kant, Hegel, Goethe, and Nietzsche was the most important influence on Benjamin in his student years.[45] In August 1912, during his summer vacation at Holzmünde and after his first semester at Freiburg, Benjamin, who was twenty years old at the time, noted that he often discussed Zionism with Kurt Tuchler, a friend who attempted to introduce him into his "Zionist conceptual framework," while Benjamin attempted to convert Tuchler to the ideas of Wyneken and his model Free School Community at Wickersdorf.[46]

That fall Benjamin felt compelled to take the problems of Judaism raised by Buber more seriously, both personally and philosophically. The occasion was his now partially published correspondence with Buber's future son-in-law, the writer and poet Ludwig Strauss.[47] Strauss, enraptured by Buber's *Speeches,* had written to Benjamin— whose prominence as the most vocal of Wyneken's Jewish disciples was already resonant—asking if he would participate in the founding of a new journal devoted to German-Jewish intellectual life, which Strauss planned to edit.[48]

Benjamin's correspondence with Strauss chronicles his attempt to find his own path to Judaism, culminating in a confrontation with some of Buber's followers in a debate in Berlin the following year.[49] These letters reveal a side to Benjamin's Jewishness that has been obscured and overshadowed by his later meeting and friendship with Scholem, whose reminiscences of Benjamin have perhaps contributed to a neglect of his earlier position. Scholem's characterization of Benjamin's early attitude toward Judaism in his *Story of a Friendship,* as "tortured," gives the misleading impression that Jewishness was not a matter of central concern at that point. Moreover, Scholem also refers condescendingly to the young Benjamin as "the most gifted intellect" among the Jewish followers of Wyneken "for whom that fact [Jewishness] was of little or no practical significance."[50] Other scholars have readily accepted Scholem's verdict on Benjamin's earlier contact with Jewish ideas, and there has been an overemphasis on Scholem's influence on the formation of Benjamin's subsequent attraction to Kabbalah and mysticism, especially during the war.[51]

However, Benjamin's letters to Strauss demonstrate a clear and sensitive attitude toward the issue of Jewishness as early as 1912, and an equally clear distance from both Buber and Zionism. More important, they show that his convictions about the "Jewish Question" were already quite developed by the time he met Scholem and were altered very little by their encounter. Benjamin's meeting with Scholem intensified the esoteric and intellectual side of Benjamin's thought, bringing him closer to Kabbalah and Jewish mysticism, but it did not change his mind about Zionism or about the role of the Jewish intellectual in German politics and culture.

Strauss's plans for a new Jewish-German journal were directly connected to an intellectual event that took on extraordinary political dimensions within the German-Jewish milieu in the spring of 1912. In that year Moritz Goldstein, a young unknown Jewish writer and editor of the influential cultural journal *Der Kunstwart,* published a now famous sharply written and highly provocative article entitled "Deutsch-jüdischer Parnass" that articulated for the first time the dilemmas faced by the German Jews in Wilhelmine Germany. Goldstein argued that Jews were in the impossible position of "administering the spiritual property of a nation which denies our right and our ability to do so."[52] To make matters worse, Goldstein adopted the terms of Werner Sombart's argument in *Die Zukunft der Juden,* which cited the disproportionate influence of the Jews in liberal culture, especially the arts and the press. For Goldstein, assimilation was an illusion, intensified by the stubborn refusal of the Jews themselves to openly admit either their rejection by German society or their power in the world of culture—a power readily noted by the anti-Semites—in the fear that such acknowledgment would lead to even greater injustices toward them. When it came to the Jews, Goldstein concluded, "Europe is not just, . . . but characterized by a truly barbarian lack of justice."[53] If "German culture was to a not small extent, Jewish culture," the relationship of Jews to Germany "is that of an unrequited love."[54]

Goldstein's article provoked an unprecedented furor in Jewish political circles. It broke the taboo on publicly speaking (especially in a non-Jewish pronationalist journal edited by Ferdinand Avenarius) of the

German-Jewish "dilemma" and announced a new bravado in the expression of Jewish "interests" in regard to German cultural life. But while the Zionists enthusiastically embraced Goldstein's article for its unabashed avowal of a Jewish "character" and Jewish intellectuals, Jewish liberals were furious, denouncing its pessimism about assimilation, pointing to the difficult and painstaking evolutionary process of Jewish self-development toward full citizenship in Germany.[55] The Goldstein article led to heated and even violent exchanges between the Jews of the liberal Central Verein and members of the German Zionist organization, the Zionistische Vereinigung für Deutschland (ZVfD), and ultimately to a complete break between the Zionists and the anti-Zionists within the Jewish community.[56]

Ludwig Strauss had been one of the most active participants in the intensive debate that ensued in the pages of the *Kunstwart* later that summer. In his pseudonymous reply to Ernst Lissauer, who offered a strong defense of Jewish assimilation and liberalism, Strauss countered that Lissauer and the liberals had denied "the national substance in German Jews" and argued that there was a "Jewish nationhood" evident in "an inner difference" that inhibited assimilation and made the Jews appear "alien" and unacceptable.[57] Citing Buber's *Speeches,* Strauss spoke of the Jews as a community of blood and inner experience and called for a "national Jewish movement in Germany" oriented toward Palestine and toward a new Jewish literature, in which Jews would become a "closed cultural circle" with their own literature and art, and perhaps ultimately even with "their own language (Hebrew)."[58] Most important for the immediate occasion of his letters to Benjamin, Strauss affirmed Goldstein's call for a German-language journal that would be the focal point for all creative Jews.[59] He too saw in the *Kunstwart* debate the moment for establishing a "central organ for Jewish writing in the German language." In contrast to the official Zionist periodicals, which placed "national regeneration in the foreground," the new journal would permit "the Jewish spirit to show itself more clearly and confidently."[60]

Strauss inquired as to Benjamin's reaction to the *Kunstwart* debate, which Benjamin said he had followed in its entirety and discussed with a few Zionists (apparently Tuchler) who had been in Holzmünde during his stay. Benjamin also castigated the German liberal "philosemitic press," especially the *Berliner Tageblatt* for passing over the polemic in silence.[61] "The manner in which the *Kunstwart* attacked the problem from the literary side was the most satisfactory," he added. Benjamin was also positively disposed toward Strauss's plans for a new journal: "Precisely for the Jewish Question we need an area where the Jewish spirit can be isolated and reveal its nature." Since "Jewish religious life ... [was] inadequate," Benjamin agreed that the *Kunstwart*'s motto of "expressive culture" (*Ausdruckskultur*) provided the suitable forum. Therefore, Benjamin notes, "in accordance with the implications of your plan for a journal of Jewish spiritual life in the German language, I am completely on your side. Not only for the Jewish Question, but for those who are outsiders to it [*die Aussenstehenden*], it promises a great deal."[62] Benjamin also approved of Strauss's suggestion of appropriate themes, all obviously directed at assimilationist German Jewry: "Jews and Luxury; Jews and the love of Germany; Jews and Friendship." For the first time "we will see the literary circles and the Jewish money aristocracy from the standpoint of Jewishness." "If we are indeed two-sided, Jewish *and* German," Benjamin concurred, "up to now all of our enthusiasm and affirmation has been directed toward the German! The Jewish side was perhaps only a foreign (worse, sentimental) Jewish aroma in our production and our lives. No individual, not even an artist, knows how to balance this dual spirit. But we will discover it."[63]

Benjamin obviously shared Strauss's enthusiasm for the possibility of bringing Western European Jewry "to self-consciousness" before "the valuable forces in Jewishness" are "lost through assimilation." But he did not share Strauss's view that "the only salvation is in a Jewish state." Perhaps, he added, "that [view] could be accepted when we think about the East European Jews. They have as little occasion to reflect on where they will end up as a man fleeing a burning house." Benjamin questioned the consequences of a state comprising both eastern and western Jews: "Is the unification of two cultures, like the western and eastern Jews not something like a *Salto-mortale* in the natural, in chaos." Moreover, Western European Jews "are no longer free *as Jews*." They can only become part of a "Jewish movement," insofar as they are "tied to a literary movement." The Jews are "committed to Internationalism."[64]

For Benjamin, this is the "strange" position of the Jews in Western society: "In most circles the word 'literati' has a derogatory undertone," but it is for him only the Jewish literati who "take the intellectual and spiritual as seriously as Tolstoy took the culture of Christianity. The 'literati' draw the consequences of our famous Enlightenment and lack of prejudice." Jews therefore have the "serious mission," not of creating art, which they cannot do, but rather of "drawing from art Spirit for the life of the epoch."[65]

In short, the intellectualist mission of the Jews is the Western alternative to Zionism. This "modern asceticism," as Benjamin called it, even determines the "forms" in which Jewish cultural life appears. What he means is evident: "even the Café." The Jew, to continue in the idiom of Christian discourse, "is called," according to the "new social consciousness," to be what " 'the poor in spirit, the enslaved and the meek,' " were for the first Christians. "The best Jews today are linked to a valuable process in European culture, and though this does not mean that political Zionism is antithetical to Jewish cultural work, in practice it is quite distinct from it and lacks any intrinsic relationship to it."[66]

Benjamin's subsequent letters to Strauss are more explicit and less conciliatory in tone. They mark a growing distance from Buber's views, particularly his central idea of Judaism as a personal experience, and they demonstrate his impatience with Strauss's efforts to make political Zionism an integral part or goal of the renewal of European Jewry. On October 10 he wrote to Strauss that he too believed "that which is Jewish is an essential core," but he emphasized (using a distinction that Buber adopted from Goethe and Dilthey and—completely inverted—became crucial to his mature philosophical work) that his position toward Judaism was not formed through an inner Jewish experience (*Erlebnis*) but solely through the experience (*Erfahrung*) of ideas in relation to the world. Benjamin conceded that he "recognizes" and "in a certain sense supports Zionism." But, he adds, "this support extends only to contributing to Zionist organizations." Zionism, he admits, is hardly a "determining factor" in his life, whereas Jewishness is: "I see two paths for modern West European national Jewry: Zionism and one other."[67]

Benjamin reminded Strauss that his decisive intellectual experience occurred "before Jewishness became important or problematic for me." At the same time, he recognized that for the most part those who held most resolutely to the ideas of Wyneken "were Jews" and that the result was a noticeable "dualism" in them, particularly in Benjamin himself. It is "from Wickersdorf," then, that Benjamin discovered his Jewishness and led him to this conclusion: "I am a Jew and if I live as a conscious human being, I live as a conscious Jew."[68]

Whether this declaration was sufficient to convince Strauss of Benjamin's suitability for his new journal is doubtful. Benjamin continued to affirm the validity of his attachment to Wyneken, even if that meant that "what is valuable in me and in the other 'Jews' is not Jewish." He added that Zionism did not appear to him as particularly Jewish. It is "futile to ask if Jewish-Palestine work or Jewish-European work is more urgent," and among the Zionists, he found, "the Jewish was a natural impulse, but Zionism a matter of political organization. The inner core of their personality was not determined by Jewishness: they propagandize Palestine and [speak][69] German. Perhaps these people are necessary: but it is least of all they who should speak of Jewish experience [*Erlebnis*]. They represent half-humans. Have they ever thought through, school, literature, inner life, or the state in a Jewish manner?" "I see three Zionist forms of Jewishness [*Judentum*]," Benjamin concluded, "Palestine Zionism (a natural necessity); German Zionism in its halfness; and cultural Zionism which sees Jewish values *everywhere* and works for them. Here I will stay, and I believe I must stay."[70]

That Benjamin was concerned with the question of Jewishness at that time, and with religious and secular identity in particular, is also apparent in one of his earliest literary efforts, "Dialog über religiöses Gefühl unserer Zeit," which he wrote during the exchanges with Strauss and included with his letter of October 10, 1912.[71] This highly esoteric text presents an imaginary debate between a modern post-Enlightenment pantheist (for whom religion has become the culture of aesthetic forms in the Simmelian sense) and the defender of a religious-social ethic, who is closer to Benjamin himself. For the protagonist, the sober defender of a tragic modernist culture, there is only an elegy (*Nachtrauer*) for the disappearing value of metaphysics and at the same time a newfound freedom in the release from the "superfluous use of energy consumed in relating everything to metaphysics." Benjamin, by contrast, identifying with his opponent, sees in his Enlightenment interlocutor only "the degradation of human beings into "work-machines," and he advocates— along the lines of Wyneken's philosophy—a Goethean religiosity, "an inner striving for union with God."[72] His theme, the identification of the literary intellectual with religious purpose, was the subject of the first letter to Strauss. For this reason Benjamin's prophets at the time were "Tolstoy, Nietzsche, and Strindberg," the beacons of a "new man."[73]

Benjamin's third salvo to Strauss, written on November 21, 1912, began on a provocative note: "You are, I assume, aware that my correspondence with you in the matter of Zionism has a programmatic meaning for me."[74] Abandoning the "careful attitude" of his earlier letters, Benjamin attempted to articulate his "Jewishness" against the ideals of Zionism. "My experience," he wrote, "brought me to the insight: the Jews represent an elite in the party of the intellectuals [*geis-*

tigen]." But, as a prescriptive morality, or, in Benjamin's Kantian language, as a "maxim" that expresses the categorical imperative in the concrete world, "Jewishness" provides no guide. "For me Jewishness is not in any sense an end in itself, but the noble bearer and representative of the intellect." Again, he reiterates that a commitment to Zionism is impossible for him, because it would betray the ethical universalism of Wyneken: "I could come closer to the active Zionism, if it were less important. If it was something purely technical. But it is much more, it also contains a formal and definitely worked out Jewish attitude." He adds also that "an idea that is rationalized, freezes to a large extent life, cleans out the instincts."[75]

Instead Benjamin maintains his advocacy of ideals of youth in the Wyneken community—as cultural resistance, which he finds, in the works of an obscure Chinese writer, Wu Huang Ming, whose book *China: Verteidigung gegen europäische Ideen* represented a "radical cultural will." European culture in need of Oriental Despotism? Benjamin does not completely dismiss the idea: "Goethe says there is no true culture without despotism. Nevertheless, even if that may be correct, it is also worth striving for the despotism to be transformed from a physical one into an ideal one." Since today "no thoroughly cultivated and privileged ruling caste can be recognized, it is implicit that our cultural consciousness forbids us *ideally* from ever restricting the concept of culture to any single part of humanity."[76]

These reflections brought Benjamin, for the first time, to the question of the meaning of politics for Jewish intellectuals. In contrast to Buber/Strauss, he concluded in his third letter that there could be no satisfactory relationship between politics and ideas, "that politics are the consequence of intellectual principles no longer carried on by the intellect."[77] To politicize an idea was to deprive it of its ethical and spiritual validity. The idea loses its symbolic element, and it becomes simply "one's" idea; or as Benjamin put it, "out of God develops a fetish."[78] Sullied by politics, ethical ideas lose their substance and become simply agonistic forces in the arena of conflict. Activism was the death of the idea, and, conversely, as he later formulated it, "truth is the death of intention."[79]

Zionism, therefore, was an alternative *only* if it remained in the sphere of ideas—as the utopian promise of cultural universality, not politics: "For me Zionism was until now an idea, a *something,* which concerned me in a particular intellectual province. . . . But you want me to transform this idea into a political imperative." "I cannot make Zionism into my political element," he concluded, "because politics is the choice of the lesser evil, the idea never appears in it, only the party."[80]

Obviously aware that it meant the end of their relationship, Benjamin told Strauss that he would now fight against Zionism in the future. Zionism, he claimed, threatened to rob western Jews of their cultural potential. Zionism "as it exists, and as it can only exist," has as its "highest value nationalism," and the spiritual Zionism of Max Brod, or of Strauss himself, remains therefore "only an idea, and is thoroughly esoteric."[81] Politically, only the left was a real alternative (Social Democracy), not because it represented European culture, but because it alone could combat the nationalism that directly threatened that culture. Benjamin's confrontation with Buber's ideas led in the end not to a mutual embrace but to a distancing, first from personal Judaism, against which Benjamin posed the universal idea of intellectual culture, and second against political Zionism, which was compromised by its own nationalism. Benjamin, at the time, according to Scholem (they did not meet until July 1915), "thought little" of Buber's *Daniel: Dialogues of Realization* which appeared in 1913, and he was publicly critical of Buber during his appearance at a meeting of the Free Student Association in Berlin.[82] For Benjamin in 1913–1914, still the passionate advocate of the Wyneken youth culture, school reform (according to Wyneken's principles) was "a conviction [*Gesinnung*], an ethical program for our time."[83]

Benjamin closed his last lengthy communication to Strauss with the unequivocal statement that from the standpoint of "liberal culture," Zionism had to be rejected.[84] Judaism only plays "a partial role" in the complex "of my attitudes," and "the National-Jewish [attitude] of Zionist propaganda is not as important for me, as is the contemporary intellectual literary-Jew." Nevertheless, he conceded that he had not yet provided a definition of what he meant by "the creative culture-Jew." Benjamin's definition is "more of an image than a series of thoughts." It is an inverted tower of Babel: the people of the Bible pile stone upon stone, but the tower does not grow downward. The Jews, he wrote, "handle ideas like quarry stones." But they "build from above, without ever reaching the ground."[85]

IV.

It is striking that at the same moment, 1912, Ernst Bloch reached very similar conclusions. Paraphrasing Buber's metaphors of illness and

health from the *Speeches* in the sections of *Spirit of Utopia* composed
in that year and entitled "Über die Juden," he too found himself opposed to the rationalism and "liberal poison" from which the Jews of
Europe became "sick" and which left assimilated Jewry completely
"self-less."[86] Already in his 1908 doctoral dissertation on Heinrich
Rickert, which Bloch wrote under Hermann Cohen, he criticized Cohen
for his attachment to the postulates of a priori reason and for his inca-
pacity to grasp the transcendent imperatives of history. Cohen, he
charged, not only reduced "the spiritual life of man" to reason, but God
as well.[87]

Bloch also rejected Buber's idea of Judaism as a purely inner experience. It is not clear whether Bloch had known Buber, but both attended
Georg Simmel's private seminar in Berlin and had a mutual friend in
Margarethe Susman.[88] Bloch's critique of Buber also retains something
of Simmel's defense of the Jewish intellectual "Luftmensch," which was
Simmel's answer when, in 1909, Buber confronted him with his view
that the Jewish spirit rested on a "biological foundation."[89] Also influenced by Max Weber, Bloch cast Jewishness in terms of a cultural idea
or ideal type, a Jewish "world-feeling" that contains three elements: (1)
an attitude of enthusiastic and completely willful opposition to the
world (the position of Jewish intellectuals since Spinoza); (2) a utopian
impulse to transform life into purity, intellect, and unity—toward a just
world; (3) a vision of history that is explicitly messianic.[90] Bloch's dissertation concludes that "God's appearance at the end of history" is
dependent on "the daring of humankind to defy history," which requires "a knowledge of the eschatological end."[91] History for Bloch is
predicated on a future-oriented knowledge that transcends the empirical order of things, that does not take flight in false images or fall prey
to naturalism, but is directed beyond the existing world toward a yet
unrealized "messianic goal."[92]

Bloch also rejected Zionism because it threatened to negate the central cultural content of European Jewish experience, its messianism, by
reducing the idea of Judea to a completely prosaic rendering of the Jewish mission, "to an Asiatic Balkan state." The "assimilation addiction"
of liberal German Jewry had given way to "Zionism grounded in the
state," or to a denial of Jewishness in its entirety, a situation expressed
by the two poles of "modern Jewish false consciousness" embodied
in Karl Kraus and Martin Buber. On the one side was Jewish self-hate
and on the other Jewish nationalism, the amour propre that abandoned
the terrain of Jewish intellectual conflict with the Western tradition.

Both attitudes, "Jewish self-hate and the national flag," represented for Bloch "secondary reckonings in Jewish stock-taking," a retreat from the depths of Judaism and from the painful *Lehrjahre* of Jewish intellectuality.[93]

In contrast to Zionism, for Bloch messianism was the product of the great paradox of Jewish history: assimilation *and* a fanatical refusal to abandon the religious-cultural character of Judaism. Even early Christian communism and the Christian evangelium of the Second Coming are for Bloch essentially Jewish elements. Zionism also threatened to negate the central Jewish experience of "chosenness," a key to the messianic idea. Though he expresses it in the prophetic nonsequitur of his early writings, the measure of the estrangement of the Jews from Europe is their oppositional intellectualist culture, "the secret of Jewish history."[94] Bloch traces the origins of this radicalism through the epochs of Jewish wandering, which resulted in "a latent gnosticism," a clear opposition of "the good and the illuminated against everything petty, unjust and hard." Not Jesus, Bloch exhorted, but this negative Jewish message has remained dangerous because it is so completely uncompromising.[95]

Bloch's and Benjamin's confrontation with Buber and with Zionism affirmed a Jewish ideal that was at once secular and theological—and which represents an intellectualist rejection of the existing order of things. The messianic idea, though more pronounced in Bloch's early writings than in Benjamin's—which were preoccupied with Kant and grappling with Nietzsche—still comes through in their common emphasis on the limits of rationalism, the need to transcend ordinary modes of perception and experience through the utopian, and the restorative nature of the "language-work" of the intellectuals. As Richard Wolin points out, as early as 1914 Benjamin articulated a conception of history remarkably close to Bloch's: "The elements of the end condition are not present as formless tendencies of progress, but instead are embedded in every present as endangered, condemned, and ridiculed creations and ideas. The historical task is to give absolute form in a genuine way to the immanent condition of fulfillment, to make it visible and predominant in the present. . . . [H]owever, it is only comprehensible in its metaphysical structure, like the messianic realm or the idea of the French Revolution."[96]

The purpose of philosophy or criticism is not merely to point to the failures of rationalism to grasp the totality, it is to reveal through language the missing dimension of cultural experience, to restore the ellipse of Reason. For both Bloch and Benjamin, the Enlightenment represented a radical foreshortening of experience, the reduction of the rational to the real and vice versa. To create a post-Enlightenment philosophy meant finding an alternative to positivism that could fulfill the promise of returning thought to the realm of experience denied by rationalism. Nowhere is this purpose more clearly defined than in Benjamin's 1918 "Program of the Coming Philosophy," which points to the limits of Kant's notion of experience:

> But this is precisely what is at issue: the conception of the naked, primitive and self-evident experience, which, for Kant, as a man who somehow shared the horizon of his times, seemed to be the only experience given, indeed the only experience possible. This experience, however, . . . was unique and temporally limited. Above and beyond a certain formal similarity which it shared with any sense of experience, this experience, which in a significant sense could be called a *worldview,* was the same as that of the Enlightenment. In its most essential characteristics, however, it is not all that different from the experience of the other centuries of the modern era. It was an experience or a view of the world of the lowest order.[97]

For Benjamin, the "philosophy of the future" had to be concerned with demarking the provinces of experience denied or ignored by Kantianism, with its blindness to religion, the irrational, and history.[98]

The modern world was not simply disenchanted, in Weber's sense of the term, it was infinitely impoverished and lacking in a discourse that could adumbrate the nature of experience. Since language is also the origin of that experience for Benjamin, the new philosophy must not only analyze the fall of experience through language, it must discover a language that brings experience into being. This language, however, because it unraveled the secret of the present—its inner hope—had to remain esoteric. As Nietzsche exclaimed in his *Fröhliche Wissenschaft,* "One does want to be understood when one writes but just as surely *not* to be understood."[99]

Enlightenment could only be redeemed through a "higher concept of experience," one that could take into account the prerational, the magical, and even madness through images of a world beyond mere sense experience—the messianic world. For Bloch, too, the Enlightenment created a "hollow space" in which religion becomes an objective "other," an alien phenomenon rather than an authentic desire, resulting in the false authority accorded to reason in the modern age.

Margarethe Susman, who was close to Bloch in Berlin during that time and also attended Simmel's seminar, described him as "a man for whom the future burned like a great light on his forehead."[100] Simmel noted that he "had Eros" (*der hat den Eros*) in his thinking. He assumed a prophetic style in his mannerisms, gestures, and physiognomy. He personally tried to embody the ideal of a prophetic, anti-Enlightenment figure in his personal relations and "self-consciously tried to break through the conventional life forms, and expected the same from every human being whom he recognized as kindred."[101]

Bloch's posture irritated some acquaintances, especially the members of the famous Weber circle in Heidelberg, which Bloch attended in those years. Marianne Weber noted Bloch's appearance at the seminar as follows: "Suddenly a new Jewish philosopher was there—a youth with an enormous head of black wavy hair and equally enormous self-consciousness, he apparently considered himself to be the precursor of a new Messiah and hoped that everyone would recognize him as such."[102] Max Weber was so vexed by Bloch's prophetic manner, his outwardly religious amalgamation of Catholic, agnostic, apocalyptic, expressionist, and above all Jewish attitudes, that he said "the man cannot be taken seriously in scientific matters." His student, Maria Bernays, author of one of the first sociological studies of factory work, recalled Weber remarking, "I would like to send a porter to his house to pack his trunks and take them to the railroad station so that Bloch would go away."[103]

V.

Missing in the writings of Bloch and Benjamin before August 1914 is the radical and apocalyptic aspect of modern messianism. In this regard the war obliged them. After 1914 we see in both Bloch's and Benjamin's writings an attempt to find a secular and theological philosophy that can embody the messianic impulse in relation to a *real* apocalypse and to translate the promise of European culture into the promise of political redemption. Like so many intellectuals of their generation, the war was interpreted in terms of the collapse of Western culture and the triumph of technology and civilization. Though many embraced the war as the harbinger of a new and more violent modernity, Bloch and Benjamin were among its most resolute opponents and perceived the war as a total conflagration that threatened to consume all of bourgeois culture in the name of its own destructive values.[104] Benjamin's messianic theory of language, which he developed during the war, and Bloch's theological-messianic anarchism, embodied in *Spirit of Utopia,* are both

expressions of the powerless deracinated, universalistic, and cultural
Jewish philosophy in the face of its potential annihilation. The war gave
political shape to the idea of redeeming European culture and to the
implication of language in its crisis.

Benjamin's involvement in the Berlin Free Student Movement lasted
until the outbreak of the war, more specifically, until May 1915 when
his final break with Wyneken occurred.[105] Benjamin describes August
1914 in his *Berlin Chronicle:* "It was in that café (Café des Westens),
that we sat together in those very first August days, choosing among the
barracks that were being stormed by the onrush of volunteers. . . . I
duly appeared on one of the following days, no spark of war enthusiasm
in my heart."[106] After a few days on the endless queue, Benjamin gave
up trying to enlist. But it was the protest-suicide of his close friend Fritz
Heinle in August 1914 that moved him to reject the chorus of war ju-
bilation. In the "strongly willful" moral gesture of Heinle's act, Benjamin saw the meaning of a phrase that he had written but *not* delivered
in his speech to the youth movement in Breslau in October 1913: "This
epoch does not have a single form which permits us silent expression.
But we feel ourselves enslaved by speechlessness. We despise the facile
irresponsibility of written expression."[107] In his final letter to Wyneken,
Benjamin quotes this phrase against Wyneken's prowar *Der Krieg und
der Jugend* (1915), noting that his loyalty to Heinle now moved him to
refuse to speak to those who "write those lines about war and youth"
and who are guilty of "sacrificing youth to the state which has taken
everything from them."[108]

The war not only brought the final rupture with Wyneken but also
with Buber, with personal mysticism, and with German *and* Jewish nationalism. His important essay, "On Language as Such and on the Language of Man," written in November 1916, in the darkest hour of the
war, must be read between the lines as an esoteric response to Buber's
prowar and pro-German position.[109] Already in his 1912 letters to
Strauss, Benjamin identified the Jewish intellect with "expressive culture." In 1916 he returns to this theme to discuss the essence of language in its "immanent relationship with Judaism and in its relationship to the first chapter of Genesis."[110]

Benjamin's decision to "situate the crisis in the heart of language"
was occasioned by and coincided with the appearance of Buber's new
journal, *Der Jude,* in May of that year.[111] Benjamin's extremely negative
response to Buber's request for a contribution repeats some of the motifs of his earlier encounter with Strauss, but even more decisively.

Strauss too, it should be noted, also embraced the war with the remark that national Jews were no worse patriots than national Germans.[112] Benjamin, by contrast, noted the "intensity of opposition" that so many of the contributions to *Der Jude,* especially those concerned with the European war, elicited in him. He wrote that his "relationship to this journal is, and can in reality be, nothing more than what it is to all politically effective writings which the onset of the war finally and decisively opened for me." It was not simply that politics resulted in "writing and language that was powerless, denigrated to a pure means."[113] Nor was it only that with the war, "the relationship between word and deed has become a mechanism for the realization of the right absolutes."[114] What was at stake was not the war itself but the intellectual complicity of the Jews in their own betrayal as the "bearer and representative of the intellect." Here Benjamin articulates the political sense that his 1916 essay on language expressed in far more esoteric form.

> It is a widely noted, in fact generally accepted dominant opinion that writing can influence the moral world and the activities of human beings, insofar as it provides concrete motives for actions. In this sense language is only a means for a more or less suggestive *preparation* of motives, which are determinant in the inner soul of the actor. It is characteristic of this view, that it in no way takes into account the relationship of language to the act, insofar as the first is a means to the second.[115]

Language degenerates into "an impoverished, weak act" whose sources lie outside of itself, in political or ideological motives. Writing can be understood in a variety of ways, from prophecy to simple matter-of-factness, but the essence of language can be comprehended "only *magically,* that is im-*mediately.* Every salutary effect of the written (of the word, of language) that is not in essence deprecating rests in its secret. No matter in how many different forms language can be effective, this does not occur through the mediation of contents, but through the pure disclosure of its dignity and its essence."[116] "My conception of straightforward and at the same time highly political style and writing," he wrote to Buber, "is to indicate that which fails words; only there, only where this sphere of wordlessness reveals itself in its unspeakably pure power, can the magic spark between word and deed arise."[117]

Years later, in his ill-fated *Habilitationsschrift, The Origin of German Tragic Drama,* Benjamin returned to the theme of speechlessness as an antidote to the powerlessness of language as political discourse that preoccupied him in regard to the war and Fritz Heinle's fatal "gesture." Benjamin found in Franz Rosenzweig's theory of tragic silence confirmation for his own view of the stance of the tragic hero condemned to solitude and powerlessness. Drawing on Rosenzweig's *Stern der Erlösung,* Benjamin quotes him to the effect that speechlessness is the essence of the tragic self: " 'For this is the mark of the self, the seal of its greatness and the token of its weakness alike; it is silent. The tragic hero has only one language that is completely proper to him: silence.' "[118]

Benjamin's objection to Buber is not to his prowar stance per se but to his propagandistic self-annihilation of the intellectual—which he explicitly identifies as political. The task of the intellectual for Benjamin is "the elimination of the unspeakable in language," through writing that is suggestive of the actual relationship between word and act in linguistic magic.[119] Esoteric language is akin to the silence of the tragic hero, in the unsuccessful attempt to break out of its solitude. As the medium of truth, rather than as an instrument of politics, language is always doomed to a kind of speechlessness. "In his silence the tragic hero burns the bridges connecting him to God and the world, elevates himself above the realm of personality which in speech, defines itself against others and individualizes itself, and so enters the icy loneliness of the self."[120] This is a political stance, "since the community of the nation denies these achievements [of the tragic hero], they remain inarticulate."[121]

In short, the esoteric theory of language developed through Benjamin's encounter with Kabbalah and with the linguistic theories of the romantics and Johann Georg Hamann, set forth in the essay of 1916, represents a programmatic antipolitics. The esoteric language of the intellectual Jews is directed against the language of political instrumentalism. The expressive quality of language carries the hidden promise of redemption from power and judgment, a reminder of "the absolutely unlimited and creative infinity of the divine word."[122] Expressive culture, then, retains only a weak remembrance of the originary "paradisic language of man," he wrote. That language "must have been one of perfect knowledge, whereas later all knowledge is again infinitely differentiated in the multiplicity of language."[123] After the Fall, language is reduced to a "mere sign," to an instrument of judgment, and to abstraction: "Man abandoned immediacy in communication . . . and fell into the abyss of the mediateness of all communication."[124] The debasement of language from this Adamic state is identified with the fall of language and culture in the war, the catastrophe of war with the catastrophe of the word. What is lost is what he later described as the messianic world: "a world of an all-sided and integral actuality."[125] The traces of that world can still be felt in the power of naming, a mimesis of God's original act. The human capacity to create an identity between name and thing retains the memory of the original correspondence of object and signifier, initially present in the language of God and ultimately preserved in a kind of onomatopoesis, the imitation of the objects to which they refer.

In contrast to modern linguistics and Ferdinand de Saussure, whose *Course in General Linguistics* appeared in the same year, Benjamin does not see the arbitrary character of the sign as the "true nature" of language as an object of scientific study, but as the expression of the fallen world, the disenchantment of experience.[126] The loneliness of language gives its esoteric character a decisively tragic cast. Benjamin invests language with a messianic power precisely at the moment of its fall, its disintegration into propaganda. At the end of 1916 he wrote despairingly to his school friend Herbert Belmore, "We are in the midst of night. . . . The war threatens to take everything, art, truth, justice, out of our hands."[127] At the same time, however, he recognized that this power is not destined to win: "I once tried to fight it [the night] with words . . . but then I learned that whoever fights the night must remove the deepest darkness in order to yield *its* light, and in this great effort words are only a station."[128]

Georg Simmel and Max Weber played an analogous role for Bloch that Wyneken and Buber had played for Benjamin. Bloch later recalled that "in Heidelberg or among the elite intellectuals it was naturally assumed that one rejected the war and saw Wilhelm II, as before, as a disaster for Germany and the world."[129] But when Weber appeared in uniform and Simmel gave a lecture at Heidelberg that Bloch, his admiring student, attended, Bloch was horrified. "It was a prowar lecture, all-German to excess [*alldeutsch* bis zum exzess]." "That this friend of Bergson, the lover and admirer of French culture, of French kitchens and of French wine, participated in the war; and that he, the *Privatdozent* with the title 'Extraordinary Professor,' because as a Jew he could never get a University position in Berlin . . . , *even he* capitulated, *the man* who said to me: 'Future history will reveal two great disastrous epochs for Germany: the first, the Thirty Years War, the second Wilhelm II.' That was incomprehensible to me."[130]

In a letter that echoed Benjamin's to Wyneken and Buber, Bloch wrote to Simmel, "You have never sought a definite answer to anything, never. The absolute was always something completely suspect and inaccessible to you, as was the striving for the absolute. And praise to you! But now you have finally found it. Now the metaphysical for you is the German trenches."[131]

In 1917 the family fortune of Bloch's wife, Else Bloch-von Stritzky, collapsed, and the pair emigrated from Munich to Switzerland, first to Bern, then to Thun and Interlaken. Emigration was an act of "decisive" refusal to participate in the war and actively join the antiwar cause. Having completed *Spirit of Utopia,* Bloch undertook a study of "political programs and utopias in Switzerland" for Weber's *Archiv für Sozialwissenschaft und Sozialpolitik.*[132] Bloch joined the ranks of the "anti-Kaiser Germans" in Bern, where he was in close contact with a virtual who's who of the German exile intelligentsia in World War I. Along with Annette Kolb, Carl v. Ossietzky, and his close associate Hugo Ball, Bloch wrote for several exile newspapers including René Schickele's *Die weissen Blätter* and the *Freie Zeitung,* which he and Ball helped edit.[133] Bloch wrote literally hundreds of articles, under a variety of pseudonyms, covering an extraordinarily wide range of topics, most of them political.[134] He was supported financially by his wealthy friend, Dr. Johann Wilhelm Muehlon, the former Krupp attorney and diplomat whose antiwar writings in Swiss exile included revelations of secret government war preparations in July 1914, published as *Die Schuld der deutschen Regierung am Krieg.* Bloch's political engagement in those years, when he was still an anarchist and a pacifist and under frequent police surveillance, when as late as 1918 he called Lenin a "Red Czar," remains one of the most interesting and least unexplored periods of his entire career.[135]

Like Benjamin, Bloch too saw light in the depths of the night: ultimately the defeat of Germany would bury forever the feudal values of the Prussian upper classes and bring a kind of religious but democratic socialism to Germany. In 1918, the year that *Spirit of Utopia* appeared, Bloch published a pamphlet entitled "Would Military Defeat Help or Hurt Germany?"—answering, of course, in the affirmative. Though we might believe it could not be worse, Bloch wrote, the apocalypse was the only source of hope: from the external military defeat, the inner economic, political, and spiritual resurrection of Germany, "our hope remains . . . that Germany must first freely undergo the destruction and defeat of its military autocracy in an 'unhappy' outcome of the war, if its deeply buried currents of beclouded, dreamy piety . . . are to come to consciousness."[136]

The appearance of *Spirit of Utopia* established Bloch's reputation as the theologian of the German revolution. But its distinctive voice is not that of a systematic theologian but "of a great, angry, god-obsessed prophet." Bloch himself claimed that it was Simmel who recommended its publication because its originality so overshadowed "much that is incomprehensible, very subjective, fantastic, and inorganic."[137] Appropriately, the concluding chapter is entitled "Karl Marx, Death and the Apocalypse." *Spirit of Utopia* announces the messianic redemption that awaits the end of the war, a redemption that also brings about "the fruitful harvest of the apocalypse." A redeemed world without death and suffering could only be found in the ruins of the old order.[138] "There can be no image of that which lies above," he wrote, "without first brushing against death; it makes us blanch and removes the weightiness from our words."[139] Only in the cataclysm of the war could the promise of culture be realized in "an anarchist-expressionist determined world." For Bloch there was no contradiction between the arrival of a "spiritual aristocracy" and the communal production of goods, between elite culture and democracy, between socialism, anarchism, Marxism, Christianity, Judaism, and Eastern religion—all of those dichotomies evaporated in the "hour of death." The messianic and the political are completely identical: the radical idea of a community of the just and this-worldly redemption is simply one side of the otherworldly longing. The revolution reveals the singular truth that evil exists through God, "but the just—God exists through them, and in their hands is the salvation of the name, God's capacity to name is itself given to them."[140]

VI.

The parallel intellectual trajectories that brought both Bloch and Benjamin to Switzerland made their first meeting in 1919 an obvious occasion for enthusiasm. Both had begun a philosophical journey that passed through the apocalypse of European culture, and both had made a language of esoteric intellectualism the expression of a secular-theological messianism. In March or April 1919 the twenty-seven-year-old Benjamin was introduced to Bloch by Hugo Ball, the Dadaist and anti-Prussian republican exile, whom he had befriended, along with Ball's companion, Emmy Hennings.[141] At the time Bloch, who was seven years older than Benjamin, was working on his never completed magnum opus, the "System of Theoretical Messianism." Benjamin was immediately taken with his personality, finding him "receptive to questions of Judaism."[142] But the meeting and friendship of these two carriers of the messianic idea also revealed a substantial area of conflict: politics. In their conflict the ethical dilemma inherent in the messianic idea surfaced with uncharacteristic sharpness. By 1919 Bloch had become a socialist. He had spent the two years in Switzerland deeply embroiled in the politics of the exile community. Yet he was still far from fully embracing either the Russian or the German revolution. For him the direction of the antiwar left symbolized by the Zimmerwald movement (after the conference of September 1915, which upheld the idea of class war and international socialism against all the belligerents) labored under the illusion that there was no distinction to be made between the Entente democracies—America, England, and France—and the German autocratic state.[143] Though he placed his hopes in the democratic powers, France and America, and though he was skeptical of both the Russian experiment (state socialism) and the potential for socialism in Germany, Bloch had already begun his own path to Marxism.[144]

Benjamin's rejection of politics was equally emphatic. Though both Bloch and Ball tried to convince Benjamin of the necessity of political activity, he remained unmoved, despite his concern for friends, especially Gustav Landauer, caught up in the maelstrom of the Munich revolution. His philosophy of language was an antipolitics; his rejection of Buber's personal Judaism for the idea of redemption through the word barred the path to action. The messianic idea for him was, as Scholem put it, "*a life lived in deferment,* in which nothing can be done definitively, nothing can be irrevocably accomplished."[145] For Benjamin, the instrumentalization of language in all political judgment made it complicit in violence. Already in 1917, he condemned Hegel as "an intellectual man of violence, a mystic of violence, the worst sort that there is."[146] Bloch, in contrast, despite his professed pacifism, was hardly shy about revolutionary violence. *Spirit of Utopia,* for example, contains the phrase, "It is necessary to oppose established power with appropriately powerful means, like a categorical imperative with a revolver in your fist."[147]

Benjamin's first reaction to Bloch's *Spirit of Utopia,* which he read in 1919, was therefore one of disappointment for both political and philosophical reasons. Writing to Ernst Schoen, he noted that Bloch himself was "ten times better" than his book, but he also remarked that this was the only book against which he could compare himself, "a truly contemporary and synchronous expression."[148] Elsewhere he is similarly ambivalent, noting his impatience with the book but also that his kinship (*verwandtschaft*) with Bloch stirs him. For him, the most interesting passage is a quote from the Kabbalah (misattributed by Bloch to the Zohar), which he cites from *Spirit of Utopia* in a letter to Scholem.

> Know that there is a double view for all worlds. The first shows its external side, namely the general laws of the world according to its external form. The other shows the inner side of the essence of worlds, namely the essence of the human soul. Accordingly there are two levels of acts, works and the orders of prayers; works are there to perfect the world in accordance with the external, the prayer, however, is there to place this world in the other and to raise it up toward heaven.[149]

Though his review is presumed lost, it is clear that Benjamin resisted the strange blend of Christianity and Jewish messianism entwined in Bloch's this-worldly eschatology and his optimistic utopianism.[150] We also know that Benjamin devoted the conclusion of his review to a critique of Bloch's epistemology.[151] Benjamin remarked (somewhat exaggeratedly) that the book made him mistrustful and that although he saw some of his ideas confirmed in it, "it nowhere corresponded to my idea of philosophy, but rather is diametrically opposed to it."[152]

Scholem also found much to his distaste in *Spirit of Utopia*. In a letter to Benjamin, he noted his dissatisfaction with the Jewish sections of the work (which Bloch subsequently omitted).

> The following remarks are based mainly on the sections entitled "Über die Juden" and "Über die Gestalt der unkonstruierbaren Fragen" [The Form of the Unconstruable Questions]; to the extent that I have understood these correctly, I most violently reject them. I have the impression that here Bloch encroaches, in the worst fashion and with inappropriate means, upon an area whose boundaries the book might at best define. With the gesture of a magus (and, woe, I know the sources of this magic!) he makes statements about the stories of the Jews, history, and Judaism, which clearly bear the terrible stigma of Prague (in my linguistic usage, that meant Buber); it's no use, even the terminology is from Prague. The Jewish generation that Bloch has invented does not exist; it exists only in the intellectual realm of Prague.[153]

It is interesting that Scholem identifies the influence of Buber in Bloch's renderings of Jewish mysticism in *Spirit of Utopia,* but the above-mentioned "source" is probably Johann Andreas Eisenmenger's two-thousand-page anti-Semitic work on Jewish mysticism published in 1701, which Bloch told Scholem he had read from "the opposite point of view" during his first meeting with him in May 1919.[154] Scholem went on to criticize the amalgamation of Jewish kabbalistic and Christian motifs in the work, an intermingling of testimonies that he found "indiscriminate."[155]

Benjamin noted that he was in "full agreement" with Scholem's comments on the Jewish chapter, particularly as far as a certain "impalpability of distance" that characterizes the work.[156] Benjamin also found Salomo Friedländer's review of *Spirit of Utopia* in Kurt Hiller's journal *Ziel* "highly interesting" and affirmed that it "brought to light its weaknesses with real thoroughness."[157] Here Benjamin meant what Hiller called its "undiscussable Christology," its exultant "schwärmerisch" metaphysics of pure inwardliness, and above all its confusing amalgamation of the first, second, and third testaments that was the butt of Friedländer's scathing sarcasm.[158] Friedländer, himself an extraordinary figure on the fringes of the Oskar Goldberg circle of modern Jewish "Kabbalists" was a Jewish Nietzschean whose book *Schöpferische Indifferenz* (Creative Indifference) is a form of Jewish apocalypticism of another stripe.[159] The identification of the messianic breakthrough with both Jewish and Christian redemption, the mysticism of the Russian revolution as the "breakthrough of the power of love," galled Friedländer's Nietzschean soul: "This is the melody that the music of this book makes . . . to tastelessness and absurdity, Christian, un-Zarathustrian, un-Dionysian."[160] *Spirit of Utopia* was a work of clever obscurantism that created the appetite for a new church: "Its most noble sentiments lead, without reason, without logical law, to babble, to chaos."[161]

Compared to the statements of the Zimmerwald left, the political program of *Spirit of Utopia* was manifestly vague. Bloch's apocalyptic religiosity stood in marked contrast to Lenin's famous rejection of the Second International pacifism and his readiness to see the war as the opportunity to initiate a class war and bring about revolution. Indeed, Bloch's *Spirit of Utopia* was so lacking in any "indices for practical application" that the wartime censor judged it "harmless."[162] Still, Bloch's enthusiasm for the Russian revolution, along with his negative evaluation of Lenin and Bolshevik methods, is often more prescient than that of many of his compatriots, acknowledging the truth of the rumors of terror and warning of the Bolshevik fetishism of central authority and power. By 1918, Bloch's hopes rested not with Lenin and the Bolsheviks but with Woodrow Wilson and the Entente, for a peace secured by an "armed pacifism." Those hopes were soon dashed, however, and the German revolution of November 1918 brought a change in Bloch's evaluation of the chances for socialism in Germany. The war had so ruined *all* of the German classes, he now speculated, that the basis for socialism was created. Once again the redemptive moment arises from the destructive power of war.

Behind Bloch's political pamphlets and articles of 1918–1919 we can see a volatile though not always clear-sighted thinker whose redemptive politics were constantly confronted with unanticipated revolutionary events. Unlike Benjamin, who had thus far evaded the essential question of violence posed not only by *Spirit of Utopia* but also by the events of that crucial year in German history, Bloch was adamant that politics could not be avoided, certainly not in 1918–1919. Some twenty years later Bloch reconstructed the argument that seemed to him most persuasive: Bloch was determined not to reenact "the misfortune which had beset even greater spirits of the past, . . . the many German poets and thinkers who wavered at the time of the French Revolution."[163]

That it was Bloch who provoked Benjamin to reflect on the nature of politics is evident from a letter to Ernst Schoen: It was "more than his [Bloch's] book, but also his conversation that was so often directed against my rejection of *every* contemporary political tendency, that finally caused me to immerse myself in the matter." Bloch, he added, "was the only person of importance who I met in Switzerland."[164] This letter marks the beginning of his writings about politics—and not, as is sometimes claimed, his "conversion" to Marxism after his famous meeting with Asja Lacis in Capri in July 1924. Wolin has suggested, for example, that Sandor Rádnoti's comment that Benjamin stood largely outside the revolutionary events taking place in his German "homeland" is misplaced since, as a Jew, he did not consider Germany his homeland.[165] While it is true, as Wolin points out, that Benjamin's philosophy of history "condemns history *in toto* as categorically *incapable of fulfillment*" and therefore finds little consolation in the vicissitudes of everyday politics—even revolutionary politics—his argument still operates within the terms of a sudden, overnight turn from "unpolitical messianism" to Marxism in 1924. As I have suggested, Benjamin conceived, as did Bloch, of esoteric messianism as a form of politics—as a politics against politics in the prewar and war epoch. To search for the reasons for Benjamin's lack of *engagement* in the years from 1919 to 1924 may be a question *mal posée*.

After meeting Bloch in the fall of 1919, Benjamin's writings reflect a profound inner battle with the problem of violence and activism in general, and with the writings of Georges Sorel in particular. As his 1916 essay on language was a confrontation with the war and the Jewish response to the war, his political essays of the early 1920s (unfortunately, the most important may be among those missing) are a confrontation with the German revolution and the Jewish response to it. Benjamin characterized his position in those years as "theocratic anarchism," which "was the most sensible response to politics."[166] In his September 19, 1919, letter to Schoen he speaks of "thoughts" he had written down on the subject of "politics."[167] In April 1920 he mentions a note entitled "Life and Violence" written, he says, "from the heart."[168] Probably even more important is the lost essay on politics conceived as a response to the Blochean challenge. But even the names of the titles of the "second part," mentioned in a letter to Scholem, are evocative of the spirit of the essay: entitled "True Politics" it contained two subtitles, "Demolition of Violence" and "Teleology without Goal."[169] In conjunction with the planned work on politics, during the new year 1920–1921 Benjamin became more acquainted with Sorel's *Réflexions sur la violence* (1906–1908), which plays a crucial role in the only significant essay to survive this period, "Critique of Violence." Benjamin began reading Sorel, according to Scholem, "as a result of his conversations with [Hugo] Ball and Bloch," after which "coming to terms with Sorel occupied him for a long time to come."[170] In addition to the work by Sorel, Benjamin praised a little-known work by Erich Unger, a member of the Oskar Goldberg circle of Berlin Kabbalists, *Politik und Metaphysik*. Benjamin considered Unger's book "the most important writing on politics of this time."[171]

Once again in esoteric form, Benjamin considered the problem of revolution from the heights of a messianic philosophy of history that in principle rejected any intrinsic relationship between "activism" and utopia. According to Scholem, "Critique of Violence" contains "all of the motifs that moved him during his time in Switzerland," and along with the short piece later entitled "Theologisch-Politisches Fragment" remain the only important sources for his thinking on the question of violence at that time.[172] As the war found its esoteric-allegorical expression in the essay "On Language," the revolution found its expression in the "Fragment" and the essay on violence. Announcing what appears to be a challenge to Bloch's promiscuous amalgamation of apocalyptic history and messianism, the "Fragment" begins with the sentence, "Nothing historical can relate itself on its own account to anything messianic." But also here for the first time the problem of redemption is posed in the political realm.

Benjamin's debt to Bloch is openly acknowledged in the "Fragment," but in a very ambiguous sense. The laconic sentence, "To have repudiated with utmost vehemence the political significance of theocracy is the cardinal merit of Bloch's *Spirit of Utopia*," can be read against the grain of Bloch's own revolutionary messianism, which amalgamates politics and messianism in a way that Benjamin explicitly rejects. The preceding sentence, "Therefore the order of the profane cannot be built up on the idea of the Divine Kingdom, and therefore theocracy has no political, but only a religious meaning," seems to inveigh against Bloch's most fundamental political sensibility, the fusion of hierocratic and secular politics.[173] The programmatic rejection of politics is clearly emphasized. "The order of the profane should be erected on the idea of happiness," Benjamin writes, but this idea is the very antithesis of the messianic order of things. The messianic idea cannot tolerate the earthly Kingdom: "the Kingdom of God is not the telos of the historical dynamic." Yet the "Fragment" also places the relationship between revolutionary violence and messianism in another, perhaps more sympathetic light. Though "the quest of free humanity for happiness runs counter to the messianic direction," the actions of human beings can, "just as force can, through acting, increase another that is acting in the opposite direction, so the order of the profane assists, through being profane, the coming of the messianic Kingdom." It does this by bringing about misfortune and suffering, which, in its transience, presses toward the messianic epoch. "For Nature," Benjamin writes, "in contrast to history, is messianic by reason of its eternal and total passing away."[174]

The tenor of these essays might be described as "anarchomessianic," in sharp contrast to Bloch's embryonic Marxism. This is evident, not only in the lengthy paean to Sorel's revolutionary syndicalism in the "Critique" but in the complex ways those essays acknowledged the affinities of revolutionary thought and action with the messianic idea while pitting the messianic idea against legitimate state-sanctioned power and violence. As Bloch was rapidly moving toward Marxism, Benjamin was approaching the messianic anarchism espoused by Bloch at the time of their first meeting.

Though Benjamin's letters rarely reveal much about his political opinions on contemporary issues, Scholem mentions the importance of events in Russia and Germany for Benjamin in 1919, as well as the November 1919 General Strike in Switzerland, "which the Swiss government put down by force of arms." Scholem also recalls the importance for both Benjamin and himself of the problem of revolutionary dictatorship, particularly for the events unfolding in Russia. According to Scholem,

> I represented the more radical point of view and defended the idea of dictatorship—which Benjamin then still completely rejected—provided that it was a "dictatorship of poverty," which to me was not identical with a dictatorship of the proletariat. I would say that our sympathies were to a great extent with the Social Revolutionary party in Russia which later was liquidated so bloodily by the Bolsheviks. We also discussed the question of republic and monarchy, and to my surprise Benjamin opposed my decision in principle in favor of the republic. . . . Even under present conditions a monarchy might be a legitimate and acceptable form of government.[175]

In the end, however, Benjamin reaffirmed his rejection of the connection between history and the messianic impulse. Yet history is somehow implicated in the coming of messianism, if only negatively, through its completely profane character. This image of history as a catastrophic "second nature," which can be attributed to his reading of Lukács's *History and Class Consciousness,* will continue to play an important role in Benjamin's philosophy.

That image is even more evident in the final pages of "Critique of Violence" where the discussion of the origins of violence and of law in myth and history ends in a disavowal of mythic and historic force, and in the affirmation of divine violence, which represents justice and is the negation of force and power: "Lawmaking is power making, and, to that extent, an immediate manifestation of violence. Justice is the principle of all divine end making, power the principle of all mythical lawmaking."[176] Benjamin counterpoises two closely aligned conceptions of force in Western culture, the constitutive violence that establishes (*rechtssetzend*) and maintains (*rechtsherhaltend*) law—originating in the mythic violence of the Greek gods—with the divine violence (*rechtsvernichtend*) that negates and destroys the legally sanctioned violence of the state. The direct analogue to this conception of divine violence in contemporary politics is explicitly acknowledged as Sorel's rendition of the proletarian violence of the General Strike. When Sorel exclaims that "the revolution appears as a clear, simple revolt," Benjamin adds that "against this deep, moral, and genuinely revolutionary conception, no objection can stand that seeks, on grounds of its possibly catastrophic consequences, to brand such a general strike as violent."[177]

In both the "Fragment" and the "Critique" the messianic idea stands outside of and opposed to any immanent historical activism that might bring about its realization. Benjamin rejects both the natural right jus-tification of revolutionary terrorism derived from the French revolution and the gradualism that seeks to replace one form of state power with another. At the same time, both essays have a decisive affinity to anar-chism, the first in its Sorelian praise of violence opposed to power and the second in the idea that the quest for happiness, because it is doomed to bringing about unhappiness, aids the "task of world politics, whose method must be called nihilism."[178]

In both essays the conflict between the Jewish messianism that rejects politics and still sees language as the one "nonviolent sphere of human accommodation" and the new radicalism of the German revolution that embraces revolutionary violence are only roughly reconciled. These essays reveal an impossible dilemma: the attempt to find a point of continuity between Benjamin's abhorrence of the German reaction re-sponsible for the death of a much admired and kindred spirit, Gustav Landauer, and the collapse of the Munich Räterepublik, and a Jewish messianism that situates redemption in language rather than in the vi-cissitudes of revolution, history, and the time-space continuum.

The dilemma reappears even more strongly in Benjamin's essay on Dostoyevsky's *The Idiot*, occasioned in part by his reading of a volume of Dostoyevsky's political writings published in Munich in 1917.[179] Benjamin called the volume "the most important political work that he knew."[180] Dostoyevsky was also the figure who tied Bloch (as well as Lukács) to the Russian revolution, albeit for different reasons. Bloch and Lukács greeted the Russian revolution as a profoundly Dostoyev-skian event. As Bloch later recalled, "I myself participated in this gen-eral feeling when I wrote in *Spirit of Utopia* that the Russian revolution was the act of a new Praetorian guard who enthroned Christ as em-peror for the first time." "For us," he added, "this was Russian Chris-tianity, the spiritual universe of Tolstoy and Dostoyevsky."[181] For Lukács too it was the "ethical" implications of Dostoyevsky that con-vinced him of the higher morality—above all of the spiritual commu-nity and suffering—that the Russian revolution embodied.[182] "If the revolution had broken out in France, it wouldn't have had the same im-pact on him," Bloch said of Lukács. "It would have been a simple affair of the brain. But Russia was an affair of the heart."[183]

Significantly, what interested Benjamin was not Dostoyevsky's essay on the Jewish Question, about which he is oddly silent, but rather the theme of the redemptive and pure humanity of the Russian people in its childlike youthfulness: "As the political doctrine of Dostoyevsky constantly declares the regeneration in the pure *Volkstum* to be the last hope, so the poet recognizes in this book (*The Idiot*) the child as the only salvation for the youth of their land."[184] Despite his clear differences with Bloch and Lukács about the problem of violence and the ethics of revolution, Benjamin shared their emotional attraction to Russia as the antithesis of Western rationalism with its ethical pantheism and primacy of economics over life. The revolution in Russia, he intimated, revealed a "proletariat with a child-soul," which paradoxically justified both a democratic communitarianism and a *deep* elitism, mirrored, for example, in Bloch's belief that the revolution would create a "spiritual aristocracy," or in Lukács's parallel view that the new higher ethic of the revolution would bring about a new moral caste.[185] But for Benjamin it was not *only* the spiritual dimension of Dostoyevsky, but his perspective of the abyss that was paramount: "The immeasurable depth of the crater, out of which the most powerful forces of human greatness can release themselves with singular enormity, that is the hope of the Russian people."[186] For that reason he applauded the far more pessimistic conclusion that "because nature and childhood are absent, mankind is destined to arrive at a catastrophic self-destruction."[187]

VII.

Both Bloch and Benjamin embodied what Leo Baeck once called "messianic irony," the certitude of redemption and the bleak pessimism that such certainty demands: "Only those who are imbued with this pessimism, this mockery, this protest and this irony are the really great optimists who hold fast to the future and lead the world a step further toward it."[188] Yet the tensions in the messianic tradition are not easily suffered. Bloch and Benjamin ultimately represented the antinomies of messianic politics: on the one side, the rejection of the world and violence in an apocalyptic vision; on the other, a radical affirmation of the new and creative destruction of the old order in what Bloch called "a colorful explosion of forms."[189] The tension here is not simply between action and passivity but between the normal politics of terrestrial beings and a politics that transcends any spatial dimension. Language is the medium of redemption, but history is the showplace of catastrophe. Esoteric intellectualism as a Jewish response to personal and political Zionism—and as a negative response to the war—could not compete with the demands of political culture in the revolutionary epoch. The claims of Jacobinism, with its dialectic of political disaster, were too strong, the politics of "Eastern Marxism" too persuasive to resist. By 1920 Bloch had turned the messianic vision into a political identification with the revolutionary left, while Benjamin adopted a theocratic anarchism that upheld the ideal of "pure violence" not directed at specific political ends but rather at the destruction of all legal violence that is mythical and unjust. This is only a single step from embracing the sectarian messianism of the revolution, which Benjamin apparently took in 1924. Nonetheless, as his *Moscow Diaries* demonstrate just two years later, he never took that step unequivocally, and just as often stepped away from it.[190]

The consequences of Jewish messianism for the legacy of critical theory are not difficult to imagine. Adorno summed up Benjamin's impact: "As a critic of violence, Benjamin as it were breaks down the unity of the subject into mythic turmoil in order to comprehend such unity as itself being only a natural condition; with his philosophy of language oriented on the Kabbalah, Benjamin saw subjective unity as scribbling of the Name. That links his materialistic period with his theological one. He viewed the modern world as archaic not in order to conserve the traces of a purportedly eternal truth, but rather to escape the trance-like captivity of bourgeois immanence."[191]

In the 1920s and 1930s, Bloch and Benjamin represented the warm current in the cold sea of an increasingly Sovietized European Marxism. The "anarchic breeze" of Jewish messianism blew fresh air into the house that Lenin built. True to tradition, of course, they both ended up as Marxist heretics. Bloch and Benjamin were practically unique in recognizing that orthodox Marxism could not be genuinely concerned with the fate of European culture because it was unable or unwilling to envision the possibility of its destruction. As the heir to the Enlightenment, the Marxism of the Second and Third internationals was tied to a view of history that could not admit that a total eclipse of reason was possible. Marxist productivism participated in the cultural hegemony that it claimed to contest, even more uncritically embracing the industrial ethos than did the bourgeois ideologists of the nineteenth century.

For Benjamin and Bloch, only an authentic messianism, which did not see history as the progressive unfolding of the rational, which was attuned to the poverty of experience that they maintained Enlightenment left in its wake, and which accepted the possibility of apocalypse could recognize in fascist politics a false reenchantment of the world. For this reason it was clear to both Bloch and Benjamin that fascism could not be defeated by denouncing it as false consciousness, that as a socially powerful myth of redemption it could fill the "hollow space" that a Marxism divested of utopia could not even imagine.[192]

Nor did Bloch and Benjamin join Lukács and other orthodox Marxists in a rationalist rejection of aesthetic modernism.[193] They understood that expressionism (Bloch) or surrealism (Benjamin) represented genuine challenges to the false promise of autonomous art—the creation of a world of beauty above labor or violence. A decade later the messianism of these thinkers was subsumed into aesthetics by the critical theory of the Frankfurt School, which retained from the messianic idea only the premise that art was the repository of utopian images. Benjamin, and later Adorno, clearly understood that the tragedy of the modern was its condemnation to the "eternal recurrence of the new as sameness," the leitmotiv of Benjamin's unfinished work on the Paris of Baudelaire. For Benjamin, the modern, unlike classical antiquity, represented the "new in opposition to the eternal return of the same."[194] Baudelaire, Blanqui, and Nietzsche discovered, each in his own domain, the secret of the modern, that the promise of the new was eternal sameness, a substitution of a transitory *Erlebnis* for real experience. The result was the melancholia of the modern, the price of reinventing itself at every moment. The promise of modernism was only the ephemeral fleeting moment of redemption that is consumed instantly.

It is its openness to catastrophe that gives modern messianism its fire and its urgency about culture. Redemptive critique is never personal, always universal and historical, since only a true reading of the past can present the image of the future—even if the present is bent on destruction. But precisely because of its radical utopianism, the messianic idea is fundamentally unreliable in the world of "facts and exigencies." Its political claims are dubious because of its propensity to "otherworldly" esoteric reflection, on the one side, and the magnetic draw of revolution, on the other. For this reason the messianic idea always threatens to subvert itself into a Machiavellian disregard for civil liberties or ethical norms in the name of virtue. As Ferenc Fehér observed in his perceptive comments on the young Lukács, but which applies to Bloch and Benjamin as well, "Without the norm of Enlightenment—which includes respect for dissenting opinions, so marked in Luxemburg and so totally lacking in Lenin—there is no way of forecasting whether the romantic rebellion will follow Lukács' or Heidegger's political path. Without this norm it can only result in destructive consequences, however different they may be."[195] In this sense both Bloch and Benjamin never resolved the dilemma of the early 1920s: how to transform a fundamentally Janus-faced vision of utopia into a clear program of political emancipation. This is the negative side of utopia, one which parallels the negative side of Enlightenment so clearly diagnosed by the messianic vision.

If messianic Jewish philosophers like Bloch and Benjamin have become out of date, it is not because the "culture of redemption" is exhausted, or because the reparative project of art requires a devaluation of experience.[196] The philosophical currents represented by Bloch and Benjamin in the first part of the century contemplated all things as they would present themselves from the standpoint of redemption, because they conceived of the apocalypse as a historical event. They believe, as Adorno pointed out, that "knowledge has no light but that shed on the world by redemption." From that perspective, "the reality or unreality of redemption itself hardly matters."[197] It may well be the case that because we have learned to live with the apocalypse, messianic thinking is not radical any longer. And if the apocalypse is no longer terrifying, there is no point in creating an image of what might come afterward. As Nadezhda Mandelstam once wrote, "Fear and hope are bound up with each other. Losing hope we lose fear as well—there is nothing to be afraid for."[198]

The Inverted Nationalism of Hugo Ball's *Critique of the German Intelligentsia*

I.

Hugo Ball's *Critique of the German Intelligentsia* is simultaneously a historical document and a provocation. A passionate indictment of the German intelligentsia for its chauvinism in the First World War, the *Critique* is also an extraordinary example of the messianic politics that inaugurated the epoch. Above all, it is the consummate performance of its author's extraordinary career, which in only a few years took Ball from Munich's expressionist avant-garde to the founding of Dada in Zurich to theological anarchism and antiwar politics in Bern and, only a year and a half later, to the spiritual refuge of Catholic faith.

First published in January 1919, the *Critique* is a passionately argued historical account of how German religion and philosophy conspired with dynastic absolutism and militarism to produce the disastrous betrayal of August 1914. Conceived in part as a counterstatement to the "Manifesto of the 93 Intellectuals" of October 1914, in which the elite of German arts and letters signed a statement that denied German responsibility for the war and condemned the West, the *Critique* offered a brilliant refutation. But in esoteric counterpoint to the work's insightful and critical dimension was Ball's uniquely theological politics, culminating in an apocalyptic vision in which Bakuninist anarchism, French romantic poetry, and chiliastic revolt combine to restore the originary ideal of Christian justice sacrificed to throne and altar. In Ball's words, Luther's revolt "betrayed God to authority" and sanctioned subordination to the nation, while Kant's categorical imperative fashioned a "divine foundation for this devilish reality." Catastrophe and anticipation thus fuel the *Critique*'s mood of rhetorical urgency and its desire for a final conflagration of the German "spirit" that would usher in a new order of things.

From the perspective of the anti-utopian revolutions of our own time, the *Critique*'s messianism as well as the arguments that Ball mustered against what he regarded as the heritage of German intellectual authoritarianism seem somewhat antiquated. Yet Ball's astonishingly accurate prediction that the failure of German intellectuals to grasp the reasons for the defeat of 1918 would soon have disastrous consequences, intensifying rather than diminishing the nationalist currents of the war years, was certainly prescient enough to warrant taking his indictment seriously. Nor has the *Critique*'s central theme—the cultural and political distinctiveness of the German intelligentsia, the corrupting influence of Germany's intellectual isolation from Western Europe and America, its lack of a democratic ethos—lost any of its relevance. Considered obsolete only a few years ago, the question of whether Germany will gradually return to its traditional role as a Central European "land of the middle" and perhaps eventually abandon its identification with Anglo-Saxon democratic culture has returned as a frequent journalistic theme. As they did in 1918 after Unification, some German intellectuals have even taken to the podium to disavow democratic commitments and responsibility for past crimes as expressions of a "national masochism" inhibiting the emergence of a self-conscious nation.[1] Even the much praised democratic stability and lack of a strong nationalist or xenophobic fringe, characteristic at least of the Federal Republic since the 1960s, can no longer be taken for granted.

Certainly the *Critique*'s single-mindedly theocentric approach to German history has not withstood the decades of historical debate. If Ball's assertion that Lutheranism and classical idealist philosophy conspired to sanction blind subservience to autocratic politics by splitting conscience from obedience was an original insight in 1919, it has long since become a dubious historiographical cliché. Nor is Ball's revolutionary insurrectionism, or his radical revival of romantic and Catholic spirituality, consistent with his political enthusiasm for the Entente and Wilsonian democracy. As the previous chapter has demonstrated, the German exile writers of the *Freie Zeitung* were often reacting to political events in ways that sometimes underscored the limits of their own messianic philosophy. Typically, Ball's arguments on behalf of the Anglo-American and Anglo-French achievement of human rights are often betrayed by the book's illiberal judgments, "fin du fin" rhetoric, querulousness, and unabashed anti-Semitism.

Throughout the text the catastrophe of the war is identified with a German spiritual apocalypse, with a tradition of thought that—from Luther to Marx—led inexorably to 1914. Ball's insistence on an equivalence here is highly ambiguous. We might apply Derrida's ironic comment that the apocalyptic tone does not easily allow us to disentangle "who, or what, is directed to whom," since it is precisely this uncertainty about who is speaking and to whom that makes it apocalyptic. The presumed linkage between anarchism, democracy, antidynastic politics, the language of redemption, and the metaphysics or "onto-theology" of a historical catastrophe bears witness to the confusions and fissures in the mental makeup of the revolutionary antiwar opposition in Swiss exile. Finally, though it has much in common with other Jewish and Protestant esoteric and metaphysical doctrines of catastrophe and redemption typical of that particular historical moment (and discussed in the previous chapter), Ball's curious brew of Catholic messianism and Germanophobic Bakuninist anarchism is marred by a degree of anti-Semitism that, for reasons that will become clear shortly, was either ignored or went unacknowledged in the considerable scholarly writing on Ball that has appeared since his death in 1927.[2]

Ball himself repudiated much of the *Critique* after his reconversion to Catholicism in 1920, and in 1924 he published a heavily revised version reflecting his unpolitical Catholicism under the title *Die Folgen der Reformation*. In 1970 an expurgated and sanitized edition of the *Critique* appeared in Munich. The edition published by Suhrkamp in 1980 was unaltered, probably inadvertently. Consequently, the adulterated version is the only form in which the *Critique* is available in the German language today. Brian Harris's first English-language translation, published in 1993 by Columbia University Press, is an event of considerable scholarly significance insofar as it restores all of the excised passages, making it the first authentic version of the *Critique* to appear since the original edition under Ball's own imprimatur of the Freie Verlag in Bern in 1919.[3] Those restored passages reveal that the anti-Semitism of the original text was not merely an incidental embarrassment, but that Ball's Judeophobia was integral to his rejection of the war, the German revolution, and the nationalist intelligentsia of the late Wilhelmine era. With the missing passages reinstated, what emerges is not merely a complete text but also the highly problematic and ambiguous relationship of the *Critique* to the political culture of the democratic West and the very German ideology that it purports to criticize.

II.

Hugo Ball wrote the *Critique of the German Intelligentsia* when he was thirty-three years old. Completed with a rapidity that astonished even its author, it was conceived in the fall of 1917 and published in January 1919. The circumstances of the *Critique*'s genesis is not inconsistent with a life full of quixotic reversals, sudden leaps, and steep emotional ascents and descents. Of Ball's intellectual biography it might be said that the only thing predictable is its disjointedness. By 1919 Ball had distinguished himself as a leading expressionist poet and playwright, as a theoretician of the Munich avant-garde, as the founder of Zurich Dada, and as an indefatigable antiwar publicist. The *Critique* was Ball's first full-scale venture into sustained intellectual activity, an attempt to harmonize his political opposition to the war with his odd philosophical blend of radical anarchism and Catholic gnosticism. The *Critique* can thus be viewed as a single station on the strange artistic and political itinerary that finally ended in August 1920 in the village chapel of Agnuzzo, where Ball found what he called the "solution to the question of guilt" and returned to the devout Catholic orthodoxy that he sustained until his premature death in 1927.[4]

Born in the town of Pirmasens in the Rhineland Palatinate in 1886, Ball grew up in a large and deeply religious Catholic family. His lifelong companion, Emmy Hennings, whom he met in 1913, recalled that Ball's mother taught him only "to stand, to walk, and to pray."[5] As a student in Heidelberg and later in Munich, Ball was scornful of the strictures and dogmas of his childhood, evident in his enthusiastic embrace of Nietzsche, the subject of his never completed dissertation written at the University of Munich in 1910.[6] Somewhat mistitled "Nietzsche in Basel: A Polemic," it presents the view of the philosopher then prevalent among the Munich avant-garde. Nietzsche stood for the "emancipation of the passions, of the drives, of nature, including a correspondingly magnificent subjugation through art."[7] The expressionist avant-garde elevated Nietzsche's Dionysian dimension to an aestheticist glorification of the artist-Übermensch isolated from the ordinary lives of the masses.[8] Yet however much Ball sought to subordinate conventional morality to what he called Nietzsche's aesthetic "cosmodicy," he nonetheless re-

mained, psychologically, a moralist, not least in his assertion that a new
type of "philosopher-artist" was to be the harbinger of the regeneration
of German culture.[9]

The work on Nietzsche was casually abandoned in Ball's abrupt departure from Munich in the summer of 1910, a move apparently occasioned by the seductions of the theater and Berlin society. Such abrupt
exits would become a distinctive character trait from that point on:
bolting the scene, for whatever reason, was Ball's trademark. During the
fall of 1910 he studied briefly in Berlin with Max Reinhardt who noted
his gifts as a director and dramaturge. In 1912, after a short stint as
director of the State Theater in Plauen, he returned to Munich, where
he frequented expressionist circles and wrote poems and prose for
Franz Pfemfert's *Die Aktion, Der Sturm,* and other radical journals of
the Munich avant-garde. In October 1913, along with the playwright
and poet Hans Leybold, Ball founded *Die Revolution,* which carried on
its masthead Erich Mühsam's slogan "Lässt uns chaotisch sein" (Let us
be chaotic). *Die Revolution* proclaimed its opposition to everything
in the German cultural scene, and, predictably, its first number was
confiscated by the authorities because of Ball's irreverent poem, "The
Hangman." Not untypically, the short-lived journal extolled Dionysian
destructivity and the negation of all values, but, in contrast to the other
journals of the expressionist avant-garde, Ball's writings also emphasized spiritual regeneration through the "inner necessity" of the works
of the ascetic artist. Of his discovery of Wassily Kandinsky in 1912, he
wrote enthusiastically, "If we speak of Kandinsky and Picasso we don't
refer to painters but to priests; not craftsmen but to the creators of new
worlds, new paradises."[10]

Ball's 1910 characterization of Nietzsche could also serve as an accurate self-description: art was Ball's "undertaking, his calling, his
muse, and the determining factor in his life."[11] He was a ferocious auto-
didact, a compulsive talker, and a chain smoker who frequently es-
chewed food and abjured alcohol. The odd combination of hedonism
and asceticism is not insignificant. Ball's attraction to asceticism and
spiritual quietude was a constant accompaniment to the excess and ex-
haustion of Dionysian revolt. In 1915, during his first year of Zurich
exile, he wrote of his fascination with yogis and Jesuits: "I have seen
enough. To sit in a cell and say, here is closure, no one may enter."[12]
Certainly before 1914 Ball showed little interest in the supremacy of
the deed, or in any sort of political action, unless one counts his rather
frivolous proposal to boycott bookstores that carried works that diluted

Nietzsche's radicalism. After 1914 his somewhat contradictory embrace of both revolt and spiritual quietude allowed him to equate the libertarian anarchism of Bakunin with Kandinsky's "purity of color and grandeur of intuition" and to see both as the "Last Ramparts" of Russian romanticism. For all his Nietzschean gesturing and hyperbole, Ball consistently maintained that asceticism was the true sign of creative genius: Kandinsky was the modern monk who gave the age "its strongest artistic expression."[13]

In August 1914, not unlike many other young artists and intellectuals caught up in the electric atmosphere of Berlin in the *avant guerre,* Ball enthusiastically volunteered for military service. Art now appeared to him ridiculous since, as he then wrote, "war is the only thing that excites me."[14] After three successive rejections on obscure medical grounds, he abandoned his military aspirations, which seemed to increase his despair about his artistic ones, rejecting first the "pathos of the theater" and subsequently repudiating the expressionist milieu. Ball's 1914 diary entries trumpet his new conviction that "action" was preferable to art. In November 1914, after a brief unauthorized visit to the Belgian front, he formulated the war's impact on his thoughts: "It is the total mass of machinery and the devil himself that has broken loose now. Ideals are only labels that have been stuck on. Everything has been shaken to its foundations."[15]

Ball's return to Berlin was marked by still greater estrangement from the literary avant-garde and, at the same time, a new interest in the Russian anarchists, Bakunin, Kropotkin, and Merezhkovsky. His "proto-Dadaist" diatribes against the *bohème,* against "beauty, culture, poetry, all spirit, taste, socialism, altruism, synonym," took on an increasingly cynical and nihilistic tone.[16] Ball quickly turned against the war, claiming that his patriotism "does not go as far as sanctioning an unjust war," a view that owed much to his renewed affiliation with Franz Pfemfert and Kurt Hiller, whom he greatly admired as opponents of the war and antipatriots.[17] Above all, the death of his closest friend, Leybold, in a hospital at the Belgian front in October 1914 helped to affirm Ball's decision to emigrate to Switzerland in May of the following year.

The first eight months in Zurich were a time of severe economic privation, in part in self-conscious emulation of his anarchist idols, but also the result of a psychological crisis culminating in what was probably a suicide attempt in October.[18] In exile, Ball's attraction to anarchism mellowed, despite his continued enthusiasm for its antistatist and theocratic doctrines. Ball's biographer, Philip Mann, points out that he frequently expressed doubts about his previous anarchist ideas of natural goodness and that he was ambivalent about the expressionists' idealization of the proletariat, which he once called "a godless barbarity."[19] Though he admired Bakunin, he emphatically rejected his atheism and was appalled to discover that the anarchist had enthusiastically supported Bismarck's campaign against German Catholicism. Finally, Ball's idiosyncratic brand of theocratic anarchism came into focus at that juncture, along with his newfound republican belief that the Declaration of the Rights of Man was sacrosanct. For Ball, "supplementing human rights with divine rights" was integral to any notion of revolution as the extension, but never as the abolition, of the legacy of the French revolution.[20]

These philosophical and political convictions did not diminish when Ball, toward the end of 1915, began to conceive of the Cabaret Voltaire, which opened early the next year and where the first Dada soiree was held on July 14, 1916.[21] In its Zurich phase, Dada adopted the now-famous public posture of chaotic abandon. The studied nihilism or frivolity of Dada fiercely competed with Ball's wartime gravity and pessimism, a tension that occurs often in the same diary passages. Zurich, he wrote, was a respite from Germany where he could enjoy the "life that pulsates here, fresher and less bound up, because one knows no inhibitions." Yet at the very same time he cautioned that "one should take care, not to call time and society by their real names. One should simply pass through, as through an evil dream; without glancing left or right, with lips pressed together."[22] This paradoxical stance, which might be described as at once uninhibited and stoical, is an underlying motif of Dada, which Ball often explained as a mirror of the pathological release of the instincts in the face of a bankrupt civilization.

Ball's hopes for the cabaret were expressly political since its main purpose was to become a collecting point for the artistic and intellectual émigrés in Zurich, "a delirious playground of crazy emotions" in which "all of the styles of the last twenty years came together." Dada's main poetic innovation was the famous "sound," or simultaneous, poems that intentionally break up and release language from syntax and meaning. In these poems the clamor intentionally overpowers the human voice or the "soul." "The noises represent the background—the inarticulate, demonic companions. The poem tries to elucidate the fact that man is swallowed up in the mechanistic process. In a typically compressed way it shows the conflict of the *vox humana* [human voice] with a world that threatens, ensnares, and destroys it."[23]

Pushing expressionism to its breaking point, the sound poems abandoned the language of signs for an "Adamic language" of innocence, resurrecting a speech that is utterly beyond all war and catastrophe.[24] It is perhaps not a coincidence that at almost the same moment Walter Benjamin formulated his own highly esoteric and theologically inspired theory of a primal language, preserved in his 1916 essay, "On Language as Such and on the Language of Man." For Benjamin, human language was only a faint echo of a "paradisiacal" language, but it still retained something of its earliest mimetic character, the onomatopoesis of nature that evinces God's, not man's, power to name things. As we have seen, in 1916 he wrote that those who had permitted words to sink to the level of propaganda could only be opposed by recalling the earliest "naming" of things, in which language evinced its originary messianic intensity. Several years later Benjamin became Ball's next-door neighbor in Bern, and it was through Ball that he first met Bloch in March or April 1919. It is not too far-fetched to see in Ball's sound poems and in Benjamin's reflections on language and catastrophe the same impulse to retrieve the primal mimetic purpose of all language in the face of the politically motivated debacle.

During the Dada period Ball refined his philosophical reflections on anarchism and intensified his search for certain "secret" strands in the history of Catholic theology, even if his passion for the militantly anticlerical Bakunin remained for him something of an exception in this regard. What attracted Ball to the Russian thinkers, however, was not merely that some of the anarchists considered the New Testament a "revolutionary book," or even their exemplary spirit of sacrifice and the "imitatio Christi" of their poverty. Rather, like Benjamin (see chapter 1), Ball saw in the chaotic and childlike naïveté of the Russian writers a sense of freedom and "right of negation" that seemed to parallel his self-definition of the Dadaist as a "childlike, Don Quixote–like person."[25] Ball once compared Dada's public infantilism to the practices of certain medieval gnostic sectarians, who as adults placed themselves in the cradle and, trembling, allowed themselves to be suckled and swaddled like the Christ child: "Dadaists," he concluded, "are similar infants of the new epoch."[26]

To this admittedly overintellectualized image of Dada as a self-consciously pre-Oedipal gesture, we should add the often ignored caveat that the cabaret was first and foremost a performance troupe. Ball played piano, Hennings sang ditties, and Richard Huelsenbeck bellowed poems to an often unappreciative and sometimes barely conscious clientele. This world of Dada is described in Ball's 1916 *Flametti*, an auto-biographical novella that depicts the frustrations of the cabaret but also its "true circus nature."[27] Ball's disappointment with Dada, which he characteristically punctuated with a flight from Zurich, was registered shortly after the first Dada soiree of July 14, 1916, and had many mo-tives: personal quarrels, political ineffectiveness, and, last, Ball's own celebrity. Dada failed because it had become yet another art movement.

Returning to Zurich in November 1916, Ball rejoined the Dadaists— Huelsenbeck, Marcel Janco, Hans Arp, Tristan Tzara—and on March 17, 1917, the new Galerie Dada opened. In this second phase of Zurich Dada, Ball began to exhibit a more reverent attitude toward "the Rus-sian Ramparts," which would become even more pronounced in the months leading up to the writing of the *Critique*. Once again, radical nihilism and an anti-Western gesture are set off against deeply Christian asceticism. In a lecture on Kandinsky (whose art he then called "libera-tion, solace, redemption and becalming") Ball asked rhetorically if "Russian Christianity is not the strongest and final bulwark of Roman-ticism in Europe today."[28] In his novel *Tenderenda der Phantast,* it might also be noted, Ball depicted Dada as "Satanopolis," a demonic and nihilistic mirror of the war's own chaotic destruction, while the author seems to identify most with what he calls "peace, stillness, and Latin absence."

Perhaps Ball's most astonishing aperçu in the Zurich phase concerns the well-known coincidence that in the same street, directly opposite the Cabaret Voltaire, a certain Russian exile called "Mr. Ulyanov-Lenin" had taken up residence. Ball recalled, "He must have heard our music and tirades every evening; I am not sure with what pleasure and profit. And, as we opened the Galerie in the Bahnofstrasse, the Russians traveled to Petersburg to set the revolution on its feet. As both sign and gesture is Dada the counterpoint to Bolshevism? Does it oppose the completely Quixotic, pointless, and incomprehensible side of the world to destruction and consummate calculation? It will be interesting to ob-serve what happens here and there."[29] Did Ball, we might also ask, whose own aesthetic and political avant-gardism were constantly at odds with each other, and with his Catholic spirituality, recognize in Lenin and Dada the two sides of his own avant-gardism, its political destructiveness and its quixotic purposelessness? Nonetheless, less than a year later Ball's antipathy to Bolshevism had solidified while Dada was cast off to the reliquaries of the bohème. Skepticism once again took the form of a flight to the Tessin, culminating in his final break with Dada in May 1917 and in his move to Bern, the center of German exile anti-war activity.

In stark contrast to the carnivalesque cosmopolitanism of Zurich, Bern was the headquarters of espionage, Entente propaganda, and organized resistance to the German war effort. A remarkable group of émigré intellectuals had gathered around the central organ of the anti-Kaiser Germans, *Die Freie Zeitung,* founded in April 1917. Its prestigious list of contributors included Annette Kolb, Alfred Fried, Carl v. Ossietsky, René Schickele, and Hermann Hesse. As we have noted, Bloch, who would become one of Ball's closest friends and admirers, wrote hundreds of articles for the paper between October 1917 and August 1919.[30] Politically, *Die Freie Zeitung* supported the Entente and Wilson's Four Points, while it consistently denounced German militarism, nationalism, and the corrupt Prussian autocracy. *Die Freie Zeitung* also rejected the socialist antiwar position taken at the Zimmerwald Conference of 1915, which maintained that since the war only served the interests of international capital, all and none of the belligerents were responsible. For Ball, Bloch, and the other contributors to *Die Freie Zeitung,* the fact of German war guilt was paramount, as was their support for the democracies, since, despite the Russian anomaly, only an Entente victory could guarantee the collapse of the dynasty and the triumph of democracy in Germany.

Die Freie Zeitung was often accused of being in the pay of the Entente—even by Bloch himself—though the evidence is largely circumstantial. It was, of course, an instrument of Entente propaganda to the extent that it accepted, as did Ball, the principle that autocracy and absolutism were responsible for the war and that democracy and the moral imperative were on the side of the anti-German coalition.[31] For Ball, the war represented "the final phase of a permanent, commensurate with its nature, barbaric protest of Germany against the Western Spirit."[32] Paramount, in this regard, was Ball's distinction between the "humanitarian liberalism of the Western democracies" (Britain, America, and France) and the "dreamy humanism" of the later German Enlightenment philosophers Johann Gottfried Herder, Alexander von Humboldt, and Johann Gottlieb Fichte. In a notation of June 1917, Ball compared the German constitution of 1848 with the Declaration of the Rights of Man and found the inadequacies of the former "striking."[33] As the *Critique* expressed it, 1914 was the apotheosis of the accumulated complicity of decree and idea by which Potsdam sought to excuse Weimar and Weimar, Potsdam.[34]

If the politics of *Die Freie Zeitung* were pro-Entente, its philosophical atmosphere was more attuned to Russian spiritualism and Bakuninist apocalypticism. In 1918 Bloch explained the emergence of this apocalyptic-messianic mood as a self-conscious response to the official bureaucratic religiosity of the Prussian state. "Thus," wrote Bloch, "a new mystical Imperium (Reich) emerges, an imperium of fighting Christianity, an *ecclesia militans* opposed to this infernal system of power."[35] In this messianic and expressionist worldview, all contingency, progress, and power were simultaneously subject to contempt.

When Ball visited Bern in early September 1917 he at first felt himself "abandoned" in an "alien city," which he immediately recognized as the "political half" that corresponded to Zurich, his "aesthetic half." Ball's dilemma was acutely registered: "I feel so divided in my interests that I am actually at the point of sacrificing the aesthete to politics."[36] A few days later he resolved to remain and engage in the antiwar resistance, a decision he called a "not only just, but highest duty."[37] "I don't want to make cabaret any longer," he wrote in November 1918. "I prefer to write, that was always my goal."[38] Soon after his arrival, Ball—whom Bloch then called a "Christian Bakuninist"—became the paper's most charismatic figure.[39]

Despite his newfound resolve to remain, Ball frequently complained of Bern's "dry milieu with all its rationalists." Yet he admitted that the city's overall intellectual quality was remarkably high: "Today it is the best political library which can be found in Europe, and it becomes more so, from day to day."[40] Overnight Ball became a political journalist, writing regularly for *Die Freie Zeitung* as well as for other émigré journals. Mann divides Ball's prodigious writing into four somewhat arbitrary subject areas: (1) criticisms of the Prussian state and its intellectual epigones from Luther to Hegel; (2) satirical articles and parodies of prowar mentality; (3) articles exposing German war aims and underscoring the absence of a liberal or democratic tradition; and (4) articles defending the Entente, attacking pacifists, and documenting German war guilt.[41] If this were not enough, Ball was also hard at work on his "Bakunin Breviary," a planned two-volume work that he envisaged as a vindication of the Russian thinker against Marx and his Marxist critics.

By 1917 Ball's political thinking was increasingly preoccupied with those theological-metaphysical reflections. He was convinced that the isolation of Germany from the rest of Europe (both from Russia and the West) could only be countered by a new European church of the intelligentsia, as opposed to the parochial Prussian spirit. True communism, he believed, had to be grounded in a new evangelium, the "this-worldly realization of all that which comprises the godly essence of Christianity."[42] Perhaps this conviction, and his disappointment with Bakunin's atheism, led him to finally forsake the Bakunin project, which, like the long-abandoned Nietzsche thesis, remained unfinished.

Instead, in early November 1917, a different idea began to germinate, quickly assuming first place in Ball's crowded writing schedule, a book that would synthesize his religious and political philosophy with his antiwar politics. According to Ball, the inspiration for the *Critique* came from René Schickele, editor of the exile literary journal, *Die Weissen Blätter,* who proposed that Ball write a book on "German intellectuals" for Schickele's press. When he finished the exposé on November 14, 1917, Ball registered his enthusiasm for the new project: "The ideas were whirling around in my pen. It was supposed to be a book about the modern intellectuals, especially about the authors of *Die Weissen Blätter,* and it has become a sketch of German development and more like a draft against the 'Manifesto of the 93 Intellectuals,' the rallying of the intellectuals to the war effort."[43] But Ball also saw the *Critique* in more personal terms: as "a hygiene for myself. A certain lightness and enthusiasm give me a wholly peculiar intense and energetic style."[44]

The basic themes of the *Critique* were already outlined in many of Ball's articles for *Die Freie Zeitung,* and Ball needed only this "encouragement" for his "entire inner self to draw itself together."[45] The *Critique,* he said, had to be written in simple and clear prose, and be "productively effective."[46] Above all, it was directed at a German audience, with Ball refusing even to permit a French translation. The *Critique* would explain why Germany had become insular, unreachable, and, above all, universally despised. His comment on the day of the German revolution, November 9, 1918, makes this point.

> When I consider that Germany has been cut off from the great currents of life, that we here in Switzerland register new convulsions daily, while over there every free gasp of breath is suppressed, then I ask myself how a reconciliation can still be possible when the borders suddenly come down. The West communicates its experiences, plans and arrangements, the world association [League of Nations] has actually come into being, but Germany plays the role of the despised, with all the terrible consequences.[47]

Only after the *Critique* was finished, he promised, would he then compose a very different kind of "manifesto for freedom," one without any knowledge or science, "entirely subjective and personal."[48]

III.

Ball's *Critique* documents the momentary confluence of two distinct political and intellectual currents among German-speaking exiles in Switzerland at the end of the First World War. First, it repudiates the German autocracy and the nationalist intelligentsia while proclaiming unequivocal support for the political ideals of the "West": republicanism, democracy, and liberalism. Its implicit polemic against the intellectual legacy of writers like Heinrich von Treitschke, Houston St. Chamberlain, Max Scheler, Werner Sombart, and, even more important, Thomas Mann is carried out by historically situating them at the end of a long line of German philosophers and writers who slavishly bowed their thoughts to the dictates of the Prussian monarchy and its politics.

Second, the core idea of the *Critique* stems from Bakunin's remark, "The source of all evil lies in the Reformation."[49] This emphasis on the missing dimension of "Godly" as well as "human rights" in Germany links the theocratic politics of the *Critique* to the broad current of theological anarchism that we have already described as it flourished among Swiss émigrés during World War I. The central texts of this tradition are Gustav Landauer's *Aufruf zum Sozialismus* (1919); Ernst Bloch's *Spirit of Utopia* (1918); Walter Benjamin's anarcho-theological writings of 1920–1921; and Gershom Scholem's early efforts at reconstructing an authentic Jewish esoteric tradition from the Kabbalah.[50] The *Critique* promotes a chiliastic and messianic politics of spiritual regeneration and divine justice by invoking such figures as Thomas Münzer, who represents the antipode to Martin Luther and Protestantism, and Wilhelm Weitling, who is contraposed to Karl Marx and Ferdinand Lassalle.

The elective affinity of these soon-to-diverge currents in German intellectual history, confused as it might appear, can be explained by the encounter of these intellectuals with the catastrophic experience of the war, which was, not surprisingly, interpreted in theologically inspired apocalyptic terms. The bitter and ironic tone of the first pages of the *Critique* reminds us that the intellectual "betrayal" that provoked Ball was not merely the chauvinism of the nationalist ideologues but the prowar stance of some of the most respected thinkers in Wilhelmine Germany. It is not surprising, therefore, that among those young German intellectuals who fled to Switzerland, many were shocked to discover that some of the figures they most idealized had signed on to the war. As chapter 1 shows, Bloch, for example, saw Max Weber and

Georg Simmel in this light; Walter Benjamin broke decisively with his formerly revered teacher, Gustav Wyneken; and for Gershom Scholem the negative exemplars were Martin Buber and Hermann Cohen. For Hugo Ball, the philosopher Max Scheler and his former teacher Max Reinhardt played a somewhat analogous role.

The year 1916 was the war's darkest period, when mass death and mechanized killing seemed to triumph over all the spiritual and intellectual achievements of the Occident. The year 1917, however, marked the beginning of the end of the German war effort: the March Revolution in Russia, the Bolshevik Revolution, the entry of the United States into the war. And 1918 saw the rapid collapse of the German military effort and the dynasty. From the perspective of the German antiwar exiles around *Die Freie Zeitung,* the choice between Wilson and Lenin was unproblematic: the traditions of the Prussian military and the dynasty fell together; Germany was forced to choose between West and East, democracy or revolutionary dictatorship, Marxism or liberalism. For Ball, as for Bloch (Bloch's Swiss democratic phase is often obscured by his later autobiographical revisionism), the victory of Bolshevism in Russia and the stirring of revolution in Germany added communism to the list of political disasters that the war had produced.[51] It was the obligation of intellectuals to choose liberal democracy over Marxism. But if Marxism, especially in the first flush of the Soviet experiment, represented the triumph of "Red Czarism" (Bloch's phrase), liberalism was judged inadequate to inspire the zeal required to realize its political destiny. It lacked precisely the kind of spiritual energy that theology had long invested in more conservative enterprises.

For this reason, Ball decided to place perhaps even greater emphasis on the *Critique*'s theological politics than on exposing the conspiracy of spirit and sword, on the collusion between Weimar and Potsdam. A critique of the intelligentsia, he wrote, had to "mobilize the secret forces of the nation," and he dedicated himself to removing "valuable fictive forces and instincts from profane heroic history and regaining them for one with religious overtones."[52] The peculiar German agony that "paralyzes the spirits," he once noted, is either "fruitless aestheticism" or a "fatal belief in progress," both of which he claimed "succumb to an overwhelming system of profanation."[53] For Ball, inventing a trope that was to be echoed in many different forms, Luther represented Germany's disaster. In Germany the Enlightenment and its critics, Kant as well as Nietzsche, represented a different aspect of the political testament of the Wittenberg theology professor and his "superstitious text-fetishism." Luther had consecrated the union of throne and altar, Luther had sanctified the violence of the state against the poor, and Luther had exorcised the mystery from Christianity. To combat this profane system it was not sufficient to merely embrace republican or liberal ideals. Liberalism's emphasis on natural rights was not up to a world irredeemably divided into Good and Evil, Christ and Antichrist. A fallen, catastrophic world required a restoration of Catholic spirituality, "the church of the intelligentsia, that society of the select who carry freedom and consecration within themselves."[54] Only a spiritual elite initiated in the "secret teachings of Christianity" could participate in the difficult inner struggle required to be an "authentic Catholic," a struggle that Ball saw most strongly personified in the Catholic thought of De Maistre, Bonald, and Chauteaubriand. Ball compared these great French writers with the deficiencies of "furor teutonicus," which prevailed by reconciling and balancing "Dionysian exuberance with law and logic."[55]

Ball did not deny the close connection between romanticism and conservative political traditions in Germany. But he also did not associate romanticism with irrationalist or nationalist politics, as was common after the Second World War. Rather he defended French or Russian romanticism for its Catholicizing and cultist impulses, while arguing that the characteristically Protestant repudiation of the Catholic core of romanticism—especially in Hegel, Goethe, and Nietzsche—was marked by a fatal loss of universalism. The collapse of the Prussian monarchy in 1918 would, he hoped, not only weaken the spiritual authority of the Reformation in Germany but also revive the spiritual forces long silenced by its modern incarnation in the university and the military. The political collapse would "redeem romantic longings" by ushering in a return to the "ecclesiastical ideal of discipline."[56]

Ball proudly referred to the engraving of the sixteenth-century theologian and radical Thomas Münzer which hung over his writing desk. He wrote Hennings enthusiastically of his discovery of the South German theologian Franz von Baader (1765–1841), a contemporary of Kant and Schelling who tried, by means of critical philosophy, to provide German Catholicism with a sound metaphysical foundation. Ball found in Baader a kindred spirit who displayed "many great things that are in harmony with my opposition to the things which I am against."[57] Baader's universalism, he believed, grounded in love, goodness, and humility, is at once the spiritual basis for the struggle for intellectual and social freedom and the struggle against the Antichrist. Consequently

Ball could assert, the cult of Reason and the terror notwithstanding, the ideals of 1789 remained "profoundly Christian and divine."[58]

Although Ball had apparently not yet read Thomas Mann's *Reflections of a Nonpolitical Man* (1918), the *Critique* can be read as a counterstatement to Mann's famous ennobling of German culture and its opposition to Western *zivilisation*.[59] Like Mann, Ball too considered Germany's estrangement from the West decisive, though for Mann it justified the war on cultural grounds, while for Ball the war was the direct result of the absence of a Christian political culture.[60] The estrangement of Germany from the West was not merely an estrangement from liberalism but an estrangement from the pillars of the true church—French and Russian. Mann's much-acclaimed antithesis of culture and civilization, he claimed, was only possible in Germany because its overtheologized concept of culture completely rejected the "godless, mechanistic industrial world." Ball excoriated Mann's prowar essays and in April 1918 ironically commented that the "smartest people today are plagued with decorously separating these two words" (culture and civilization), adding that the German cultivation of the concept of culture "crassly contradicts the facts as they now stand."[61]

Ball seemed to disavow his own Dada phase when he said that the style of the *Critique* had to be emphatic and rigorous. "In Germany," he wrote, "there is no use gesticulating. The Germans require arguments."[62] Before turning to politics in 1917, Ball could still be moved by Nietzsche's image of the artist as an "ascetic priest" who stood in opposition to society like the medieval heretics. But the prophet of a cultural renaissance praised in Ball's dissertation soon gives way (in the *Critique*) to the "Pastor-Son," to the Nietzsche who sows moral confusion by conflating goodness with its misuse by the omnipotent state. Nietzsche now appears as a late-blooming idealist and as the court philosopher of the post-Napoleonic glorification of violence and force. Already in October 1917 Ball accused Nietzsche of trying, by means of his doctrine of genius, to destroy the cult of Reason, the state cult of the Reformation. "But," he added, "genius itself is a classical concept," which ultimately leads to paganism, to "antique nature-mysteries, to the unleashing of drives."[63] In a Catholicizing gesture, Ball inverted Nietzsche's contempt for ascetic priests, praising the ascetic will to sacrifice in Münzer, in Giuseppe Mazzini's campaign against the papacy, and in the authentic mystics from Jakob Böhme to Tolstoy.[64]

Despite Ball's emphasis on the "invisible" as opposed to the "visible" church, it seems excessive to assert, as does Philip Mann in his critical study, that the *Critique* "can be seen as relinquishing both the radical modernist critique of culture and the revolutionary remedies and espousing a conservative ideology which, rejecting the present age as fallen and decadent, looks backwards to an idealized Golden Age and forwards to a future Utopia when the Golden Age will be reestablished."[65] Certainly Ball's Catholic mysticism and his apocalyptic radicalism appear to clash with his political support for the Entente. Yet there is little evidence of conservatism in the *Critique,* which is the work of a republican radical for whom the Rights of Man and democracy are not incompatible with Christian anarchism and revolutionary gnosticism. As late as July 1920 Ball delivered a speech in which he clearly rejected all rightist "stab in the back legends" and laid blame for the German defeat squarely on the "moral superiority of the opponents."[66] Ball's vision is that of a holy Christian revolution and of the *unio mystica* of a democratically liberated world: "The new democracy that we believe in and whose principles are being fought for by the world today has not drawn the conclusion that 'freedom in God' can coexist with an absence of freedom in the law, with the use of force in the state. . . . [N]or has it concluded that a German parliamentary system modeled after Western democracies will resolve all conflicts which currently separate Germany from the rest of the world."[67]

In a note on Rousseau, Ball once called Switzerland a land "where aesthetic and political enthusiasm meet."[68] The *Critique* is no exception, and it is as misplaced to regard it as the encapsulation of Ball's expressionist and Dadaist avant-gardism in political form as it is to see it as a work of conservative Catholicism. Reading Ball either forward from the standpoint of the wartime anarchist, Dadaist, and revolutionist or backward from the end point of his Catholic quietude is to miss precisely the extraordinary artistic, philosophical, and political amalgam that the *Critique* represents. The event—the end of the dynasty, the German Republic, the revolution and its (for Ball) betrayal—can be read in the text itself. Nor is it incidental that the publication of the *Critique* coincided with the breakup of the exile community around *Die Freie Zeitung.* From that world, Ball once said, "my *Critique* is a break, a flight toward the imprecise designation of the causes of this flight." Writing the *Critique* seemed to have exhausted him completely, "as if he had used up and expended all his force" on it.[69]

Ball's sudden reconversion to Catholicism in the Church of Agnuzzo the following year was not, at least not primarily, motivated by political disappointment, though it bears comparison to the equally precipitous embrace of communism by any number of radical avant-gardists at the same time. This time the decision proved not to be another impetuous flight. The Church, he noted in 1917, was the only place that romantic individuals could still "find the inner space that they miss in modern life."[70] His conversion was once explained by Emmy Hennings as a turn from "critique of conscience to the fathoming of conscience."[71] Political conservatism, it seems, played little role in Ball's decision, nor does it surface later, even in his apparent admiration for the Catholic jurist Carl Schmitt, who later emerged as the prophet of decisionistic politics on the German right, and whose *Political Theology* Ball sympathetically reviewed in 1924.[72] Ball's praise is reserved for Schmitt's repudiation of both left- and right-wing versions of political romanticism and irrationalism. After 1920 politics remained distant for Ball, whose post-*Critique* works are primarily taken up with the psychology of religious conversion and the exemplary asceticism of the saints, a theme that preoccupied him up to his premature death from cancer on September 14, 1927.

IV.

When the *Critique* appeared on January 15, 1919—Ball notes it arrived on the day of the Spartacist Karl Liebknecht's assassination—it was attacked, as Ball predicted, by patriotic writers who regarded it as the work of a traitor or worse. But even within the intimate circle of *Die Freie Zeitung* its initial reception was cool, the reviewer judiciously noting that one does not have "to subscribe to all its conclusions" to recognize the "fullness of its premises."[73] Several contemporary judgments demonstrate that, despite Ball's later recollection, the *Critique* was neither ignored nor universally praised, even by more sympathetic critics. Fritz Brupbacher, the anarchist and historian, called it "a devout book in a nicely irreligious style," underlining the point in a personal note to the effect that he hoped the style would kill Ball's religion.[74] Bloch's laudatory review in *Die Weltbühne* proclaimed that "like no German ever before him, [Ball] had comprehended the secret causes of the blasphemous state as they are in themselves."[75] But Bloch also warned elsewhere that the *Critique*'s exaggerated denunciation of idealist metaphysics made it impossible to admit to its own esoteric claim that precisely an "incomparable" need for metaphysics and transcendence could alone usher in the age of true freedom, of "transsocialist anarchy, the multiversum of liberated humanity."[76] Gershom Scholem recalled

that he and Walter Benjamin were initially "impressed with the acuity
of its [the *Critique*'s] hatred" but that its "immoderate attacks on Kant
only made us shake our heads."[77] The Viennese critic and pacifist Hermann Bahr playfully mocked the *Critique* by listing Ball's philosophical
and theological excesses: a new romanticism in the spirit of Baader, a
mystical union of Germany and liberated Europe, republicanism and
social Civitas Dei, the reunification of the eastern and western Church,
and so on. Bahr's compendium was so catholic, and so deflating, that
Ball readily conceded, "I can see from this compilation that I tried to
link the different European slogans of yesterday and today, and thus
committed the patriotic mistake of wishing to see them all realized in
Germany in a single attempt."[78]

Finally, Ball's anti-Semitism cannot be disentangled from these excesses, nor can he be posthumously exonerated by indefensible scholarly
practices, as has been the case since the 1970s. The restoration of the
deleted material in the 1993 edition makes clear that from its opening
passages the *Critique* intends to document "a conspiracy of Protestant
and Jewish theology (since Luther) and a conspiracy of both with the
Prussian powers (since Hegel) seeking to subjugate Europe and the
world, and bent on the universal destruction of religion and morals."
Ball concludes that "this conspiracy is more firmly and deeply rooted
than is commonly believed. To underestimate it is not in the best interest of mankind or the German people."[79]

Ball leaves no doubt that from his perspective the great intellectual
betrayal of 1914 can ultimately be traced back to the principles of the
Old Testament venerated by Luther and that the Protestant conception
of the state as an instrument of power is ultimately derived from Jewish
theology. It is this doctrine of power and the sword that Luther used to
suppress the revolt of the poor and the disenfranchised whose true and
authentic voice was Münzer; it is the same doctrines that led Germany
to its disastrous defeat in 1918; and finally, it is this doctrine that continues to triumph after 1918 in the form of Social Democracy. German
Social Democracy is the product of "two Jewish intellectuals, Ferdinand
Lassalle and Karl Marx." For Ball, German Social Democracy represented a "Jewish-German agreement" particularly "in as far as Marx
succeeded in uniting the Jewish international with the socialistic one
and in placing German-Jewish Messianism at the head of both, and
in as far as Lassalle at the same time linked the proletariat to Prussian-
ism, then, hypothetically, the dictatorship of German-Judaism, the Jew-

ish-Junker world rule, was on solid ground."[80] Ball approvingly cited Bakunin's remark that "the Jewish sect today represents a more ominous power in Europe than do the Catholic and Protestant Jesuits. They reign despotically in business and finance alike. . . . Woe to anyone who is clumsy enough to offend them."[81] The Jews represent a secret diabolical force in German history, evident in Ball's phantasm of Jewish power, his contempt for the Jewish industrialist Walther Rathenau, whom he regarded as a tacit ally of Marx and Lassalle, and his diatribes against the German-Jewish philosopher Hermann Cohen. Though Ball explicitly disavowed the charge of anti-Semitism, he ultimately believes that the catastrophe was "the price that Europe had to pay for the advances gained by Judaism: the surrender of the social ideal to the messianic *antisocial,* Prusso-German concept of the state as power and success; the instigation of the most horrible of all wars; the annihilation of twenty million human beings; and the ruination of Germany."[82]

Despite his disclaimers, the fact of Ball's anti-Semitism was already well established before the *Critique* appeared and was apparently the cause of strains in his relationship with Bloch, who not surprisingly reacted strongly to one such instance, Ball's editorial in *Die Freie Zeitung* on November 16, 1918. The offending passage contains the following statement about the dissolution of the monarchy and the role of Social Democracy in the founding of the German republic.

> They send anational Israelites forward, in order to achieve the most advantageous liquidation. This too is wrong. The soil of the Israelite Republic is the promised land, not Germany. We gladly work alongside these people, as long as they unambiguously dedicate themselves to the moral deed. The legend of the chosen people is triumphant. Berlin is not Sinai. We want a German nation, a German Republic, we want a German National Assembly, which disavows the business makers and the opportunist, and declares itself for the resurrection of a great, truly purified nation. Only thus can we win back the trust of the world.[83]

Bloch's shocked reaction to Ball's assertion that once again alien Jews are holding Germany hostage is evident from a letter written to his patron and fellow wartime Swiss émigré, Johann Wilhelm Muehlon, only eight days later: "I have something else to say that is important for me. It concerns the astonishing concluding sentence of Ball's editorial. I wrote Ball immediately that this sort of anti-Semitism is scandalous, no matter how he means it."[84] If Bloch and Ball were "completely at one in the explicit denunciation of the Ludendorff war," by November 1918 their friendship was shaken, though not entirely ruptured.[85] Bloch added that he planned to write *Die Freie Zeitung*'s editor, Hans Schlieben, about the affair so that he doesn't appear as a "buffoon" (*Hanswurst*) when his own article appeared in the next number of the *Freie Zeitung,* which now looked like a "pogrom sheet": "Ball knows full well, and Schlieben has never been in doubt, that I am a completely racially conscious Jew, and that I am proud of my old, secretive people, and that I am, in my best aspects, at home in Jewish blood and the great religious tradition of my people."[86] Bloch also planned to inform both Ball and Schlieben that he would not write another single line for the *Freie Zeitung* if "such a simple-mindedness" is repeated. It should be added that Bloch did not consider Ball to be an anti-Semite, at least not before the incident ("otherwise he could not be my friend"), but he now saw that the "complexities" and "inconsistencies" of Ball's attitude toward the Jews could hardly be discerned in the "short telegram sentences" of the egregious editorial. Bloch himself obviously excused a great deal of Ball's eccentricity, having even agreed at one point to write a preface to a proposed critique of nineteenth-century Jewry, so that Ball could not be suspected of vulgar anti-Semitism (Schmutzverdacht des gemeinen Antisemitismus).[87] It is apparent that Ball's editorial was the final straw and the "not very pretty reason" for Bloch's subsequent decision to part from the paper in December of that year.

It is perhaps possible to attribute the anti-Semitism of the *Critique* to Ball's anti-Protestantism and Catholic resentments. It is more plausible, however, that by the end of 1918 Ball's anti-Protestantism was fueled by his belief that statism, amorality, and authoritarianism were essentially Jewish theological inventions and that a "Jewish-Junker conspiracy" also aligned the German Revolution to the Bolshevik Revolution. The November 1918 reference to "Israelites" whose interests are those of a "stateless people" and who are as dedicated to obstructing a Catholic community of Christian renewal as are the Protestant militarists and national chauvinists takes the theme of a Prussian and Social Democratic conspiracy to an absurd conclusion. Ball's desire to "mobilize the secret powers of the nation" against this conspiracy turns him into yet another protagonist of the German "special path" between East and West. Against his best intentions, Ball ultimately shared with his prowar opponents, for example, Treitschke and Thomas Mann, the conviction that neither Western liberalism nor Russian Bolshevism could end the spiritual malaise of Germany. By this route, Ball's anti-Semitic and radical vision of the apocalypse, and his monochromatically theological standpoint, makes him one of the best examples of the system he is out to expose.

Ball's strange odyssey through gnostic revolt and anti-Semitism raises yet another question. Did Ball's remark about his "patriotism" in his comment after Bahr's review, or his 1914 avowal of a "patriotism" that did not extend to sanctioning an unjust war, remain an unacknowledged motif in the *Critique*? Did Ball not see himself as the spokesman for that very same "secret Germany" that had been suppressed and hounded by the conspiracy of crown and altar, Junker and Jew? Was *Die Freie Zeitung* the equivalent of Weitling's League of the Just? And is the *Critique* not, as one critic recognized, a book that remains after all "stuck in nationalism, even if in a negative one"?[88] How else can we interpret the remarks about the "chimeric nationality of the Jews" or the "internationalism of the moneymen and businessmen." It is precisely the idea that the Jews represent a barrier to national self-identity that most strongly reveals this dimension of the *Critique,* which for all its hostility to German militarism and national chauvinism, harbors its own peculiar, inverted nationalism. The inverted nationalism of the *Critique* was also confirmed by a letter Ball sent Hennings as he worked on it: "I am nevertheless completely German, German in my essence. Can I adopt a standpoint, that does not somewhere coincide with things against which I have turned?"[89] Hennings too acknowledged that the *Critique* was the "outburst of a desperate German, an unhappy patriot, who had to exit from nationalism, even if he himself resisted it."[90] Several years earlier Ball had written in his diary, "I tend to compare my private experiences with those of the nation. I attribute to my conscience the need to perceive a certain parallel there. It may be capricious, but I cannot live without the conviction that my personal destiny represents an abbreviation of that of the people as a whole."[91]

Reviewing the *Critique* in 1920, Bahr rightly underscored this parallel as the essence of Ball's book: "He believes in a Germanness that can fulfill the meaning of the war: the integration of a nation rebelling against society."[92] The redemption of Germany's authentic Christian spirit as a restitution of the secret tradition of Münzer, Böhme, Baader, and Weitling is the resurrection of that "other" Germany and simultaneously the end of the abyss separating it from the rest of Europe. The inverted nationalism of the *Critique* was encapsulated by Ball in his Hamburg lecture in 1920: "In this way we want to restore Germany— Religion. And this is the most important German task of present and future, which contains the meaning of all other national tasks."[93] The

Critique offers a striking reminder that nationalism comes in many forms, not the least in the form of hostility to militarism, materialism, and, above all, "Jewish" cosmopolitanism.

V.

In light of these excesses, to what extent can Ball's thesis that classical German philosophy and criticism was compromised by its historic collusion with absolutism be affirmed? It is by now well established that the relationship between German critical philosophy (Kant, Hegel, Fichte) and Prussian absolutism is neither as simple nor as one-sided as Ball claims. To be sure, the German philosophers of the Enlightenment were equivocal in their political allegiances. But Ball's judgments about the inherently cynical marriage of dynastic power and Luther that inspired philosophical Machiavellianism have not withstood the scrutiny of modern scholarship. Before the French Revolution, for example, Kant's commitment to constitutionalism was tempered by his belief that enlightened absolutism seemed to offer more freedom of public debate than revolutionary democracy; obedience to rational law permitted the development of universal principles. If in 1784 Kant still supported the monarchy, he would soon judge the French Revolution to be that singular "event of our time" through which the enlightened public could enthusiastically bring about and extend the principles of morality and natural law. Ball's wholly negative portrayal of Kant, the "archenemy" who "raises Prussian reason of state to Reason," cannot do justice to the philosopher's admittedly paradoxical refusal to sanction the right of rebellion while giving his wholehearted support to the French Revolution. It should also be noted that much of Ball's interpretation and polemic rests heavily on popularizations of Kant in the German academic philosophy of the later nineteenth century.[94] By contrast, the German philosophers themselves understood full well, as Kant himself put it, that though they might well live in an age of enlightenment, they did not yet live in an "enlightened age."

It is more plausible, as the historian Reinhart Koselleck argued, that the emphasis of late eighteenth-century German idealism on subjective reason could hardly keep pace with the historical events and political exigencies of the age. As a result, the burden of demonstrating the rationality of human freedom was increasingly placed on history and its secular plan of salvation. Paradoxically, the attempt to ground freedom in political action and the need to give politics a higher purpose placed the morally self-conscious individual in a void and made a virtue of necessity.[95] This fusion of morality and history did at some moments sacrifice justice to the state, but at others it easily placed the state in the docket of the "court of world justice."

Ball's assertion that Prussia was the omnipotent master of Germany's intellectual legions effaces the tension between "Potsdam and Weimar," power and spirit. His intemperate fusion of Potsdam and Weimar is only the reverse side of the well-known argument of prowar German liberals like Friedrich Meinecke, Max Weber, and Ernst Troeltsch that the unity of Potsdam and Weimar would protect Germany from becoming a ruthlessly imperialist power. Ernst Bloch recalled in the 1960s that the *Critique* "claimed or tried to prove that Potsdam and Weimar actually conspired with each other apologetically, to the extent that an unknown, non-Potsdam Germany existed, but that it was consistently suppressed in coordination with Weimar. This good Germany, the good spirit, [Ball] views as opposed to the triumphant Potsdam. [. . . .] Now, this is highly exaggerated, Potsdam and Weimar were not to that extent apologetically linked."[96] The paradoxes, contradictions, and deep inner conflicts in the German idealist tradition are entirely invisible in Ball's optic.

As should be evident, the *Critique* is infuriatingly inconsistent in its political loyalties. Ball's commitment to the Entente and to republicanism coexists uneasily with his emotional and critical allegiance to French Catholic romanticism and Russian autocracy. If Ball praises the Rights of Man and Wilson's Four Points, he simultaneously insists that the French Revolution was an essentially Catholic event. Moreover, his assertion that German romanticism was divided between "pagans" like Goethe, Kleist, Wagner, and Nietzsche and antiautocratic authentic Catholics like Baader, Novalis, and Beethoven is at best confused, especially in light of Baader's support for the post-Napoleonic German restoration and in light of Novalis's poetic exaltation of the mystical essence of death and warfare. Finally, Ball's defense of the democratic and republican ideals of the West carries far less weight than his defense of Russian and French mysticism.

These observations reveal some of the limits of the *Critique,* but they also enable us to appreciate Ball's unacknowledged affinity to the very traditions he disparages. His antipathy to classical German philosophy and to Enlightenment as a system of values is not fundamentally different from the arguments made by many of the conservative nationalists and liberals who supported the war. As the historian Fritz Stern pointed out several decades ago, it was not the myopic racists and hard-core reactionaries who explain the allure of Germany's cultural remove from the traditions of the West. Rather, this stance was the achievement of an elite and educated mandarinate, which considered itself unpolitical and was dogmatically opposed to utilitarianism, liberalism, and materialism.[97] Finally, Ball's own theological criticism perpetuates and reenacts the very link between religion and politics that he ostensibly rejects, vitiating his own argument that theology, not politics or culture per se, lies behind German rationalism's nihilistic and Machiavellian impulses. The *Critique* recapitulates the theologization of politics that, according to Ball, is Luther's first sin. Ball's attempt to offer an account of Germany's solipsism and isolation from the West does not—especially in its own inverted nationalism and anti-Semitism—escape from that very solipsism and intellectual isolation.

VI.

After World War II, German intellectuals like Friedrich Meinecke, Karl Jaspers, Theodor Adorno, and Günter Grass reframed and restated many of the arguments of the *Critique* in their own rejection of Germany's militarist and nationalist past (without, of course, Ball's eccentricities and excesses). For this later generation, as we shall see in Jaspers's case, the critique of the German intelligentsia is motivated far less by an apocalyptic vision of political redemption than by a deeply ethical sense of trauma, and by what Primo Levi once called "remembrances of emergencies, of suffered or inflicted offenses."[98] Above all, for the postwar intellectuals there was an unequivocal recognition that the fact that democracy came to Germany late, that it was not the product of a strong tradition of bourgeois liberalism, and finally that it was introduced by the allied victors deprived it of strong emotional connections.

To be sure, the broad thesis of German exceptionalism, to which Ball subscribed, has frequently been challenged by comparative analysis of other European societies (above all, Britain and France) that remained strongly conservative in outlook and stratified in social structure until well into the twentieth century. If the simplistic view that National Socialism was "preprogrammed" by social, economic, or intellectual preconditions has been largely corrected, the fact remains, however, that the repudiation of modernity and the liberal political culture of the West was considered a respectable hallmark of the educated *Bildungsbürger* in Germany until (and to a large extent after) 1933. Nor, as the

Critique itself demonstrates, was this kind of criticism limited to conservatives and the antidemocratic thinkers of the political right. Rather, the inverted nationalism of the *Critique* leaves little doubt that there were currents of political irrationalism and anti-Semitism on the left of the political spectrum as well. Thus it may not be far-fetched to conclude that the most disturbing element of the *Critique* may be its most instructive lesson. If conservative ideologies of German nationalism and militarism have been discredited, and if the culture of obedience and loyalty that prompted Ball to excoriate German intellectuals during the First World War has all but disappeared, in certain circles a kind of inverted nationalism may have indeed resurfaced as a consequence of German unification.

VII.

The dissolution of communism in East Central Europe was accompanied by popular revolts that were not merely opposed to a totalitarian system but implicitly opposed to the principle immanent in all prior twentieth-century social revolutions including the anticommunist uprisings of 1956 and 1968: the promise of a higher order of democracy and a morally superior socialism. From the anti-utopian perspective of this century's end, Hugo Ball's theological anarchism and the messianic vision of his "utopian friend," Ernst Bloch, appear as anachronistic alternatives to the Machiavellian politics of Prussian and Bolshevik power. What remains of the utopian potential of 1918–1919 is not so much the messianic intensity of those thinkers but the "weak" messianic power of a normative or regulative idea of democratic rights and the expansion of personal freedom. Unlike the anticommunist revolutions in Hungary, Poland, and Czechoslovakia, which took place in the framework of subjugated but largely intact national political cultures, however, German unification has provoked the fear that a greater assertion of Germany's political role in European politics could indeed strengthen the already expressed desire of some politicians and intellectuals for positive identifications with cultural and historical traditions that up to now have been suspect. Since at least the 1960s, most responsible German public opinion accepted the judgment that an end of the German nation-state tradition was a welcome liberation from the burdens of a discredited past. The division of Germany was sanctioned not merely as a postwar fait accompli but also in some sense as a just and legitimate dismantling of a largely negative national identity. Unification has raised the question of whether the minimal and non-nationalist "constitutional patriotism" identified by Dolf Sternberger as the basic premise of postwar German political culture is sufficient to bind Germans to a more powerfully sovereign state. Germany's commitment to the intellectual and democratic traditions of the West, many observers point out, has been hegemonic only since 1945, and only in the western half. The question remains: Is this commitment part and parcel of Germany's limited postwar sovereignty, or will it extend to the era of a unified Germany?

Or, as some fear, will the democratic and benign Western orientation of the Federal Republic and the Marxist-Leninist dogmas of the East both be regarded as political imperatives unjustly imposed by the cold war and coercively required by the respective blocs? Will a united Germany continue to assume responsibility for the suffering of the Nazi epoch while healing the more recent wounds that forty years of division and communist rule have inflicted?

Since unification these perplexing questions have aroused much debate and provoked a "far-reaching crisis and the self-understanding of public intellectuals."[99] As Dan Diner has observed, "The West that is once again spoken of in a very different way than it was during the cold war, no longer stands opposite an ideologically clearly defined East."[100] The concept of the "West" is once again being defined in cultural and political terms, and with the end of Soviet and East European communism, the apocalyptic rhetoric that accompanied the Gulf War controversy and revelations about the penetration of the German Democratic Republic state security apparatus into public and private life contributed to an uncertainty about Germany's relationship to the West that in some ways recalls the situation Ball confronted in 1918–1919. Yet unlike the intellectual atmosphere that surrounded the genesis of the *Critique,* the crisis faced by the German intelligentsia is today in no small degree a product of the antinationalist spirit that Ball's work first attempted to articulate. At least since the early 1960s, the liberal left in the Federal Republic was able to mobilize political and cultural resistance to the authoritarian and patriotic traditions of the German mandarinate. Today, however, it is precisely that antinationalist consensus so clearly embodied in figures like Jaspers, Adorno, Jürgen Habermas, and Grass that has become the source of controversy. Moreover, those intellectuals most closely identified with the opening to the West and the democratic culture of the Federal Republic, Grass and Habermas among them (as well as most dissident intellectuals of the German

Democratic Republic), were also early opponents of unification and the most vocal advocates of a "two-state solution." From the perspective of the intellectuals, the unification process was too rapid and controlled by executive fiat, lacking in adequate constitutional legitimacy, and above all too forgetful of the heritage of nationalism in German history. As Grass warned, "A reunified Germany would be a complex-laden colossus."[101]

Since the "Turn" of 1989–1990, these judgments have come under fire from critics like the novelist Robert Walser who have drawn the line from the antinationalist consensus of the Federal Republic through its pro-Western and pro-American stance to point to the conclusion that West Germany's attachment to the West was a temporary arrangement. They condemn the left intelligentsia for imposing a strict taboo on the idea of unity in the face of an irrepressible reality.

In an article aptly entitled "Some People Can Even Sleep Through an Earthquake," the novelist Peter Schneider included himself among those guilty of the charge that Germany's left political culture was too complacent and oblivious toward the harsh dictatorship in the Eastern half and with keeping faith in the dogma that anticommunism was merely a mask of West German capitalism.[102] To be sure, what for some critics, like Schneider, serves as a critical reassessment has for others become a new myth that accuses left intellectuals of lacking a "positive basic decision for unity."[103] In the fierce debates over the 1991 Gulf War, which were to some extent a public controversy over national unification manqué, the apocalyptic rhetoric of the antiwar protesters spilled over into an anti-Americanism unprecedented in postwar West Germany, a stance that recalled what Thomas Mann once called the German "nonrelationship" to politics.

Ball's *Critique* was a sometimes confused and sometimes lucid case for a return of Germany to the spiritual traditions of Catholicism, and a warning against the perils of nationalism and the dangers of abandoning the West for a solipsistic political course. But Ball's own case underscores the opposite risk: that of an inverted nationalism of the left, of an antiwar sentiment that sees the struggle between power and justice in Manichaean terms, and can be as dangerous as a resurgence of the malevolent right-wing nationalism of 1914 and 1933. Any account of the *Critique* today must also consider this dilemma, since Ball exemplifies the paradox of an intellectual who repudiated the nationalism of the right while seeing Germany's salvation in an apocalyptic and inverted nationalism that believed German politics was held hostage by a mysterious "Jewish" power. The parallels to today's arguments against German involvement in global politics and the perverse idealization of Germany as the "spiritual" nation of a higher morality, along with the recognition that this mentality has its historical antecedents in the antiwar politics of 1918, may in fact be the *Critique*'s most important legacy. In this sense, the dilemmas that German intellectuals have encountered in the aftermath of the epoch ushered in by the revolutions of 1918–1919 continue to resonate from the *Critique* to the present.

PART TWO

1946-1947

CHAPTER 3

Heidegger's "Letter on Humanism" as Text and Event

I.

Written in the fall of 1946 and first published in France in 1947, the "Letter on Humanism" was initially a response to questions put to Heidegger in a letter written by a young French lycée instructor, Jean Beaufret.[1] As the first and most cogent statement of Heidegger's postwar thinking, it has had far more influence than any other expression of his thought, including perhaps even his masterpiece, *Being and Time*. Hannah Arendt called the "Letter" "an eloquent summing-up and immense clarification of the interpretive turn he had given the original reversal."[2] Heidegger's critics, most notably Theodor Adorno, were not so charitable, citing its "anesthetizing" effect on thinking and referring to it as a "haze" or "ether" that belied its own concepts.[3] His former student, Karl Löwith, commented on its style, noting that "to be able to satisfy fully the claim of Being, his apodictic language must in fact be an inspired language of revelation and a thinking that follows the dictates of Being."[4]

The "Letter" exemplifies Heidegger's characteristic ability to assume a position of the highest philosophical rigor while positioning himself in the most opportune political light. Initially intended for a French audience, the text has passed through several incarnations since it first appeared in 1947: first, as an intervention in the controversies around existentialism in the late 1940s; second, as a key text of deconstruction in the late 1960s; and most recently, during the Heidegger affair of 1987, as a refraining of the Heideggerian project of overcoming metaphysics. My interest is in this highly charged hermeneutical and political after-life, in the ways that Heidegger's "Letter" has become both text and event.

According to Heidegger's "marginalia" to the second edition published in 1949, "The Letter" was "not first thought out at the time of its writing," but "rests on the course of a path" (*Gang eines Weges*), which began in 1936.[5] Despite that assertion, the circumstances of its drafting and publication reflect Heidegger's precarious situation at the moment of the collapse of the Third Reich, the French occupation of Baden, and the negative judgment rendered by the Freiburg University faculty in his case.

When Heidegger returned to Freiburg in the summer of 1945, the University Senate commissioned a panel to deal with the most prominent of National Socialist "functionaries" on the faculty, its first "Fuhrer-Rector."[6] Moreover, according to the inter-Allied *Basic Handbook,* the occupation guidebook, Heidegger was already notorious as "a 100% Nazi, a dangerous intellectual, to be eliminated."[7] The French military authorities essentially concurred with that judgment, confiscating his house and library. A few days before Christmas 1945 Jaspers delivered the coup de grâce, his negative letter of evaluation to the Senate committees.[8] At that time, Louis Sauzin, who was responsible for the administrative affairs of the French zone of occupation, wrote to his former professor, Dilthey's translator into French, René le Senne, that Jaspers was "categorically brutal toward his former friend."[9] At the end of December 1946 he was prematurely "pensioned," losing all rights to participate in university activities, with compensation for only one additional year. The final decision arrived from the university only shortly after the "Letter on Humanism" was sent to Beaufret.[10] Several weeks later, in February, Heidegger suffered a nervous breakdown and entered a sanitorium in Badenweiler where he was entrusted to the care of Victor Freiherr von Gelbsattel, a physician and psychiatrist.[11]

These circumstances should make us aware of the extent to which the "Letter" combines personal, philosophical, and strategic elements. The problem of exoneration looms large in the composition of the text, particularly in the obvious effort to create the impression of a philosophical continuity from the pre-Rectorate period to his postwar thinking. Yet it also represents Heidegger's first utterances on the defeat of Germany and—indirectly—on Heidegger's own fall from grace. As I hope will become clear, it is this conflation of self-exoneration and political defiance in the face of catastrophe that ultimately defines Heidegger's text and its relation to the event that is at its center. Heidegger's effort to philosophically excuse and explain his complicity with Nazism circumscribes and informs several strands of its argument, and this combination of philosophical and strategic considerations has continued to weigh heavily on the legacy of its reception up to and including the reading given the "Letter" by contemporary French thinkers. First, I will briefly examine the text and its strategy; second, I will discuss some of its political implications (including the overlooked aspect of the "humanism problem" in National Socialist ideology); finally, I will consider its contemporary reception and some of its implications for Derrida's reading of Heidegger.[12]

II.

The "Letter" begins with Heidegger's famous distinction between the essence of man and the essence of truth. Only thought concerned with Being, never "action or praxis," can reveal the latter. Neither man's existence nor will, but Being itself, is the source of action. Occidental thought has reversed this relationship, substituting essence or existence for the truth of Being. The source of this fatal reversal is a primordial event: at an early stage in the development of Western "logic" and "grammar" metaphysics "seized control" and posited subject and object as appropriate terms to define the human condition. The "Letter on Humanism" is an attempt to "liberate language from this grammar," to forgo Western metaphysics and return to the essence of thought, which is the truth of Being. Its most famous sentence asserts that this thinking occurs in language, which is "the house of Being."[13]

The grammar and thought of the West are entirely responsible for the "homelessness" of modern man; they are the root cause of the "forgetting of Being." This homelessness is manifested in many forms: in communication, in technology, in the "market of public opinion," and in such "illusory" notions as public and private. Ideas of aesthetic or moral responsibility are further indications of an ever-increasing fall of language. Heidegger sees humanism—which he defines as any conception that places "man" at the center and privileges man's essence—as implicated in this forgetting. All "humanisms" have as "their ground" the projection of some essential characteristic onto man. The apparent differences, which Heidegger elaborates through the examples of Greek, Roman, Christian, Marxian, and contemporary existentialism, are ultimately without distinction. Diverse as their notions of "freedom" might seem, and "however different these forms of humanism may be in purpose and in principle, in the mode and means of their respective realizations, and in the form of their teaching, they nonetheless all agree that the *humanitas* of *Homo humanus,* is determined with regard to an already established interpretation of nature, history, world, and the ground of the world" (LH, 202). The history of metaphysics is the history of a decline (*Verfallsgeschichte*), the devolution of this anthrocentric and foundational hubris in which man's essence or existence is always prior to Being.

Similarly, metaphysics, which inquires into the nature of the knowable, or the "real," "not only does not pose the question concerning the truth of Being, but actually obstructs it, insofar as metaphysics persists in the oblivion of Being" (LH, 224). Nor can it even pose the question of man, since the distinction between essence and existence "completely dominates the destiny of Western history and of all history determined by Europe" (LH, 208). As such it blocks the recognition that man's being is a matter of "Ek-sistence," which can only occur in language as the "lighting-concealing advent of Being itself." The facticity of *Dasein* in *Being and Time* is transformed into the ecstatic determination of *Sein.*

III.

The language of the "Letter" extricates thought from action so that the truth of Being, "primordially sheltered in Being itself and removed from the domain of mere human opinion" (LH, 216), can be thought. To stand "in the openness of Being" suggests both a different orientation and a rethinking, so Heidegger says, of "man" who "is never first and foremost man on the hither side of the world, as a 'subject' " (LH, 229). We can imagine "man" in this sense as forgoing a pretense to mastery, control, worldly being. Humility is invoked by nurturent terms such as "shepherd," "care," and "guardian," and by the awe suggested by such phrases as standing in the "openness," "clearing," or "light of Being." Yet the "Letter" is in no way as naive as its rhetorical humility intends.

The "Letter" also includes the author's guide to reading Heidegger from the perspective of the "turning," or *Kehre,* toward Being, which Heidegger dates as occurring as early as 1930, for example, prior to the Rectorial Address and the other statements attesting to Heidegger's enthusiasm for the Nazi revolution.[14] It explicitly suggests that Heidegger began to think in these terms *before* his involvement with Nazism (which may have begun as early as 1931) so that Nazism could not in any way be considered the outgrowth of his philosophical thinking. However, in 1949 Heidegger added the sentence, "Since 1936 the advent [*Ereignis*] has been the leitmotiv of my thinking" (*GA* 9, 316). This claim places yet another marker in the story line, this time between the period from 1933 until 1936, when, as he now contends, he broke openly with the "worldly" conceptualization of Dasein, for example, with a politicized conception of "man." Thus opposition to National Socialism is also emphatically inserted into the revised narrative of Heidegger's thought. If we combine the two dates—1930 and 1936—the text puts forward two alternative periodizations: the myth of Heidegger's immunity to Nazism and the myth of the great philosopher's brief but fateful descent from the realm of thought to the realm of worldly affairs, from Being to being, and back again.

In the "case" of Heidegger there are many well-established strategies for confronting the problem of the "relation (or nonrelation)," as Richard Bernstein nicely puts it, between the philosopher and politics, or the question of the unity of "work and person," as Habermas has put it.[15] Victor Farias and Hugo Ott are primarily concerned with the events of Heidegger's career and consider his philosophical work only insofar as it illuminates biographical elements. Richard Wolin and Tom Rockmore, although differing over whether Heidegger ever ceased to be "a Nazi," have tried to establish the set of connections between Heidegger's philosophical preoccupations and his political choices.[16] At the other end of the spectrum, Hannah Arendt and Richard Rorty have tried to surgically disconnect work and person, so that there is no necessary connection between Heidegger's philosophical achievement and the fact that, according to Rorty, he "was a rather nasty piece of work—a coward and a liar, pretty much from the first to the last."[17]

There are of course those who still deny Heidegger's involvement in Nazism, or who maintain, as does the *ancien provocateur* Ernst Nolte, that his Nazism was entirely justified, even admirable, given the political choices available to him as a German in the epoch of European civil war.[18] Heidegger also has his critical defenders, those like Philippe Lacoue-Labarthe and Gianni Vattimo, who still argue that only a radicalization of Heidegger's philosophical impulses can illuminate (not merely his) Nazism—as a kind of hyper or "archi" fascism, in Lacoue-Labarthe's words, "the last attempt at 'mythizing' the West,"[19]—or, in Vattimo's words, demonstrate that "he was acutely aware of the power that suprapersonal structures have over the individual, indeed more radically aware than anyone else, perhaps even more so than Marxist thinkers themselves."[20]

Wolin, following Karl Löwith's lead, has elaborated on the ways that *Being and Time,* with its contempt for the "everyday" and its rhetoric of "authentic resolve" and "decision," though not explicitly political, already pointed toward Heidegger's later "collectivist," organicist thinking during the Rectorate.[21] That continuity is very much in dispute, however, no more so than in the "Letter" itself, where the decisionism and extreme voluntarism of *Being and Time* are confined to a misunderstanding or misinterpretation of the early Heidegger, but one that was legitimate enough for Heidegger himself to have subscribed to it. The "Letter" is the first statement of what has been referred to as Heidegger "II," a somewhat awkward way of periodizing Heidegger according to a schema encouraged by the philosopher himself. It refers to the works that postdate the Kehre, or turning, that he dates at a juncture prior to the fateful involvement with Nazism. According to Heidegger's own interpretation, the chief cause of Heidegger's National Socialism was a residual and "fatal" attempt to reverse the course of Being's destiny though the actualization of philosophy; a metaphysical "act" of historical engagement, a profound lapse from the achievement of *Being and Time,* and "a humanistic deviation in his earlier philosophy."[22]

In no other text does Heidegger deal as extensively with a contemporary philosopher. Directed at a French audience during the height of Jean-Paul Sartre's postliberation philosophical prestige, the "Letter" attempts to distance Heidegger's thinking from the latter's existentialism: "Sartre's key proposition about the priority of *existentia* over *essentia* does, however, justify using the name 'existentialism' for a philosophy of this sort. But the basic tenet of 'existentialism' has nothing at all in common with the statement from *Being and Time*—apart from the fact that in *Being and Time* no statement about the relation of *essentia* and *existentia* can yet be expressed since there it is still a question of preparing something precursory" (LH, 209). Sartre's "Existentialism Is a Humanism," a lecture delivered in 1945, conveniently serves the "Letter" as a kind of "straw" version of Heidegger I, since Heidegger obviously recognized that Sartre appropriated themes of "being-there," "authenticity," and "decision" from his own earlier work. At the same time, it is an effective demonstration of the inadequacies of what Heidegger regards as Sartre's misreading of his earlier philosophy solely from the perspective of a philosophy of the existential subject, as opposed to Heidegger's larger purpose: to ground philosophy in an ontology of Being that transcends the philosophy of consciousness. In an earlier letter to Beaufret, Heidegger underlines how a common French translation of *Dasein* as "human reality" (*realité humaine*) placed that concept in an exclusively anthropological framework, whereas his intention had been to locate Dasein in the ontological realm. But Sartre's misreading is also excusable, Heidegger admits, since the "adequate execution and completion of this other thinking that abandons subjectivity" was less accessible because the third division of *Being and Time* was "held back" at that time (LH, 207). *Being and Time* is thus retroactively interpreted as a "phenomenological destruction" of the notion of subjectivity, though what Heidegger "held back" in that earlier work was the more profound "humanism" that grants man only the passive role of "the shepherd of Being," while existence is interpreted as care, as guardianship, but never as actualizing or bringing into being the essence of man or the world. As Löwith observed, by retroactively putting this "turn" prior to 1933 there can be no connection between Heidegger's philosophical development and the Nazi involvement since Heidegger's "opposition" to Nazism is already "announced" and "conceived" prior to the Rectorial episode.[23]

The "Letter" is also strategic in its odd (and unique only to this text) claim that the "Marxist view of history is superior to that of other historical accounts" (LH, 219). A bold assertion, to say the least, and one that seems so out of character for Heidegger that we shall return to this point subsequently. Finally, and most important, the "Letter" is an allegory of the author's attempt to remove himself from all ethical considerations or demands of responsibility. The narrative voice assumes a posture equivalent to that of man's "Ek-sistence," which "gains the essential poverty of the shepherd, and whose dignity consists in being called by Being into the preservation of Being's truth" (LH, 221). The marked quietism in Heidegger's stance in the "Letter" is diametrically opposed to the action-oriented heroic stance of the Rectorial Address. In fact, the entire text is structured around the opposition between "action" or "praxis" and man's "coming forward into the lighting of Being." In this way, the "Letter" is concerned with absolution, which for Heidegger takes place not in the realm of conscience but in the domain of Being. The essence of evil consists not merely in the baseness of human action but rather in the "malice of rage"—an unambiguous reference to the bad motives of the victors. Habermas has rightly called this posture "abstraction via essentialization," a process by which the history of Being is "disconnected from political and historical events."[24]

IV.

To fully understand the "Letter on Humanism," it must be considered not merely as a philosophical meditation on the hubris of subjectivity in the blinding light of Being, but as a careful reformulation and restructuring of a narrative on the event with which Heidegger is most profoundly concerned: the collapse of Germany, whose chief victim Heidegger considered to be himself. Recently, several scholars have added significantly to our knowledge of the philosophical implications of Heidegger's involvement in Nazism, particularly Otto Pöggeler, Tom Rockmore, and Richard Wolin.[25] Especially after the biographical spadework of Farias and Ott, there is little doubt, as Pöggeler notes, that Heidegger himself "placed the decision about the truth of Being as he sought it in a political context."[26] This emerging "historicization" of Heidegger's Nazism will, however, by necessity remain incomplete as long as the archives are barred to the scrutiny of scholars.[27]

Nonetheless, a plausible account of Heidegger's changing attitude toward Germany's political destiny can be gleaned from his *Introduction to Metaphysics* (1935), the wartime lectures on Nietzsche, and the courses on Heraclitus and Parmenides during the early 1940s. In 1935, less than a year after leaving his post as rector of the university, Heidegger's lectures still insisted on the possibility of a "new beginning," that "primordial event" which decided the fate of the history of the West and the essence of truth. Since the Greek poets and thinkers first produced the grammar of the West, their view of Being—as essence and existence—has prevailed. But that view, that man and not Being as Being is the essence of Truth, has led to a "flattening," to the nihilistic struggle over "values," to the reign of technology, and to having "fallen out of Being without knowing it."[28] As a consequence, the "historical destiny of the West" had culminated in a fatal "enfeeblement of the spirit," a weakness rendering it incapable of standing up to the singular task of repeating the primordial achievement of the Greeks at the outset of Western history—of constituting a new beginning.

National Socialism alone could enable Germany to fulfill its historic mission and reverse this destiny, to overcome "the darkening of the world."[29] Germany is entrusted with this "vocation" because it is "the most metaphysical of nations," because its poets and thinkers (Hölderlin and Nietzsche) are the most profound, and because "this nation, as a historical nation, must move itself and thereby the history of the West beyond the center of their future 'happening' and into the primordial realm of the Greeks."[30] In the famous *Der Spiegel* interview of 1966, Heidegger still considered this kinship to be operative: "I have in mind especially the inner relationship of the German language with the language of the Greeks and with their thought."[31]

"This Europe," Heidegger wrote in the *Introduction to Metaphysics*, "lies today in a great pincers, squeezed by Russia on the one side and America on the other." From a metaphysical point of view, "they are of course identical" (communism and liberalism) insofar as they are "the same dreary technological frenzy."[32] To break this threat Germany must wear the uniform of a ruthless and consequential nihilism (Nietzsche) to confront, through total mobilization (Jünger), the metaphysics of technology (Bolshevism, Americanism) and the "halfhearted nihilism" of England and France.[33] In his Schelling lectures in the summer of 1936, Heidegger referred to "Hitler and Mussolini, each in his own way, as having inaugurated into Europe countermovements to nihilism," but "without the actual metaphysical dimension of Nietzschean thought being acknowledged directly."[34] German "nihilism," in other words, was a "countermovement" to the nihilism of the West, by which Heidegger meant nothing less than an inner and outer abandonment of being—*Seinsverlassenheit*—"the darkening of the world, the flight of the gods, the destruction of the earth, the transformation of men into a mass, the hatred and suspicion of everything creative."[35] For all of its limitations, he considered Nietzsche's nihilistic antinihilism to be the form of thought that defined "all areas of human actuality." In other words, the "good nihilism" of Nietzsche, embodied in Nazism and fascism as Nietzschean practice, the nihilism that acknowledges the will to power as the destiny of mankind, is pitted against the "bad nihilism" of the West, which masks its will to domination in technology, in Marxism, in its projects of subjective self-assertion. Little wonder that Heidegger regarded World War II as a war of metaphysical surrogates between American "technologism," Soviet "productivism," and German Dasein in the uniform of Nietzsche's "will to power."

Still, Heidegger's commitment to National Socialism was never a conformist parroting of the slogans of the regime. Though he dismisses Heidegger's later philosophy as continuing in this project, Rockmore rightly points out that Heidegger considered his Nazism to be higher, purer, and better than the Nazi program or the rhetoric of the racist ideologues. Since there was no single doctrine that embraced all aspects of Nazism, Heidegger could not have considered it inappropriate to carefully construct what one Nazi leader complained was his own "private" version of National Socialism, even though it more than once caused close brushes with the authorities.[36] After 1934 his lectures contain critical remarks directed against doctrinaire biologism, especially that of the racial ideologues (Alfred Bäumler, Alfred Rosenberg).

During the late 1930s Heidegger expressed his dismay at the fetishism of technology evident in the propaganda campaigns for Hermann Göring's Five-Year Plan and Albert Speer's Bureau of Beauty of Labor (Amt Schönheit der Arbeit). In an unpublished June 1938 public lecture, entitled "The Legitimation of the Modern Worldview through Metaphysics" (Die Begründung des neuzeitlichen Weltbildes durch die Metaphysik), he subsumed modernity under the metaphysical gaze of Occidental man toward self and world which produced the epoch's catastrophes: science, technology, aesthetics, culture, and the flight of the gods (*entgötterung*). These dimensions of the West all spring from the same source; "the basic procedure of modernity is the conquest of the world as image." Occidental man embarked on the rational conquest of the world in knowledge and action, which culminated in the "battle of worldviews" (*Kampf um die Weltanschauungen*) for preeminence. The "ratio," in Schelling's words, becomes the "court of Judgment for the determination of the essence of Being." Nothing escapes this struggle of worldviews, and in accordance with the meaning of this struggle, human beings put into play the unrestricted power of calculation, planning, and indoctrination. Thus Heidegger's post-Rectorate reckoning with National Socialism took the form of a critique of technology that considered National Socialism as merely one expression of modernity and no longer as its "overcoming."[37]

This is a central theme of Heidegger's *Beiträge zur Philosophie* (1936–1939), unpublished in his lifetime, which frequently equates National Socialism with the reign of technology, "machinism," and "gigantism."[38] In this work Heidegger acknowledges that there would be "no countermovements to nihilism" and castigates the lack of a Herculean effort on the part of those who failed to initiate the new beginning: "The foundation of this essence demands, of course, an effort of thought, which must have been brought to completion only at the first beginning of Western thought." By contrast, he condemned those who remain excluded from this "thinking path," and who "take flight" in

" 'new' contents and preoccupy themselves with outfitting the 'political' and the 'racial' with an until now unprecedented dressing up [*Aufputz*] of the old display pieces of philosophy."[39] Yet to call this evidence of Heidegger's opposition to National Socialism, or even a "critique" as does Silvio Vietta, is nonsense, since Heidegger never believed that the actual Third Reich had anything "essential" to do with what was referred to, sotto voce, as his "Freiburg National Socialism."[40]

V.

Despite the lack of corroborating letters and personal documents, much detail about Heidegger's involvement with Nazism is now known. However, one important aspect has escaped the attention of scholars. Though Heidegger was not associated with any particular faction—and certainly not with any form of resistance—in 1940-1941 he briefly played a small part in what can be called the "humanism debate" within National Socialism. It was then that the problem of "humanism" was first posed politically for Heidegger, in a way that directly affected his own position, and his "solution" in many ways anticipates the one put forward in the "Letter" six years later.

There were several reasons why Nazi ideologues, particularly Rosenberg, became concerned with "humanism" shortly before the outbreak of war in 1939. First, closer relations between Hitler and Mussolini after the exchange of "state visits" in 1938 raised the issue of the potentially corrupting influence of Italian fascism. Fascism, it should be emphasized, was not unproblematically regarded by the leading ideologues of the Third Reich. Though considered "kindred," it idealized both elements of modernism in the arts and a Roman and Florentine past that competed with, if not overshadowed, the claims of "Nordic" doctrinaires that blood and not culture was the source of German superiority. Among the ideologues there was a good deal of concern that certain Italian intellectuals, for example, Giuseppe Bottai, the Italian minister of education and culture, were clandestinely smuggling a dangerous version of fascism into Germany which stressed humanism and nonracial ideals.[41] Nazi propagandists attacked the "ruin fetishism" of the Italian Renaissance because "the humanists were beautiful speechifyers for a *Bildung* lacking in *Volkstümlichkeit* [roots in the people]."[42]

After the war began in 1939, anti-German propaganda coming from the exiles (most prominently from Thomas Mann) persistently contrasted "the values and goodness" of the Anglo-American democracies

(humanism) with the barbaric violence of the Axis powers. Nazi propagandists orchestrated an ideological campaign against "humanism" to
coincide with the invasion of Poland and with England's declaration of
war against Germany, a campaign that was intensified after the fall of
France and during 1940-1941, as evidenced by the publication of new
"black lists" of anti-German, Jewish, and Anglo-American writers.[43]

However, if, as Heidegger argued, the war was essentially a war of
nihilistic powers, if it was merely an expression of "the will to power,"
then, as Domenico Losurdo rhetorically asks, "what is the sense of taking sides with one or the other of the parties in the struggle?"[44] This
campaign put Heidegger in the position of reaffirming his commitment
to German nihilism and demonstrating its superiority over the various
"humanisms" that constituted the thought and action of the West. Heidegger's wartime lectures leave no doubt that he was not at all indifferent to the outcome of the conflict. His enthusiasm for the expansionism
of the German war machine was—despite all criticism of technology—
often boundless, its victories the result of "a fundamental metaphysical
law of power itself," and all Allied criticism of "dictatorship and authoritarianism" hypocritical moralizing.[45] The "new beginning" is the
"unconditional domination of nihilism"; the active nihilism of Nazism
not merely the triumph of the "New Order" but a completion, destruction, and ultimate triumph over the passive, decadent nihilism of the
West and its "halfheartedness." In the summer of 1941, Heidegger
opened his lectures with the pronouncement, "History signifies here, if
again at first glance only arbitrarily, *the advent of a decision about the
essence of Truth*."[46] Heidegger's identification of this German/Greek
advent squares with his interpretation of the war as the decisive conflict
in which the "West," or Germany, would triumph over the "East" and
the non-European Americans.[47]

At that time, Heidegger found himself under increasing scrutiny by
the racial ideologues around Alfred Rosenberg for his insistence on
reading National Socialism through the prism of his "Hellenism"
rather than through the prism of race. The distinction is important, because the "Hellenism" of Nazism's leading artists, for example, Arno
Breker and Josef Thorak, was approved by Hitler, while the Nordicists
were apparently concerned that an excessive emphasis on Greece could
in fact be a Trojan horse for humanistic "ideals." The classical Greek
educational ideal (*Bildungsideal*) of the so-called Third Humanism,
which reached its apotheosis in Germany during the last decades of the

nineteenth century, was castigated as a "schoolmaster affair" in contrast to the authentic Volkisch values of the Nazi revolution. The most important of these attacks was made in 1940 by the Heidelberg professor Ernst Krieck, who accused Heidegger of belonging to a long list of "philosophers from Heraclitus and Parmenides to Hegel" who had attempted "to replace and suppress" reality by the concept rather than to describe and actively transform it.[48] Krieck further charged that a "campaign against the gods, heroes, and poets, against nature and history," was being carried on by Heidegger, which he also intimated was being orchestrated by his student and colleague, the Italian-born philosopher Ernesto Grassi. The virulence of Krieck's attack on Heidegger is significant for several reasons. First, Krieck, though Heidegger's bitterest opponent from the outset, had not been actively hostile since the Rectorate, when along with Rosenberg and the Marburg philosopher Erich Haensch he had mobilized colleagues to block Heidegger from assuming a leading position either in Prussia or in the Reich.[49] The new attack clearly signaled the onset of a potentially dangerous public campaign against him. Second, the attacks were directed, not at Heidegger's lack of fidelity to the movement's Weltanschauung, as they had been in the 1930s, but against his resistance to the "triumphal" ascendancy of myth over pure logic and ontology. Heidegger's notion of "Being" (Sein), or "consciousness," Krieck asserted, belonged to the autonomous rationalism of the last century and therefore to the "miscarriage [Ausgeburt] of universalist nihilism."[50] In other words, reading Krieck's attack politically, Heidegger could be considered a protohumanist, an opponent of the National Socialist "myth," and might potentially even be declared an enemy of the state.

Earlier in 1940, Grassi, a student of Heidegger since 1928, then teaching as an honorary professor at the University of Berlin, had published an annual entitled Geistige Überlieferung: Ein Jahrbuch (Spiritual Legacy: A Yearbook), devoted to the "illumination of the essence of humanism and the Renaissance, and the influence of Antiquity on both," which included contributions by several German as well as Italian scholars.[51] Otto and Farias have discovered that Heidegger's contribution to the scheduled second volume of the Yearbook, "Plato's Concept of Truth," which was to contain his equation of "humanism" with "nihilism" and "metaphysics" ("Der Beginn der Metaphysik im Denken Platons ist zugleich der Beginn des Humanismus"), eventually became the subject of serious conflict between Joseph Goebbels and Rosenberg, who had tried to prevent Heidegger's contribution from appearing in print. In fact, Rosenberg's academic overseers in the Hauptamt Wissenschaft had paid close attention to Grassi's academic activities, particularly since he was the Mussolini regime's unofficial mediator between German and Italian scholarship.[52] This discovery is extremely important, though hardly, as Farias characteristically exaggerates, evidence of a "pressure group that acted in favor of Heidegger with Goebbels' support."[53] Nothing could be more unfair than to saddle Heidegger with belonging to a faction of the Nazi elite. Rather, the importance of the affair is that it reveals that a number of prominent thinkers (among them Grassi, the Königsberg classicist Walter F. Otto, and the philologist Karl Reinhardt) tried sub rosa to put forward an esoteric "Hellenist" interpretation of humanism in which "the Spirit of Greek philosophy since Nietzsche speaks to us more profoundly than ever."[54]

The "humanism" affair of 1940–1941 was clearly not a well-publicized event. Grassi, who later defended Italian humanism against Heidegger's disparaging of the Renaissance as inauthentic and superficial, gingerly attempted to mark out a path between the racialists and what was then regarded as the "contemporary humanism" of the Italians, who like Bottai saw their forerunners in the Roman imperium and in the Greek-Roman spirituality of the Renaissance. The study of Greek antiquity is "the most sublime manifestation of German life," Otto wrote in his preface, and the renewal of the Greek spirit is simultaneously the creation of a German "new man." Yet the esoteric challenge of these "Hellenists" to the National Socialist "Nordicists," who claimed that their "tradition" was "Indogermanic," and that *Volk, Blut,* and *Rasse* were concepts derived from biology and not from culture, did not go unnoticed by the Office for Indoctrination, or Amt Rosenberg, which reacted in an article by Wilhelm Brachmann, an evangelical theologian. Brachmann contrasted the "contemporary humanism" of the Italians and this group of Germans with the "political humanism" of Hans F. K. Günther, the proponent of a "racial science."[55] Talk of humanism, Brachmann claimed, was a way of evading the real connection to antiquity, "the blood-determined spiritual inheritance of the Indogermanic peoples."[56] Heidegger's presence among the defenders of the cult of Nietzsche and classical antiquity appeared to Rosenberg as proof that his "position on the important problem of humanism helps to validate the Italian claims to exist and compete with German science."[57] The Amt Rosenberg demanded Heidegger's article be removed on the grounds that Heidegger was sowing confusion by supporting Grassi's efforts to import humanism "in the German spiritual world": "Heidegger went against the position recently defended by Comrade Wilhelm Brachmann in the National Socialist *Monatshefte*. His position indicates strongly and insistently that for us in Germany contemporary humanism has ceased to exist and that we oppose to the contemporary humanism a political humanism."[58]

Farias reveals that Heidegger's contribution was only finally permitted to appear at the request of the Duce, who through the Italian ambassador Dino Odoardo Alfieri, interceded personally with Goebbels. Rosenberg had to content himself with the assurance that the "press will not mention Heidegger's article."[59] In fact, when "Plato's Concept of Truth" was published in the second volume of the *Jahrbuch* in 1942, it did not coincide with either the position of the racialists, the fascists represented by Bottai, or the humanists around Grassi and Otto. Heidegger's claim that humanism—including its most radical "completion" in Nietzsche—was a fatal error in the philosophical/historical constitution of the West and that the poetic/philosophic advent is still to come avoided the reprobation of the racialists without subscribing to what Brachmann called "Erasmian, that is West European-cosmopolitan humanism."[60]

Heidegger carefully defined humanism as "the inclusive process that is bound up with the beginning, the unfolding, and the end of metaphysics, and which, in accord with any one of several differing perspectives, but each time knowingly, the human being is placed in the center of Being without therefore becoming the highest being."[61] Heidegger carefully included the typical Nazi definition of "man" among universalist, individualist, national, and ethnic "humanisms": " 'The human being,' here means, first a humanity or humanity [*Menschentum oder die Menschheit*], then an individual or a community [*Einzelnen oder eine Gemeinschaft*], then a people or group of people [*Volk oder eine Völkergruppe*]."[62] Yet Heidegger still left the door open for what the rector of the University of Göttingen, Hans Drexler, saw as a revival of Third Humanism, of a "heroic National Socialism," and—with obvious reference to Heidegger's Rectorial Address—a return to the Greek principles of "risk" and "decision."[63] In fact, the larger premise of the Rectorial Address, that "science in the ancient Greek sense will realize the Nazi goal," was conspicuously revived in the two volumes of *Geistige Überlieferung*.[64]

VI.

Several scholars have convincingly argued that the turning point in Heidegger's Nietzschean National Socialism came only after the "decision," which the war posed, was resolved at Stalingrad.⁶⁵ Russia's "metaphysical," not to mention military, triumph demanded a revision as to which "nihilism" was the most "complete." Though Heidegger still hoped for a German victory, after 1942 he now seemed to accept the possibility that "Europe" might not be redeemed by a new primordiality won on the battlefields of "Asia." Some of Heidegger's most pessimistic thoughts about politics come to light in his summer 1942 lecture cycle on Parmenides, where he unambiguously identifies National Socialism with Imperial Rome, as opposed to the authentic politics of the Greeks: the difference between the Roman *res publica* and the Greek *polis* is equated with the difference between the modern concept of the essence of truth or the Roman *rectitudo* and the Greek *Aletheia*. The metaphysical passion of today's Russians for technology is understandable, he claims, because the Russians are bringing "the technical world to power." Technology, for Heidegger, "*is* our history" (*GA*, 54, 127).

Nietzsche too is reconsidered in this light, since his evocation of the polis in Roman terms (like spirit and culture) confuses the modern "power state" with the Greek "site" of tragedy (*GA*, 54, 133). Before 1942 Heidegger saw democracy, socialism, and communism as variants of halfhearted nihilism, as opposed to metaphysical, for example, active German, nihilism. Now, after the German defeat was at least "thinkable," the latter option faded, replaced by the passivity of the philosopher who must wait patiently for Being to disclose itself. This disclosure occurs cataclysmically, through the tragic events of history: "the terror, horror, and calamity [*Unheil*]" that befall the polis.

Heidegger's interpretation of the polis as a site of tragedy explains some of the most puzzling passages of the "Letter." The unambiguous tilt toward Marxism, which Jaspers called "lethal," can be interpreted as Heidegger's concession to the new reality that the "West," for example, Germany (but also England and France), had been decisively defeated, that Stalin's victory (and America's) also signaled the collapse of the weak European democracies and their replacement by the new technological order. In the summer of 1942, during his course on Hölderlin, Heidegger noted that "Bolshevism is only a variety of Americanism. The latter is the genuinely dangerous form of the measureless, because it arises in the form of bourgeois democracy and is mixed with Christendom, and all of this in an atmosphere of decisive history-lessness" (*GA*, 53, 86–87).[66] Germans, Heidegger averred in 1943, would now be "tested" by those who "know nothing," who represent "mere modernity."

There is also a more justifiable opportunism at work here, insofar as Heidegger's sons were still in prisoner-of-war camps, and he feared Georg Lukács's attacks on him were potentially a threat to them. Ironically, Lukács's review of the "Letter," entitled "Heidegger Redivivus," acknowledged Heidegger's affirmation of Marxism, noting that he indeed understood the inner connection between the private and public spheres of modern life and their respective alienation from the essential being of humanity, but that he had turned real history into the mythical pseudohistory of Being.[67]

On May 8, 1945, the day of Germany's military capitulation, Heidegger wrote the following lines in Schloss Hausen im Donautal near where the Freiburg University philosophy faculty spent the last days of the war: "On the day that the world celebrates its victory and does not yet recognize that for centuries it has already been defeated by its own insurrection" (*GA*, 77, 240). These words close a remarkable imaginary conversation "in a prisoner of war camp in Russia between a younger and older man," obviously an allusion to Heidegger's two sons, both of whom were Soviet prisoners of war at that time. It encapsulates Heidegger's mood on the day of the war's end, as well as his reflections on the "devastation" (*Verwustung*), "evil" (*das Böse*), Nietzsche's "will to power," and what it means to be German. After a brief prologue on the healing power of the "distance" (*Weite*) evoked by the forest in contrast to the "unhealing narrowness of the camp," Heidegger turns to the matter of Germany's devastation. His concern is not with the "blindness with which our own people was led astray," since that is "too pathetic (*kläglich*) to waste time complaining about" (*GA*, 77, 206). Rather, "the devastation we are talking about does not exist since only yesterday" (*GA*, 77, 206). That devastation, he continues, "cannot be tallied in what is manifest and graspable, nor in the enumeration of the destruction and the extinction of human life" (*GA*, 77, 207).

For Heidegger, the devastation of the earth and the liquidation of the human beings that accompanies it, not the "blindness," is evil. This evil, he continues, has nothing to do with what is usually called morally wrong or ethically contemptible. Rather, the source of this evil is the "rebelliousness" (*Aufrührerische*) that rests on "wrathfulness," the boundaryless self-empowerment and "will to power" of the West. Nietzsche, whose "beyond good and evil" and "will to power" was the "counterworld" (*Gegenwelt*) to the Platonic world, still did not grasp that "will" itself is evil. Even if the "rageful functionaries of their own mediocrity" must be "held in check," they too are consequences of that devastation, but never the source of the devastation itself. " 'Devastation' means, rather, that the world, human beings, and the earth are transformed into a desert" (*GA*, 77, 211).

In this text, Germany's defeat, the victory of the Allies, even the crimes of Nazism vaguely alluded to here, are not world historical "events" in the Heideggerian sense. These ephemeral occurrences are assimilated to a nebulous global history of decline of the West, which philosophy, not history, can best comprehend: "The devastation is not the consequence of the world wars, but the world wars are already only a consequence of the devastation that has been visited upon the earth for centuries" (*GA*, 77, 211). To be German, Heidegger concludes in the very hour of Germany's defeat, is to grasp the fact that devastation is merely the completion of the nihilism that first appears in the "abandonment of being" (*Seinsverlasseheit*) and to recognize it, not the collapse of the Reich, as "a world event that encircles the earth" (*GA*, 77, 215). Germans must forgo their claim to nationality that is nothing else than the "pure subjectivity of a people" and assume their more proper role as expecting and anticipating the advent of Sein: "then the people of poets and thinkers would be in a unique sense, an expectant people [*wartende Volk*]" (*GA*, 77, 233).

In the "Letter," written more than a year later, Heidegger does not hide his contempt for the victorious nihilisms: "Whoever takes 'communism' only as a 'party' or a 'Weltanschauung' is thinking too shallowly, just as those who by the term 'Americanism' mean, and mean derogatorily, nothing more than a particular lifestyle" (LH, 220). Similarly, Heidegger once again condemned both "nationalism" and "internationalism" as mirror forms of anthropologism, equally nihilistic humanisms, with the inescapable conclusion that to conceive of National Socialism as a "worldview" is equally shallow. Viewed from the Olympian perspective of their essential, that is, metaphysical, truths, the defeat of Germany is a catastrophe—and not just for Germany but for its historical mission. The "worldview" of the movement is one thing, he noted, the metaphysical heroism of young poets in uniform quite another. How else can we interpret the lines, "When confronted with death, therefore, those young Germans who knew about Hölderlin lived and thought something other than what the public held to be the typical German attitude" (LH, 219)?

Heidegger, who had stated unequivocally in 1942–1943 that the Germans alone could deliver the West into its beginning, that this historical Volk had already "triumphed and cannot be triumphed over," feared in 1946 that the "danger" that Germany's defeat poses for "Europe" is its "falling behind" in its "provenance" to announce the new dawn. Unavoidably delayed by catastrophic defeat, the advent is postponed; "the conflict with respect to the interpretation of beings" cannot be settled, he concludes, "*because it has not yet been kindled*" (LH, 223).

The catastrophe is not the collapse of National Socialism, which itself had become a nihilism, or of Nietzscheanism, which deserved what it essentially got, but of Heidegger's conception of National Socialism, the advent of a new order of Being. National Socialism and the war were not a catastrophe for its victims, only a catastrophe for the advent of Being. What the outcome of the war decided was only the "postponement of the crisis and conflict" that leads to its "unconcealment." It is hardly accidental, then, that the "Letter" concludes with an appeal to Being's guardians and shepherds for an "open resistance to humanism" (LH, 225).

Heidegger expressed his ultimate judgment on the outcome of World War II even more clearly in 1951–1952.

> What did the Second World War decide, if we do not mention its terrible consequences for our Fatherland, in particular the tear through its Center? This World War has decided nothing, if we use "decision" here in so high and broad a sense that it pertains solely to the destiny of the essence of humanity upon the earth.[68]

The "Letter" is a gesture of defiance in the cloak of humility. Heidegger's complaints about the "peculiar dictatorship of the public sphere," the conflict of "isms," and his tilt toward Marxism reveal his barely disguised contempt for the occupation. It is also a direct answer to the call for a reckoning with the Nazi past and an opening to democracy, which Jaspers issued in *The Question of German Guilt*, and, as the following chapter demonstrates, which he and the university committee found so utterly lacking in Heidegger. The comment Heidegger sent to his former student, Elisabeth Blochmann, who had spent the war in English exile, in March 1947 is indicative of just how defiant his posture was at that juncture.

But we are now, as we have been for a long time, in the center of Europe, and as a result, the fatal consequence [*Verhängnis*] has a wholly different power over us. The "West" of course already collapsed at a time when no one spoke about it. Other "powers" have long since become *real*. But the question remains nevertheless: whether this reality is the beginning or only the end of the process that for three hundred years has determined the epoch of modernity [*Neuzeit*].[69]

What was that "power" become real, that process, and that collapse which has already occurred? Not merely the collapse of the Third Reich, or of Hitler, who, in Heideggerian terms, only functioned as a "Myrmidon" (*Schergen*). Rather, the victory of the American and Soviet armies constituted a descent into a metaphysics of the machine or, "in Marxist terms," the "power of the technical," whose first victim is Germany. The "Letter" expresses this tragedy in these terms: "German is not spoken to the world so that the world might be reformed though the German essence; rather it is spoken to the Germans so that from a fateful belongingness to the nations they might become world historical along with them" (LH, 218). In other words, the German catastrophe is globalized, insofar as "homelessness is coming to be the destiny of the world" (LH, 219).

From this point of view, it is not surprising that a philosopher whose thought centers on the "forgetting of Being," and who is frequently concerned with remembrance (*Andenken*), never publicly remarked on or even alluded to the killing of the Jews, except to coldly compare it to "motorized agriculture."[70] Heidegger's notorious remarks in a letter to his former student Herbert Marcuse which arrogantly refused to distinguish between the fate of the Jews and the fate of East Germans are entirely consistent.[71] The collapse of the one true nihilism capable of carrying metaphysics to its completion was the only true catastrophe of 1945, compared to which a few million victims was a mere sideshow.[72]

In the "Letter," National Socialism, whose essence remains unscathed by its unprecedented crimes, is transferred onto the higher plane of the "West" and joins the metaphysics of the subject, humanism, and nihilism. From Plato to Nietzsche, the error of the West turns out to be Heidegger's and Germany's error. Reduced to one wrong turn, the philosopher's error is indistinguishable from the error of all metaphysical "isms," and that error is no error at all because it belongs to the disclosing/revealing history of Being.[73] The "Letter" is a missive from Being to man, absolving its author from all responsibility. As Habermas put it, "The eventuating of Being transposes the thinker into error. He is absolved from all personal responsibility, because error it-self objectively befalls him. A mistake could be ascribed only to an in-tellectual, an unessential thinker."[74] But Heidegger's judgment, that Na-tional Socialism failed because it was essentially yet another humanism destined to obliterate the light of Sein, is not merely exculpatory. It reflects on his own hubris as well, that of the philosopher whose privi-leged access to the realm of Being now revealed to him that his own residual humanism, which just as surely led to his current historical cir-cumstances, was only the consequence of the same "devastation" that brought about the *Unheil* of World War II. What Heidegger was unable to accept was that even if the murder of the Jews was a "metaphysical" or ideological project, that did not make it any less a caesura, any less an event for the victims. Only through an acceptance of the event as a historical occurrence and not as a primordial "sending" of Being, or a postponement of the advent, can that event even begin to be thematized. Heidegger's scandal is not that he was attuned to the appeal of Being but that he was deaf to the lamentations of the earth.[75]

VII.

When he wrote the "Letter" in late 1946, Heidegger already knew that the University Committee would likely prohibit him from teaching, even if the question of his premature retirement or an "emeritus" clas-sification remained undecided. Yet he soon became aware that the French occupation of Baden might also offer a way out of his dilemma. In the spring of 1945 Heidegger proposed and was refused—"sans dou-ceur"—the right to hold a small private seminar on Pascal and seven-teenth-century religious thought.[76] In 1945–1946, Heidegger was un-characteristically generous in welcoming several young French visitors who arrived in Freiburg while still in uniform (among them, Edgar Morin and Alan Resnais), granting no less than two interviews for is-sues of *Les Temps Modernes*.[77] This German/French nexus structured the double cultural context that has accompanied the story of Heideg-ger's postwar influence during the past five decades.

    For German Heideggerians of the "zero hour," there was only "*one* theme of philosophizing, not the individual human being and existence, but only and solely Being."[78] This perspective emphasizes man's passive subordination to Being, language as the "site" of Being's disclosure, and the history of metaphysics as the process by which Being delivers the decisive message of its absence to man. By shifting the emphasis to "Ek-sistence," in Heidegger's "radical reversal" (*radikale Umkehr*) "Dasein has become Being's act" or, to put it more directly, a "revelation" of Being to man.[79]

Heidegger's involvement in National Socialism was never mentioned in these early German commentaries whose "theological ring" echoed the "silent mastery of the past" after 1945. Adorno's *Jargon of Authenticity* (1964) was directed against what might be called the "popular" Heideggerianism manifest in the sanctimonious style of public address in which Being is the ultimate ontological "alibi," and the "testimonial" (*Aussage*) "the complementary ideology to silence."[80] Yet it is also evident that the first German Heidegger controversy did center on the question of ethical responsibility. For example, in the late 1940s and 1950s, the paramount issue was whether the text should be read as the emptying of all historical and existential contents into the overarching category of Being, so that all ethical action is by definition impossible, or whether the text points toward an overcoming (*Überwindung*) of ethics. As Beda Allemann argued, the "Letter" turned to a new language after the failure of the "metaphysical" to think the ontological difference (between being and Being), pointing to a new or "second way" of regarding humanism.[81]

This German context is far removed from the reception of the "Letter" in France after the Liberation, where the situation in 1946 was more serendipitous in two respects. First, it should be recalled that Heidegger's reputation in the French-speaking world, though tarnished, was still very much intact. In April 1940, while still in the army, Sartre declared himself a "partisan of Heidegger," and the debt to him and to Husserl was frequently acknowledged by others within the orbit of postwar phenomenology (Alexander Kojéve, Maurice Merleau-Ponty, Alphonse de Waehlens, Jean Wahl, Emmanuel Lévinas).[82]

In October 1945, Alfred de Towarnicki, still in French military uniform, attempted to arrange a meeting between Heidegger and Sartre. Though the meeting never came off, Heidegger, after some hesitation, sent Sartre a letter that has since been discovered.[83] In it he mentioned that he had been given a copy of his *L'etre et le néant* by de Towarnicki: "For the first time I was confronted with an independent thinker, who from the very foundations experienced the dimension from which I think." "Your work," he added, "is dominated by an immediacy of understanding of my philosophy, that I have never before experienced." Heidegger closed with the hope for a more "fruitful discussion" (*fruchtbare Auseinanderetzung*), but also cautioned that since he had written

Being and Time twenty years earlier, he now saw many things "more clearly and more simply." More specifically, he wrote that though he found the "introduction" and "conclusion" to Sartre's work "stimulating" (*erregend*), he now regarded these questions from the perspective of a "primordial relation to history, above all in connection with the beginning of Occidental thinking, which until today is subordinated to the predominance of Platonism."[84] He concluded by inviting Sartre, in the course of the winter, to visit him in the ski hut, "and from there to philosophize together, and make a ski tour of the Black Forest." A month later he confided to his friend Rudolf Stadelmann that he had come to realize that his work had "influenced and stimulated" the thinking of the youth of France in intellectual matters but that he preferred to wait until the opportunity existed to make his work available to the Germans before he "risked having such an influence of our thinking in France."[85]

In 1945 Marxists like Henri Lefebvre were already tarring the existentialists with a "fascist" connection—above all, that of Heidegger.[86] In 1947 Sartre published an introduction to one of *three* issues of *Les Temps Modernes* devoted to Heidegger in which he claimed—in a statement that can only be read with some astonishment—that there was no more connection between Heidegger's phenomenology and his politics than there was between Hegel's dialectical logic and his politics.[87]

If Sartre wanted to protect Heidegger's reputation, others soon recognized the latter's even greater usefulness in diminishing Sartre's. In early 1945, before they met, Beaufret published a series of articles in which he invoked Heidegger to challenge Sartre's virtually undisputed preeminence over existentialism. Even Jaspers, Beaufret contended, lacked the "power" and "originality" of Heidegger, while his other French interpreters, Lévinas and de Waehlens, for example, tended to read him through a "Cartesian perspective" (*regard Cartesienne*). Beaufret portrayed himself as the only true disciple, in contrast to Sartre, who only "exacerbated confusion." To truly grasp existentialism, he wrote, it was necessary to "taste" the real thing, the "most profound and original" thought of the great philosopher "who doubles as a great writer."[88] Beaufret later recalled that in 1944, while teaching philosophy at a lycée in Lyon, a colleague burst into his classroom with the cry, "They have landed." Beaufret reproached himself for not having had the same enthusiasm for the Allied invasion as he did for "the feeling for the first time, on that 6th of June 1944, to have begun to understand something of what Heidegger wrote."[89]

Beaufret's long career as the protector of the Heideggerian flame since 1945 has been documented, a career that reached its denouement with the 1988 scandal of the posthumous publication of two private letters of support addressed to the notorious Holocaust denier, Robert Faurisson, in 1981.[90] As early as 1945 Beaufret gave a long interview to *Le Monde,* in which he falsely claimed that Heidegger had been prohibited from publishing by the Nazis for twelve years.[91] Even prior to his first meeting with Heidegger in September 1946, Beaufret defended him against Sartre's "hasty" conclusion, published in the December 27, 1944, issue of *Action,* that "Heidegger has no character, that is the truth."[92] Beaufret's explanation of Heidegger's Nazism was that Heidegger, like Rainer Maria Rilke, naively saw in fascism "an authentic philosophy of resoluteness in the face of death." His was not merely the naïveté of a "distracted intellectual," Beaufret added, but a typical and fundamentally unconscious trait of the "petty bourgeois."[93]

After Beaufret's first encounter with Heidegger in September 1946, and after his having become familiar with Heidegger's wartime publications, Beaufret published the first article to trace Heidegger's philosophical development since *Being and Time.* This study appeared as a preface to the "Letter" in the November 1947 issue of *Fontaine.*[94] Beaufret was destined to be Heidegger's messenger in France, not only because of his fidelity to his master's voice, or his willingness to do battle against any and all of his misinterpreters and maligners, but above all because of his acute sense of the strategic possibilities of Heidegger's philosophy in new, postwar circumstances.[95]

It was Marxism, even more than existentialism, that first propelled Beaufret to make a pilgrimage to the famous hut in Todtnauburg. He was led by his correct intuition that the perspective of the history of Being sanctioned Marxism's account of violence in human history. There is an affinity between Marxism and Heidegger's postwar philosophy that appealed to Beaufret because neither hypocritically condemns what Hegel called the "slaughter bench" of history, and because for both struggle and violence are the inner law of both class struggle and *Seinsgeschichte.* Originary violence is the primordial beginning of both civil society and the "advent" of Being, and as a consequence of this recognition, both Heidegger and Marx see through the masquerade of the hypocritical humanism that serves as the West's legitimation. For Beaufret, as he succinctly put it, to be a Marxist "is to be at war precisely where the enemy pretends to be at peace."[96]

This neo-Machiavellianism of the left, it should be remembered, was not unique to Beaufret's thinking in 1947. It was characteristic of many of those postwar French intellectuals who justified communist violence on the ground that it was more "authentic" and that the verdict of history alone would decide whether humanism was served by violence. Ironically, both Heidegger and the Marxists around *Les Temps Modernes* regarded Stalin's victory as proof positive that a new historical epoch had been inaugurated. The argument that Stalinism was a "humanism" and the Moscow trials were justified by the dialectical logic of history was the basis of Merleau-Ponty's arguments in *Humanism and Terror*, which appeared in the same year (1947).[97]

The famous passage in the "Letter" proclaiming that the "Marxist view of history is superior to that of other historical accounts" (LH, 219) is therefore the chief sign of Heidegger's reciprocal acknowledgment of the opening to the left. By 1947 Beaufret's main line of defense was well rehearsed: Heidegger's philosophy is the most original and profound version of existentialism; there is no connection between *Being and Time* and National Socialism; Heidegger was a victim of Nazi ideologues; and there is no reason why Heidegger's thought could not be compatible with Marxism. The French connection explains, as I have already suggested, the otherwise inexplicable "Marxism" of the "Letter."

VIII.

The "Letter" did not merely serve its author as a grand exoneration. By situating the violence of human history in the nihilistic and destructive war of subject-centered humanisms, it offered a new generation a way out of the vicissitudes of the cold war. A radical left-wing Heideggerianism was already anticipated by Beaufret in 1947, but by the 1960s it was recast with Sartre once again the iconic representative of existential Marxism, a Marxism that had itself fallen on hard times with the explosion of sectarian politics and Maoism, not to mention Sartre's own communist apologetics. Precedents for a phenomenologically oriented Marxist appropriation of Heidegger's thinking already existed: Herbert Marcuse had attempted a Marxist-Heideggerian synthesis in his *Hegels Ontologie* (1932), and in the 1960s Kostas Axelos, Enzo Paci, and Karel Kosik each attempted their own reconstructions.[98] In this new context, the "Letter," in which Sartre's voluntaristic Heideggerianism is held up as the antipode to Heidegger's postwar thinking, called into question the very origins of political commitment and once again pointed to a way out of the dilemmas of engagement.

Derrida's "The Ends of Man," written in 1968 at the height of the Vietnam War and delivered in New York in May of that year, begins with a frontal assault on Sartre's misreading of *Being and Time.* The essay faithfully replicates the procedure of the "Letter," though Derrida's criticism is aimed directly at the edifice of French Hegelianism, built on Kojéve's reading of Hegel and Sartre's purported (mis)reading of Husserl and Heidegger. This interpretive tradition, Derrida argues, is fundamentally wedded to the logic of transcendence and thus is unable to free itself from the "ontotheological determinations" of its various essentialisms. For example, Sartre's rendering of *Dasein* as "human reality" is called "monstrous" because it leaves unexamined the entire conceptual framework with which Heidegger had so decisively broken. Whereas the Heideggerian *Dasein* is bound to a situation that is anterior to the framing of such categories as subject and object, Sartre simply substitutes one ideal of man's perfectibility for another. Existentialism, so to speak, took man for granted, and, notes Derrida, "everything occurs as if the sign 'man' had no origin, no historical, cultural, or linguistic limit" (EM, 116).[99] The "magnetic attraction" of Heidegger's "archaeological radicalness" is its uncompromising refusal to leave unquestioned any metaphysical structuring of Being, its claim to look beyond "the identity or self-presence" of any unity that claims to be collectively "man." What Derrida finds in the Sartrean emphasis on some authentic or essential truth of "the end" of man is ultimately a logic of exclusion, of distinctiveness, of privilege, which a priori corrupts its own radical premise.

However, it should also be clear to anyone with a rudimentary acquaintance with deconstruction that Derrida has never shared what he called "Heidegger's hope." There is no trace of nostalgia for a moment of thinking that reaches beyond the origins of the first "false" Enlightenment of the Greek thought of Being, beyond Plato and the West, where language was pure in the light of Being, not yet implicated in false claims to logic, truth, or hierarchy or power. Here Derrida parts company with Heidegger, who still remains within the metaphysical tradition of a higher, more profound humanism of "letting be," or "listening to Being." Derrida's response to Lévinas turns Heidegger upside down by insisting not on an ethical reading of Being "as a pluralism which does not fuse into unity" but on the impossibility of returning

to a humanist ethics. Lévinas had seen that the priority of Being subor-
dinates, tyrannizes, and neutralizes the other to such a degree that "ontology as a first philosophy is a philosophy of power."[100] Yet Derrida
regards Lévinas's return to the subjectivity of the other, the face-to-face
encounter that is prior to all positing of being, as something quite impossible apart "from a hollow space of finitude in which messianic eschatology comes to resonate" (VM, 103). In short, violence in Derrida's
critique cannot be reduced to a purely ethical act without taking into
account "violence as the origin of meaning" (VM, 127).

My point here is not that Derrida succumbed to a totalitarian temptation or that Heidegger's thought be quarantined. Nor am I claiming that deconstruction is simply unadulterated Heideggerianism or, as
Tzvetan Todorov claims, that "today's Heideggerianism has simply taken
up where yesterday's exhausted Marxism left off."[101] Heidegger's project
of "overcoming metaphysics," in Derrida's essay does not take the form
of humanism or antihumanism but posits an escape or remove from the
opposition between them.[102] The power of the text to transcend its immediate circumstances and still generate—as it has for Lévinas, for
Arendt, and also for Habermas—"lasting insights" is undeniable.[103]

For Derrida, especially in 1968, Heidegger's radical critique of sub-
jectivist metaphysics would not permit him to remain content with
Lévinas's ethical nonviolence, precisely because Heidegger's postmeta-
physical thinking penetrated to "the violent relationship of the West to
its other," a relationship in which language is complicit with an ethno-
logical, economic, political, and military violence. Satisfying as it may
have been at the height of the Vietnam War, Derrida's response leaves
the more fundamental question unasked: Did not Heidegger's "original" framing of humanism as a metaphysics of the will to power level
all distinctions? How do we now evaluate the legacy of Heidegger's
refusal to distinguish among the "humanisms" of the West (which includes its most extreme racist manifestation), his flattening of the history of Being? The irony that before 1945 the majority of Heideggeri-
ans were on the right and after 1946, on the left, does not minimize the
crucial weakness in the post-Heideggerian "questioning" of the political, its "bias to denigrate public life," to define politics entirely in terms
of the exclusionary matrix of all metaphysical humanisms: "man, production, biology, race."[104] This difficulty has not escaped even those
who are sympathetic to Heidegger's thought, like Domenique Janicaud,
who has called it "a complete blurring of the ontical specificities of the
political dimension."[105]

Derrida sought to confront this difficulty in his 1987 account of Heidegger's involvement in National Socialism, *Of Spirit*.[106] Derrida contends that Heidegger, who should have known better, consciously returned to the word "Spirit" in the Rectorial Address and the texts of the Nazi period without deploying the all-important "scare quotes" that still surrounded it in *Being and Time*. This return to a metaphysics of "presence" is no mere lapsus but rather, Derrida speculates, a tactical move, by which Heidegger opposed and resisted the worst of Nazism— its racism—by sanctioning its "spiritual" project of a German/Greek resurrection of the West. This move, however, commits two sins at once: it assents to Nazism, and it restores the "subjectivism" already exercised from *Being and Time*, a linguistic regression that made Heidegger complicit with Nazism by putting a "decision" about "history" in the realm of human action. The Rectorial Address, Derrida claims, "capitalizes on the worst, that is on both evils at once: the sanctioning of nazism, and the gesture that is still metaphysical" (*OS*, 40). Heidegger's justification of Nazism was made inevitable by his having recourse to a metaphysical language that he had already once abandoned, the language of humanism.

There are three serious problems with Derrida's conceptualization of Heidegger's involvement. First, historians who are aware that Nazism never prescribed a monolithic ideology, that its political polyvalence carried over into matters of doctrine, will find his juxtaposition of "spirit and race" simplistic. As we have seen, Nazism permitted a relatively polyphonous array of ideological doctrines, and even the primacy of "race" was never wholly enunciated as an official doctrine. The "humanism debate" during the early 1940s reveals Heidegger's effort to find a middle path between his own earlier formulation of a philosophical approach to Nazism and the doctrine of racial breeding.

Second, Derrida unquestioningly accepts Heidegger's claim to having "resisted" National Socialism, a claim that even Heidegger himself revealed to be disingenuous, when, in 1945, he directed a few bitter remarks about "guilt" to those who did not—"in a secret bond"—seek, as he did, to "refine and temper" the movement that had gained power.[107] Heidegger's Hellenic-Nietzschean National Socialism was, as I have indicated, distinctive, but it could only be considered "opposed" to Nazi doctrine as a potentially influential alternative within Nazism's fundamental premises.

Third, Derrida's overemphasis on the absence of the "scare quotes" around "spirit" in the Rectorial Address does indeed point to a difference from *Being and Time,* but it underestimates the more fundamentally nationalist and activist sense of a German mission in Heidegger's Nazism. In that respect, Heidegger's vision of a German/Greek polis, the fundamentally aesthetic ideal of state construction in its originary violence, is reduced to a linguistic misstep. Here Lacoue-Labarthe's reading of Heidegger's "archi-fascism" is more consistent with his insistence on a Greek/German synthesis in the Rectorial Address. For Heidegger, a second German/Greek beginning was the true promise of Nazism: a reorientation in the interpretation of the essence of knowledge, an overturning of slave morality, a shift in the meaning of *technē*—or making real. This German Greece or "meta-Greece" (Germany, Lacoue-Labarthe says, "only exists in the distress of not existing") is an aesthetic reversal, the substitution of a poetic state for a scientific-technological one.[108]

Toward the end of *Of Spirit* Derrida poses the issue that his own involvement in the "Heidegger Affair" of 1987 brought to public attention the more serious question of the Heideggerian legacy. How do we account not merely for Heidegger's failing to perceive the essential truth of the regime he supported but for his more consequential attempt to extricate himself from his "error" by demonstrating that it was the product, perhaps even the necessary disclosure, of a more fundamental history of Being?

Derrida does not go so far as to claim, as does Lacoue-Labarthe, that "Nazism is a humanism insofar as it rests upon a determination of *humanitas.*"[109] But he does argue that Heidegger trapped himself in the fatal logic of his own metaphysical discourse by opposing spirit to race. His mistake was not merely trying to "humanize Nazism." Rather, by opposing racism with his own spiritualized "will to power" he could still believe that National Socialism—despite its ideological excesses— would be the vehicle of Being's self-disclosure. In short, in spite of its "worldview," the "Nietzschean" nihilism of National Socialism might still be Being's way of disclosing to man that the epoch of metaphysics was at an end. Heidegger's thought was still hopelessly "metaphysical," "caught in the metaphysico-Platonic-Christian oppositions of the below and the beyond" (*OS,* 33).

Only in 1953, in an essay on the poet Georg Trakl, Derrida claims, did Heidegger finally extinguish the term "spirit," consigning it to "flame." The flame, and here one can only interpret, is a sign of recognition that all metaphysical humanisms are ultimately complicit in their respective political involvements, including those they claim to resist.

This complicity is inevitable once the language of metaphysics, of the "truth of man," is invoked, even for those who did not embrace, or resisted, Nazism.

> Because one cannot demarcate oneself from biologism, from naturalism, from racism in its genetic form, one cannot be *opposed* to them except by reinscribing spirit in an oppositional determination, by once again making it a unilaterality of subjectivity, even if in its voluntarist form. (*OS*, 39)

What was attractive to Derrida in 1968 was that the "Letter" avoided the "contaminations" of an overinflated subjectivity: of revolutionary utopianism, of political commitments fallen into disrepute, corrupted by bloody regimes, terrorism, and violence. Heidegger's own complicity was relegated to the margins of the text. At the time, it appeared that only a radical refusal of metaphysics could outwit the rapid descent of the New Left into its own revolutionary apocalypse. Yet, in 1987, Derrida seemed to acknowledge that we can no longer be seduced into thinking that there is any magical formula that avoids such future "risks." This risk—Derrida says—is even there for those who opposed Nazism (he includes Heidegger) since there is a "law of commonality" that persists in any appeal to "spiritual" freedom, "threads shared by Nazism and non-Nazism, the law of resemblance, the fatality of perversion." What this means, in the final analysis, is that there can be no avoiding the contaminations of intellectual traditions—that there is very little difference between fascism and antifascism.[110]

It seems that for Derrida the circle has come round, from Sartrean antifascism, with its own lethal contaminations, to Heidegger's "solution" and once again to Heidegger's own contamination. Yet this also brings us back to the issue of the unresolved legacy. By introducing the problem of the need to establish differences and distinctions within metaphysics, Derrida seems at once to accept and to resist the conclusion that in the end the problem still remains one of "demarcations." The crucial passage deserves full quotation:

> The constraint of this program remains very strong, it reigns over the majority of discourses which, today and for a long time to come, state their opposition to racism, to totalitarianism, to nazism, to fascism, etc., and do this in the name of spirit, in the name of an axiomatic—for example, that of democracy or "human rights"—which directly or not, comes back to this metaphysics of *subjectivity*. All the pitfalls of this strategy of establishing demarcations belong to this program, whatever place one occupies in it. *The only choice is the choice between the terrifying contaminations it assigns.*

Even if all forms of complicity are not equivalent, they are irreducible. The question of knowing which is the least grave of these forms of complicity is always there, its urgency and its seriousness could not be overstressed, but it will never dissolve the irreducibility of this fact. (*OS,* 40; my italics)

If indeed the "forms of complicity" are a constant, why does Derrida foreground their "irreducibility" against the background of their non-equivalence? What does this reversal of emphasis mean? If the "only choice" is between these forms, if the urgent matter for us is to discern the ways in which they "are not equivalent," why does he bring us back finally to what is not different, not alterable, "irreducible"? Is this point of conclusion not in fact just a beginning, whose next logical step might be that *"humanisms" do not have the same face,* that some "transcendental" systems of belief—Nazism, for example—cannot be equated with humanism at all?

Is this admission not already implicit in Derrida's own construction of a Heideggerian "Spirit" as the philosopher's antipode to race, so that even within the terms of the Nazi discourse we have discussed, he makes a hierarchy of "demarcations"? Does not "Spirit" still transcend racism's natural determinations? Does Derrida not return here to the problem of "will," and "action," even perhaps to "tolerance," precisely the terms exorcised once and for all by the "Letter"? And finally, is not the legacy of the "Letter" that, by absolving Heidegger of responsibility and complicity, by making his error the error of all "humanism" since Plato, it too becomes yet another "totalizing" program? Is Derrida conceding that there is no way of *not* returning to the "metaphysics" of being, to privilege one account of "subjectivity" over another, to at once recognize that the "terrifying" side of Reason or "Spirit" is that it obliterates difference, and yet to see that obliteration in terms that do not "anesthetize" us to the contingencies of human experience?

If we can no longer revoke the knowledge of "contamination" and complicity that these critiques, Heidegger's no less than the others, have urged on us, if now we recognize the complicity of all humanisms, all projects of enlightenment, all transcendental subjects, then we are faced with the task of making a different kind of distinction. The upshot of the Heidegger question is that the question for us is no longer a simplistic "for" or "against" humanism. For if humanism can no longer be idealized except by willful naïveté and denial of catastrophe, so it can no longer be monolithically dismissed except by an equally totalizing conceptual framework that obliterates such distinctions. Such distinctions can only be made by conceding that in politics ethical considerations do matter, that humanism is not always entirely indifferent to history's victims, and is sometimes even conceived as an expression of solidarity with them.

To make this sort of discrimination returns Derrida and us to the problem distinguishing between the overpowering indifference of some projects of humanism, for example, Stalinism, and of antihumanisms like Nazism and those democratic forms that are still capable of solidarity with suffering and reflection. The problem of "humanism" is that it is not historically uniform, uncontradictory, monolithic; reason cannot be dismissed "by the yardstick of a teleological history of humanity."[111] Although it was not written with the "Letter" in mind, to have identified this problem in the same catastrophic event as Heidegger, but from the point of view of solidarity with its victims, is, as we shall see in the concluding chapter, the lasting contribution of Adorno and Horkheimer's *Dialectic of Enlightenment*.

Unlike Heidegger, Adorno and Horkheimer were able to sustain the tension between the destructive omnipotence of thought and the capacity of subjects to resist it. Their work, for all its similarities to Heidegger's in situating the catastrophe in the history of Western Reason, posed the question that Derrida now acknowledges is inescapable, the question of a possible, if partial, retrieval. Their thinking pointed to the unfulfilled possibilities of modernity, as well as to the reality of the catastrophe, rather than await a new "advent." What makes enlightenment totalitarian, they concluded, was not Reason itself but the subject's loss of the ability to distinguish instrumental reason from consciousness, the price of mental omnipotence. Given that diagnosis, they recognized that critique could no longer be expected, neither from transcendental Reason nor from the transcendental subject of history. Yet their contribution was to insist that though rationalism was itself responsible for the decline of critical thought, they never cease to ask "whether reason—as a force of domination of nature—is able to gain control of itself, to reflect on itself."[112] Their paradoxical conclusion, that only enlightenment "can break the bounds of enlightenment," is, *avant la lettre*, a response to the legacy of the "Letter."

The German as Pariah

Karl Jaspers's The Question of German Guilt

I.

A great deal has been written about Martin Heidegger's involvement with National Socialism, and still more about his notorious silence about the crimes of the regime to which he lent his support and enthusiasm.[1] As we have seen, much has been and will continue to be said about the connections between his early philosophy and his political choices. But apart from Habermas's scant references to his role after 1945, Karl Jaspers, the "other" great German philosopher of the postwar era, has received hardly any attention.[2] This is especially odd, since in the 1950s Jaspers and Heidegger were the undisputed giants of postwar German existentialism, conjoined in numerous depictions linking Heideggerian Dasein to the irreducibility of man's existence brought into relief by the "limit situation" described in Jaspers's *Existenz-philosophie*. Jaspers's name was so often coupled with Heidegger's that he once considered writing a book about their differences under an epigram from Cicero's *De oratore*: "People are always used to thinking about both of us together, and whenever people talk about us, they feel they must render judgment about us through comparisons. But how dissimilar is each from the other."[3]

Nevertheless, before 1933 such comparisons were not entirely arbitrary. In the early 1920s Heidegger and Jaspers regarded themselves as a *Kampfgemeinschaft,* a kind of philosophical duo resolutely struggling together against the official Kantianism of the day. Heidegger's *Being and Time* (1927) like Jaspers's early work the *Psychology of World-views* (1919) and his *Reason and Existence* (1935) are—despite their disparities—explorations of how being is encompassed by what Jaspers called the "immanence of the world." Only their earlier intimacy and fidelity to each other explain why Heidegger's commitment to the Nazi revolution was experienced by Jaspers as so total a betrayal.

During the Nazi years Jaspers steadfastly chose to remain in Germany, despite his well-known antipathy to the regime and his removal from the university in 1937. For his former student Hannah Arendt, "what Jaspers represented then, when he was entirely alone, was not Germany but what was left of *humanitas* in Germany. It was as if he alone in his inviolability could illuminate that space which reason creates and preserves between men."[4] Jaspers later recalled that *Die Schuldfrage* (1946) (published in English as *The Question of German Guilt* [1947]) was written at the moment when the crimes of National Socialist Germany were first made "apparent to the entire population."[5] But among German intellectuals he was practically alone in publicly acknowledging that fact. Moses Moskowitz, who reported on conditions in Germany for *Commentary* magazine in the summer of 1946, wrote, "To date no one (except the philosopher Jaspers) has arisen in Germany to exhort his people to repentance and expiation for the mass graves of Jews dotting half the European continent."[6]

After the war, Jaspers, who was then in his sixties, abandoned the traditional reluctance of the German academic philosopher to enter the public realm. As "the symbol of changed times and attitudes," Jaspers, who had moved to Basel in 1948, was frequently at the center of public controversies over rearmament and against reunification. In the 1960s he led the campaign against the German Parliament adopting a statute of limitations on Nazi crimes. Nationalists excoriated Jaspers as the philosopher of "national betrayal" (*Landesverrat*), and the jurist Carl Schmitt, whose activities on behalf of the Reich resulted in his imprisonment by the Americans in 1945, blamed him for initiating West Germany's officially sanctioned culture of guilt.[7] East German propagandists condemned Jaspers as the court apologist for pro-NATO and militarist policies of the Federal Republic.[8] In West Germany, many on the left also accused him, as did Adorno, of being the representative figure of the exculpatory "jargon of authenticity" characteristic of postwar existentialism.[9] In retrospect, all of these judgments have proven singularly shortsighted, and in the case of Adorno particularly unfair, since he did not distinguish Jaspers from Heidegger, whose *Being and*

Time Adorno considered the diabolical source of all postwar ideology. No longer a philosophical outsider, Jaspers became the "Praeceptor Germaniae" of a new postwar Germany, the public advocate of moral reversal and the repudiation of the "national state thinking" that characterized previous generations of German philosophers.[10]

In postwar Germany silence was a political statement; that Heidegger chose silence, while Jaspers spoke often, and to as broad a public as possible, is of enormous political significance. When Jaspers remarked that in postwar Germany "no one can in honesty withdraw from political activity and cooperation," he was almost certainly speaking of Heidegger's conspicuous silence.[11] Moreover, his advocacy of the "European Spirit," of the unity of Western and non-Western metaphysics, was clearly directed against Heidegger's continued insistence on the German roots of his thought. After 1945, it should be noted, Jaspers regarded Heidegger as the "obvious and substantial adversary in the reality of [his] life and conduct."[12] In his fateful report to the Freiburg University Senate Committee in December 1945, which led to the teaching ban imposed in January 1946, Jaspers noted that Heidegger "certainly did not see through the real forces and purposes of the National Socialist leader."[13]

Their differences became symptomatic of an even deeper divide in German intellectual culture: between those, like Heidegger, who experienced and interpreted 1945 as a humiliating defeat, capitulation, and postponement of Germany's cultural and political aspirations and those who regarded the liberation of Germany by the Allies as an opportunity for moral and political renewal. Whereas Heidegger did not think Germans should be made to submit to the "tribunals of the victors," Jaspers endorsed the Nuremberg trials and conceded that Germans had justly been forced to become a "pariah people," deprived of their state because of its crimes. If, as the previous chapter has shown, Heidegger regarded the outcome of the war as having "decided nothing," for Jaspers, the fact that democratic renewal and human rights were imposed on Germany by force of arms did not discredit them. The Heidegger-Jaspers relationship shipwrecked over Heidegger's complicity with the Nazi regime, over issues of German guilt, denazification, and assuming responsibility for that complicity. Jaspers's effort to rethink the role of the philosopher in Germany is bound up with his pre- and post-1945 relationship to Heidegger, and the ambiguities of that relationship are essential to answering the question of whether Jaspers's thinking was indeed a break with the philosophical style and content of

German thought before 1933. It is no accident that the protagonists of the 1987 Historians' Controversy, Jürgen Habermas and Ernst Nolte, invoked Jaspers and Heidegger, respectively, as their intellectual and spiritual forebears.

Yet these profound differences also obscure the extraordinary reticence that Jaspers showed in regard to any discussion of Heidegger in public life. Jaspers's reluctance to publicly air his dispute with Heidegger, a dispute he carried on monologically in his notes and drafts for planned but never published books and articles, highlights a weakness in Jaspers's philosophy of communication to which Arendt alluded when she commented on the "error rather prevalent among modern philosophers who insist on the importance of communication as a guarantee of truth."[14] Jaspers's presumption was that the intimacy of dialogue could ultimately become "paradigmatic" for public political discourse. My goal is not to simply document the philosophical, political, and moral difficulties that plagued their friendship, but to inquire more deeply into Jaspers's ambivalence about Heidegger, an ambivalence I contend can be best understood in the larger frame of his preoccupation with German guilt.

I propose to examine Jaspers's *Die Schuldfrage* from the perspective of the formation of a political and cultural narrative that, at least for a specific generation of Germans, had authority and plausibility. Jaspers's narrative contributed to the removal of the remaining elements of National Socialist ideology and to the intellectual reconstruction of West Germany, much as the actual ruins of National Socialist Germany were being swept away and replaced by modern, if rather conventional, edifices. This was only possible, I should add, if its source was above all the one philosopher of repute who remained in Germany throughout the entire National Socialist era, who never collaborated with the regime, who was dismissed from his teaching post in 1937, and who was married to a Jewish woman, Gertrud (Mayer) Jaspers. At the end of the war, when Frau Jaspers's imminent deportation threatened the pair, the couple prepared for a joint suicide to evade Nazi capture.[15]

Die Schuldfrage, published in 1945, is the founding text of the new narrative of the "European German," of a neutral, anti-militarist, and above all ethical Germany. Jaspers's linking of political freedom and democracy with the rhetoric of "guilt," "atonement," and "reparation" was a way of reestablishing what he called the "unconditionality" of good and evil in politics. If theoretical or practical reason proved powerless to prevent politically sanctioned murder, how then, Jaspers asked, can the nihilistic threat be removed without either opting for some new il-liberal *volonté général* or, conversely, entirely giving up on modernity and returning to a more traditional framework, for example, that of religion? His answer was an unambiguous embrace of the values of the "West," that is, of Anglo-Saxon democracy and the rights of man.[16] Jas-pers's response thus helped to produce the first contribution to what Habermas called the postwar consensus of the Federal Republic, estab-lishing the connection between a collective German responsibility and a democratic political identity.[17] For this reason it might be of interest to return to the conditions of the original formulation of this postwar document—not only for the purposes of defending its original intent but also to inquire into some of its weaknesses.

II.

A cursory comparison of the text of Jaspers's *Die Schuldfrage* published by Piper Verlag in 1979 with the first edition published by Lambert Schneider Verlag in Heidelberg in April 1946 reveals that a preface has been deleted from the later version.[18] This absence is understandable, since Jaspers's opening remarks, directed at his audience in the Alten Aula of Heidelberg University, would have been superfluous forty years later. But the fact that they *were* necessary in the winter of 1945–1946 makes us aware of the very different intellectual climate that sur-rounded Jaspers's lectures: mistrust, skepticism, and the cynical attitude that after the collapse of the Nazi regime the occupation authorities were now imposing *their* ideological and political requirements on Ger-many. Such requirements, though they claimed to be the opposite of those commonly spoken and heard in the same room for the past twelve years, were in essence the same—a kind of spiritual *diktat,* this time, however, imposed by the Americans. "It is not the way of thinking, but only the direction of the aggression, or fraudulent glorification, which has altered." To confront this mood directly, Jaspers remarked,

> All thought and scholarship is, of course, dependent on political circum-stances. But the important distinction is whether thought and research are coerced by political power and employed for its own ends, or whether they are left in peace because the authorities want to preserve the freedom of re-search.[19]

Jaspers was right to expect that his words would be greeted with scorn. According to a confidential report submitted in February 1946 by Captain Daniel Penham, "In the course of a lecture delivered by Professor JASPERS, the students started laughing and scraping their feet on the floor at the mention of democracy, in connection [with] the spiritual situation of Germany. As soon as this began, Professor JASPERS interrupted the lecture and declared that he would not tolerate such a demonstration."[20] Apart from that demonstration, public reaction to *Die Schuldfrage* was almost nonexistent, Jaspers later recalled. But privately he complained of the bitterness and isolation he encountered: "Publicly I am left in peace. But behind my back people slander me: the Communists call me a forward guard of National Socialism; the sullen losers, a traitor to my country."[21]

What interests me in this story is that Jaspers did not attempt to hide the way his own thoughts conformed to the "political circumstances." This, however, can be interpreted as both conformity and, to a certain extent, refusal to accommodate to circumstances. He was certainly sympathetic to the American authorities to a degree. He was among those present at a meeting of "reliable" dignitaries organized by the Counter Intelligence Corps (CIC) in 1945 which included Alfred Weber, Gustav Radbruch, Otto Regenbogen, and Alexander Mitscherlich, and he had the trust of Edward Hartshorne, the man responsible for German "reeducation" at the university level in the American zone.

However, in the complicated intrigues and conflicts between Heidelberg University (and its rector, the surgeon Karl Heinrich Bauer) and the CIC, Jaspers sided with the university. In the winter of 1945–1946, the medical faculty was open but the university was still closed and its ultimate fate undecided. University officials were locked in a fierce struggle with the recently arrived CIC denazification officer Penham, on the one side, and the local trade unions, on the other, both of whom demanded that the university remain closed until sufficient measures were taken against former Nazi sympathizers.[22] Penham's arrival in November 1945 coincided with growing anxiety among the American occupation authorities that Bauer's 1926 textbook on racial hygiene, entitled *Rassenhygiene,* made him unsuitable for the rectorship.[23] A prominent eugenicist whose views on "racial hygiene" (which he admitted was an ill-chosen title) were never as extreme as those put forward by the Nazi racial biologists, Bauer had advocated eugenicist measures such as voluntary sterilization in the late 1920s. It remains a matter of debate whether the controversy over Bauer's rectorship antedated Penham's arrival, but even if Penham did not ignite it, he fanned its flames by calling for Bauer's removal and demanding that the university remain closed until the matter was resolved. Penham, a German Jew, who was born Siegfried Oppenheimer and had emigrated from Frankfurt to New York where he joined the U.S. Army, combined a passionate hatred for former Nazis with impeccable academic qualifications—he was a student of the distinguished Renaissance historian Paul Oskar Kristeller—that surpassed those of most other CIC officers. Penham soon concluded that the notorious "Questionnaire" (*Fragebogen*) method was being abused by the professorate and preferred instead to personally consult what he called the "poison cabinet" of the Heidelberg faculty's writings during the previous twelve years, often with embarrassing consequences.[24] Professors subjected to Penham's lengthy interrogations bitterly complained that citing their Nazi era writings (not to mention forcing them to read them aloud) was decidedly unfair. There is no doubt that the presence of this Jewish émigré elicited fear and loathing among the Heidelberg professorate, resulting in the widely shared view that Penham was responsible for an "inquisitorial" atmosphere.[25] Penham, however, maintained that his efforts were met with far more hostility and antipathy in Heidelberg than elsewhere (Penham had previously been denazification officer at Leipzig University) and that many former Nazis and Nazi sympathizers were being protected by Bauer.

Though Jaspers's role in these intrigues remains opaque, there is little doubt that his primary allegiance was to Bauer and his efforts to reopen the university on schedule.[26] At the height of the crisis, Jaspers strongly supported (and openly took credit for drafting) the University Senate's declaration against Penham.[27] Privately, Jaspers opposed the denazification procedure and considered the American occupation "disastrous," since, as he put it, the blanket criteria of "party membership" excluded all those from political office whose competence might be useful, while the imposition of democracy from above simply substituted "for the authority of the Germans selected by you [the American army] the authority of party hacks, party bureaucrats and their dictators."[28] Jaspers insisted that the university be freed of any external control and be returned to its unpolitical "corporate" status.[29]

But apart from the university crisis, Jaspers took it upon himself to publicly advocate a moral reversal (*Umkehr*) and "repudiation" (*Abkehr*) of the nation-state thinking that characterized previous generations of German academic philosophers.[30] Even the famous Stuttgart Declaration of Guilt (*Stuttgarter Schuldbekenntnis*), issued by the Ecumenical Council of Churches in October 1945, was the result of much external pressure from Anglo-American churches, above all from the archbishop of Canterbury, and was quite limited in scope, referring only to the guilt of the Protestant "community."[31] Jaspers was therefore practically a lone voice when he called Germans to a new "organization of responsibilities," one that was only possible in collaboration with the occupying powers. He rightly recognized what was in fact a situation in which the majority of the population would not or could not accept the distinction between National Socialism and foreign occupation, and his remarks were designed not only to explain the difference but also to make that occupation useful: "Then loyal integration into the wider context of the emergent world order would be a matter of conviction and real trust."[32] But this, I believe, only helps to clarify the context of Jaspers's text. More important were the ways and means that Jaspers chose to argue his case.

In this regard I would like to pose three questions. First, how did Jaspers's self-conscious choice of a highly theological language of guilt and innocence (*Schuld und Unschuld*), law and grace (*Recht und Gnade*), evasion and purification (*Ausweichen und Reinigung*), contribute to the emergence of a profoundly important idea and reality, the self-perception of Germans as a "pariah nation"? Second, how did the "question of guilt" lead to the self-image and ideal of a nationless and cosmopolitan Germany as the "path to purity"? Third, was there, perhaps unconsciously, a transposition or "change of place" that occurs for the first time in this text, and subsequently in popular attitudes, between Germans and Jews? To put it more simply, how did it come to be that the German people, who had been a nation-state with catastrophic consequences, could, taking the historically stateless people, the Jews, as the model of a process of self-humanization, themselves reverse the process? And, vice versa, could the Jews, whose very humanity came from their condition of statelessness, in the wake of their own catastrophe, now deserve a state to protect them? Changing places: Germans and Jews; from nation-state to cosmopolitan citizenry; from cosmopolitan statelessness to a people with their own right to a nation-state. This theme, which is ambivalent at best, is the unacknowledged core of the story that Jaspers proposes.

III.

No single intellectual in immediately postwar Germany contributed more to the reorientation of German philosophy toward a reconceptualized Western humanism than Karl Jaspers. His change, most evident in his articles of 1945–1946 and in his *Die Schuldfrage,* exemplifies a unique personal reckoning and transformation in the face of the catastrophe. In what was at once a moral journey and a philosophical reorientation, Jaspers attempted to break decisively with the antiliberal, antipolitical, and anti-Western elements of his earlier critique of reason, deeply rooted in German idealism—especially in Jaspers's own prewar thought. Jaspers's student, the writer Dolf Sternberger, who, along with Jaspers, Alfred Weber, and the literary critic Werner Krauss, founded one of the first intellectual journals in postwar Germany, *Die Wandlung* (The Transformation), once recalled that "only the experience of Hitler's dictatorship made Karl Jaspers into a political philosopher."[33] Indeed, Sternberger wrote, "a different Jaspers emerged out of the obscurity of oppression."[34] The title of Jaspers's first postwar lecture series, "Von der geistigen Situation in Deutschland" (On the Spiritual Situation in Germany), self-consciously recalled and commented on Jaspers's 1931 *Die geistige Situation der Zeit.* Though its antiliberal plea for a future "respiritualization" of German culture cannnot be confused with sympathy for National Socialism, *Die geistige Situation der Zeit* exemplified the melancholic pathos of antimodernity and nostalgia for "substance" and "authority" typical of the conservative revolution of the 1930s.[35] It is worthwhile recalling, if only to underscore the contrast, that in that earlier work Jaspers condemned Marxism, psychoanalysis, and racial doctrine equally for "having destructive tendencies in common."[36] In his opening remarks to the 1945–1946 lectures, Jaspers emphasized his larger purpose: to provide a moral guideline for German reconstruction "through the drafting of an ethos, that remains for us—even if this is the ethos of a people regarded by the world as a pariah people."[37]

The possibility that the Germans are or might be regarded as a "pariah people" is perhaps the most important yet overlooked theme in Jaspers's writing during this period. An admirer and former student of Max Weber, Jaspers derived his understanding of the concept of the pariah from Weber's own admiration for the "tarrying mood" of the Jews. In his *Ancient Judaism,* Weber portrayed the ethos of the pariah people as one of social exclusion and worldliness, combined with an inner anticipation embodied in the ecstatic visions of the prophets. The suffering of the Jews in exile was the path to inner purity and national redemption.[38] Yet, as Hannah Arendt pointed out in "The Jew as Pariah," published in 1944, social isolation was not without its benefits: exclusion from power was a powerful impulse to private humanity. But, she added, the Jews paid a high price in political vulnerability and "senseless suffering."[39] For Jaspers, the Germans, in an astonishing reversal, had now become a people deprived of their national existence and excluded from the community of nations because of the enormous suffering they had inflicted on others, above all, the Jews. Jaspers's vision is apocalyptic: their state destroyed, their country under foreign rule, their leaders in flight or in custody, the Germans now occupied a position not unlike the one historically occupied by the Jews. In an ironic twist, they had begun their own political diaspora.

Unlike Weber, who believed that the nation-state was the sole ground of German political existence, Jaspers hoped that the end of a German national and political identity could bring into existence the true cosmopolitan German whose very statelessness would inaugurate the European world citizen. In a letter to Arendt in May 1947, he compared his ideal of Germanness with Weber's.

> I will never subscribe to a concept of Germanness by which my Jewish friends cannot be Germans or by which the Swiss and the Dutch, Erasmus and Spinoza and Rembrandt and Burckhardt, are not Germans. I affirmed with Max Weber the idea of a German political greatness, and at the time regarded Switzerland and Holland as German entities that fortunately lay beyond political risk and kept German qualities viable that were threatened in the German Reich (as in 1914). That this German Reich has not only failed but has also by its criminal actions brought about the demise of what is best in Germany does not destroy that other possibility, which retains its place among our noble memories (from Freiherr vom Stein to Max Weber).[40]

In an autobiographical sketch written in 1957, Jaspers recalled that he was among the few who believed that "since 1933 it was probable, and since 1939, certain, that the events in Germany meant the end of Germany. *Finis Germaniae.*" What would such a complete breakdown of the German polity represent? As Jaspers recognized, "so many German persons, speaking German, partakers in the events originating in the lost German state, would survive. What shall they do, what gives their existence value, do they remain Germans and in what sense do they have any task?"[41] Did Jaspers see the German catastrophe as the road to collective redemption? Did he regard his own voice as somewhat analogous to those Hebrew prophets whom Weber revered for securing the continued existence of the Jewish community in exile by giving "religious cohesion to a politically destroyed community"?[42]

These questions led Jaspers to his most important conclusions. First, that Germany is no longer a viable political entity and would not become one in the future. Neither the German empire nor the "Third

Reich" was more than a short-lived political episode. Second, if a liberal German identity compatible with national pride was no longer possible, the German still "lives in the great spiritual realm, spiritually creating and battling: it need not call itself German, has neither German intentions nor German pride, but lives spiritually of the things, of the ideas of worldwide communication."[43] Only by this means could Germans find solace in the "foundation of history" (*Grund der Geschichte*) and in solidarity with that which "human beings throughout the world experienced in extremis," even if those values were "despised in their own Fatherland."[44] In short, the end of German political existence can now bring into existence the true German—the universal citizen.

Die Schuldfrage is an attempt to provide a guide to the wanderings of the German spirit in this new incarnation as a stateless specter. But it also delivers a warning: if Germans do not complete a moral self-education, this condition might become permanent. Though its larger goal was to herald emancipation from the nation-state and the beginnings of a new world citizen, a politics "with comopolitan intention," it provided Germans with a program for citizenship in this new collective. As Arendt recognized, the new global human solidarity envisioned by Jaspers is a restatement of Kant's ideal of "perpetual peace," a rethinking of his history from a "cosmopolitan standpoint."[45]

> If the solidarity of mankind is to be based on something more solid than the justified fear of man's demonic capabilities, if the new universal neighborship of all countries is to result in something more promising than a tremendous increase in mutual hatred and a somewhat universal irritability of everybody against everybody else, then a process of mutual understanding and progressing self-clarification on a gigantic scale must take place.[46]

This necessary self-clarification was both internal and external: it was predicated on a break with the major philosophical traditions in the West that conceived of thought as an isolated and solipsistic process. As Arendt observed, "Jaspers is as far as I know, the first and the only philosopher who ever protested against solitude, to whom solitude appeared 'pernicious' and who dared to question 'all thoughts, all experiences, all contents' under this one aspect: 'What do they signify for communication?'"[47] For Jaspers, expression and truth were never distinct. Thinking is a practice that occurs *between* individuals; communication is not secondary to truth, not mere representation, but its essential feature. Although as a mandarin intellectual of the old school Jaspers remained somewhat skeptical of parliamentary politics, he was also a pluralist in the sense that he believed diversity and variety across cultures is the basis for universal philosophy, not evidence of its impossibility. Habermas's insistence that modern ethics takes as its starting point the human communicative potential given in speech owes much to Jaspers's emphasis on the political significance of "limitless communication" between, against, and within traditions.

Jaspers's humanism was not predicated on the formal universalism of Kant, or on the visible community of the nation, or on the language of rights, but on the ideal of a moral existence achieved through communication with others, what he called *Existenz*.[48] For this reason Jaspers always insisted on the public character of his utterances, and on the necessity of a public process of spiritual reconstruction. "Everything base in public life can be corrected only in and through public life," he remarked.[49] This is perhaps Jaspers's most important contribution to the intellectual reconstruction of postwar Germany: the insight that a public life is only possible in and through a constitutionally sanctioned liberal polity; that political freedom and public discussion were indispensable to producing the political "transformation" of Germany. Political freedom, according to Jaspers, begins when the individual feels responsible for the political acts undertaken in his or her name. Though Jaspers was far less interested in the formal elements of a new democratic parliamentary system—parties, interest groups, trade unions, and so on—he focused his attention on the moral element, what he believed was the missing element in the German experience.

Jaspers was well aware of the obvious contradiction between the historical circumstances of Germany in 1945–1946 and the message of *Die Schuldfrage*: German guilt was established by outsiders, imposed by force of arms and under political dictatorship: "We live in the situation of '*vae victus.*'"[50] Yet this situation was not one of barbarism. The opening to the West, the redirection of German politics, was governed by the fact that the political identity of the Germans was prescribed and imposed from above and outside. But the victors were peoples who recognized "human rights," indeed whose history was bound up with their very elaboration. Western values were thus imposed on Germany from outside in an authoritarian manner, but they were not discredited. A more serious inhibition to their acceptance was the condition of Germany itself. Political responsibility emerges only in authentic communication among autonomous individuals, a communication that was by Jaspers's own admission practically nonexistent in the atmosphere of ruin, hunger, grief, dissolution, hypocrisy, and four-power occupation that existed at that time.

Nonetheless, Jaspers still perceived a possibility for renewal in 1945: "We have lost almost everything: state, economy, the secure basis of our physical existence, and even worse than that: the valid norms that bind us all together, moral dignity, the unifying self-consciousness of a people."[51] This loss was accompanied by an entirely new circumstance: the disappearance of the National Socialist powers at large; the end of independent German statehood; the "dependence of all our collective acts on the will of the occupying powers, which liberated us from the National Socialist yoke."[52] But even if political initiative was limited to the narrow scope of this situation, the possibility of speech was present for the first time: "We may now speak publicly with each other, let us now see what we have to say to each other."[53] No doubt Jaspers was aware that this was a risky enterprise when he wrote those lines in the introduction to the first volume of *Die Wandlung*: "We have changed inwardly and outwardly in twelve years. We are still in a process of further change, which cannot be foreseen." This new journal was not conceived programatically; it was to permit free "meditation and discussion." But it was also based on certain principles: on a recognition of the "common origins of humanity" and on a rejection of the "true evil of nihilism," of "contempt for humanity," and of "heinous cynicism."[54]

If Jaspers might appear both excessively optimistic and naive about the potential afforded by the political and moral collapse of Germany, he was far more pessimistic about the prospects for a future German polity. He predicted that it would take at least twenty years before Germany could be ruled by men who are freely elected.[55] Jaspers did not think that the German pariah should be permitted a political life until "the power of reasonable men—who exist in Germany, and I believe in good measure—has matured."[56] What would that maturity entail, morally and politically? These are the questions first posed by *Die Schuldfrage*.

IV.

Die Schuldfrage was first delivered as part of a series of lectures at Heidelberg University during the winter semester of 1945–1946. Its overriding theme, the renewal of a German polity through communication, is announced at the beginning: "We must learn to speak with each other" (7). This process, Jaspers added, is far more than an inner-German affair. It alone could deliver "the indispensable basis to speak with other peoples" (10). Before Germany could reenter the community of nations it had to undergo a process of political and moral self-clarification, to accomplish a restoration of speech from the very ruin of language and politics. What all Germans had in common in 1945, apart from individual experiences of suffering in war and dictatorship, was only the negative experience of being a "vanquished nation (*besiegten Staatsvolk*) delivered up to the mercy or mercilessness of the victor."

Twelve years of official public propaganda created many different "inner attitudes," but permitted no common mode of speech, no public language of communication. The possibility of bringing into public speech the private experiences of the Nazi era was made possible only by the victory of the Allies. Despite the circumstances of occupation, the "opening of the doors of the German penitentiary" from outside made the "German soul dependent on this liberation." Every German suffered losses, but no loss was as great as the loss of "a common ethical-political foundation." The result was profound atomization, the absence of any social solidarity, and deep mistrust and suspicion between those who had supported and those who had feared the regime. And yet, Jaspers remained convinced, "Germany can only return to itself when we Germans find each other in communication" (14).

Throughout the text Jaspers adopts the soothing and comforting tone of a stern but sympathetic teacher. The mood is pedagogical, the familiar technique of a teacher reasoning together with his or her students. Of course, there is always something slightly disingenuous about this tactic, the sole voice. But he also adopts the collective "we," a voice that *is* conducive to communication. There is no finger pointing, no self-serving rhetoric: "Affect speaks against the truth of the speaker. We will not strike ourselves pathetically on the breast in order to insult others; we will not praise ourselves in self-satisfaction, which is only an effort to make others feel ill. But there should be no inhibitions created by self-protective reticence, no leniency via silence, no comfort through deception" (9). By depriving the reader of a judging authority, Jaspers writes as if he too belongs to his own audience: "In such speech no one is the judge of the other, each is at once accused and judge" (9).

Jaspers has a clear agenda: first and foremost the separation of political responsibility from other forms of guilt. The four concepts of guilt that take up the bulk of the text are familiar. Jaspers distinguished *criminal guilt, political guilt, moral guilt,* and *metaphysical guilt.* Each is weighted differently, and it is clear almost from the outset that Jaspers is far less concerned with the first two categories. Moreover, it is really with the third and fourth categories, moral and metaphysical guilt, that Jaspers is most seriously preoccupied. Given the persistent controversy over the legal and moral basis of the Nuremberg trials, the few sentences devoted to defining criminal guilt as "objectively demonstrable actions which transgressed against clearly defined laws" are barely adequate. Jaspers simply restates the tripartite classification worked out in the London statutes of the International Military Tribunal at Nuremberg: the crime of waging aggressive war; war crimes; crimes against humanity.

Nonetheless, it was courageous for Jaspers to defend the legality and legitimacy of the Nuremberg trials and to condemn the commonplace opinion that the trials were a national "embarrassment" or that any tribunal of victors against the vanquished was outside the framework of law. He rejects the *tu quoque* defense (that the victors committed the same crimes as the accused) and, most important, points out that the trials made manifest the most "monstrous" consequence of the crimes committed by the Nazis. Hitler and his minions repudiated Kant's famous dictum that "no act should be undertaken in war which makes a later reconciliation impossible," a crime that encompasses all the others and accounts for the irreparability of the German question.

Political guilt refers to those whose political office implies responsibility for the acts of state taken by a particular regime. But—and this is perhaps the most important aspect of Jaspers's definition—it includes every citizen of that state, since "each human being is responsible for how he is ruled" (17). Political responsibility is a direct consequence of political decisions undertaken in the name of the members of a polity whether or not they consent tacitly or explicitly: it requires "reparations" (not yet explicitly financial), or the "loss or limitation of political power and political rights" (21).

In contrast to political responsibility, moral guilt is borne only by individuals. Each individual is responsible for his or her own acts. The moral authority of the individual conscience supersedes all other authorities. "Any haziness concerning this basic fact is as much a form of guilt as the false absolutizing of power as the single determining factor in events" (19). Moral deficiency is the cause of all crime: "The perpetration of countless tiny acts of indifference, comfortable adaptation, cheap justification of injustice, indifferent promotion of injustice, participation in the public atmosphere which disseminates unclarity and as such makes evil possible," all of that constitutes moral guilt and requires both "penance and renewal" (*Busse und Erneuerung*).

Metaphysical guilt is by far the most ambiguous and difficult to grasp of the four categories. It refers to a basic *solidarity* between human beings that makes each responsible for all the justice and injustice in the world, "in particular for the crimes that are committed in their presence and with their knowledge. If I fail to do whatever I can to prevent them, I, too, am guilty." This guilt requires an even greater inner transformation than does moral guilt. It requires a destruction of pride and humility. This inner transformation "can lead to a new beginning of active life," but metaphysical guilt is borne neither by states nor individuals but "by God alone" (21).

If Germans are responsible for the political acts of the Nazi regime, they are not criminally liable for them, nor can they be made to bear their moral or metaphysical responsibility. Law might affect criminal and political guilt, but not moral and metaphysical guilt. The former are determined by the victors (as punishment, as juridical restrictions on Nazi officeholders, as proscriptions on certain organizations), but moral and metaphysical guilt remain outside the sphere of legal action since "no one can morally judge another" (23). The chief virtue of the Nuremberg trials from this perspective was to remove the burden of criminal guilt from the German people by emphasizing that the regime was acting in flagrant disregard of any known moral or legal principle—including those of the defendants themselves.[57] Collective guilt is thus a contradiction in terms: "*It is against all sense to make a whole people responsible for a crime,*" and "*it is against all sense to morally indict an entire people*" (24). Since only political responsibility is in any sense collective, collective guilt only has meaning as political responsibility, never as moral or criminal guilt. In fact, collective guilt actually removes responsibility from the Germans, while collective responsibility demands a differentiation of the spheres of guilt and individual moral reckoning with the crimes of the Nazi regime. "*Collective guilt of a people* or of a group within the people can never exist—except as political responsibility—neither as criminal, moral, nor as metaphysical guilt" (25). This distinction is at the core of *Die Schuldfrage*.

The political implications of Jaspers's distinctions are clearly stated in a brief section entitled "The German Questions." Here Jaspers repeats the widespread belief among Germans, first propagated by Goebbels, that the Allies had planned (in the famous Morgenthau plan) be-

fore war's end to "cut up Germany," to "restrict the possibility of reconstruction," and to "allow it no peace in a situation between life and
death" (30).[58] Although not directly addressed, Jaspers's argument also
seems to speak against "denazification" as an externally imposed moral
imperative. Finally, the question of German guilt is also a political question about the future of Germany: "It is the question whether it is politically sensible, rational, safe, and just, to make an entire people into
a pariah people." Although Jaspers does not fully elaborate on this
question, it is clear that his answer is that Germans are politically, morally, and metaphysically responsible for the crimes of the Nazi regime
but that the absolute majority is not guilty of any criminal act, and
therefore to declare Germany a "pariah nation," to punish its people as
"inferior, without worth, and criminal, an ejection of humanity," is unjust and inhuman (31).

This transposition is worth emphasizing. Jaspers's invocation of the
German as pariah here seems to speak not only against the notion of
collective guilt and retribution but also against the ways that the occupation might result in a humiliation of the German people. Did Jaspers
believe that the Germans were being unjustly placed by the occupiers in
the position of the Jews? Or did he welcome the new pariah status of
the Germans as an opportunity?

The two readings are not, of course, entirely incompatible. Guilt had
to be *assumed* in order for it not to be *imposed*. Germans must assume
the burdens of pariahdom to achieve the moral and metaphysical reckoning that *Die Schuldfrage* demands. In a brief commentary on the
Jewish Bible, "Von der biblischen Religion," published in *Die Wandlung* in 1946, Jaspers underscored the more optimistic sense of the pariah as a new chance: "A passion courses through the Bible, which is
effective only because it is related to God. Because they stand before
God the people of the Bible, who as human beings knew themselves to
be nothing, grew into the transcendentally human (*Übermenschliche*)."[59]
In *Die Schuldfrage* the question of German guilt is conceived as a "wager" but not one without risk. If the wager fails, the exclusion of Germany from the world community is certain; Germany would suffer a
permanent loss of sovereignty. Germany would then be delivered up to
the political whim of the victors and relegated to the permanent status
of a pariah nation. Jaspers warned of the consequence of not accom-
plishing this task: "This path is the only one which might protect our
soul from a pariah existence" (10).

Much of the subsequent text is concerned with articulating and rejecting the various apologies, excuses, and exonerations frequently invoked by Germans in the postwar years. The catalog is by now familiar and does not bear repetition. Jaspers presents the arguments against these rationalizations with great clarity and without ire. Yet he avoids a moralizing stance, citing instead the American critic Dwight Macdonald to the effect that despite the gore and mass destruction perpetrated on all sides in the war, only the Germans systematically employed modern technical means of mass murder entirely in the service of political paranoia, devoid of rational or political purpose. Here, and we shall return to this point shortly, we can also recognize the influence of Arendt's argument that the *novum* of Nazism (which she later extrapolated to Soviet Russia) was to efficiently employ political murder to no distinct political or social purpose.

Therefore, given the political responsibility of all Germans for the crimes of Nazism, those who suffered injustice as victims of the Hitler regime require assistance, and have a particular right that supersedes the right of even those Germans who suffered in consequence of the war and destruction. A leveling of this essential difference by virtue of common suffering is exculpation and a refusal to admit that it was Germany that began the war and caused the suffering. Second, clarity about inner responsibility also involved "a clarification of our new life and its responsibilities." Only such an inner "cleansing" would make possible the reemergence of Germans from their political past and establish a new basis for democracy. "Only in the consciousness of guilt can the consciousness of solidarity and responsibility emerge, without which freedom is impossible" (82).

V.

"Germany," Jaspers wrote, "is the first nation that, as a nation, has gone to ruin."[60] He later recalled that during the time of National Socialism it became clear to him that "the moral evil had its origins as early as the 1860s," with German unification.[61] This judgment, that a liberal German identity compatible with national pride was no longer possible, is the basis of Jaspers's attempt to revive the idealism of the cosmopolitan humanist tradition of the German Enlightenment. To be sure, this was an enterprise that, as Arendt remarked, "looked like reckless optimism in the light of present realities."[62]

What is clear is that for Jaspers, as for Arendt, with whom he resumed an intense and lifelong correspondence in 1945, human solidarity only becomes meaningful in the context of political responsibility (*Haftung*), for example, for the destruction of the nation-state. Regardless of any individual guilt that can be ascribed, and irrespective of moral self-scrutiny, political responsibility requires that each citizen is accountable for everything that a government or state undertakes in his or her name. However, under the shock of recognition that the nation-state is also capable of relieving mankind of its humanity—an annihilatory, totalitarian state deprives its citizens of solidarity—political responsibility extends beyond the boundaries of the nation-state. According to Arendt, this insight is Jaspers's most important contribution to the revision of Kant: "Just as according to Kant, nothing should ever happen in war which would make a future peace and reconciliation impossible, so nothing, according to the implications of Jaspers' philosophy, should happen today in politics which would be contrary to the actual existing solidarity of mankind."[63]

As an attempt to formulate the principles of post-Hitlerian political ethics that transcend the nation-state, that is, as a document of pan-Europeanism, *Die Schuldfrage* should be read in light of two other texts that Jaspers produced in the same period: "Vom europäischen Geist," a lecture on European unity that he delivered in Geneva in September 1946, and the essay in the philosophy of history, *Vom Wesen und Ziel der Geschichte* (The Origins and Goal of History) (1949). In the former, Jaspers pleaded for the "Switzerlandizing" (*Verschweizern*) of Europe in order for it not to be Balkanized.[64] In the latter work, Jaspers developed some of the themes of his philosophy of Existenz, in which he claimed that the diverse traditions of world religion and philosophy demonstrated that "metaphysical ideals are not taken as straightforwardly true, but each stands for the truth of some realm of faith." As Habermas later commented, this philosophy of history brings humanity together "coercively" in order to "grasp its chance for a fragile solidarity."[65]

But in a letter of October 19, 1946, Jaspers conceded to Arendt that the solidarity that he understood by the concept of metaphysical guilt "has nothing to do" with the kind of political solidarity—or citizenship—she had envisioned. In fact, he notes, "the demand of political solidarity can be valid only where one can depend on the cooperation of a majority of the population. It showed up often in Italy under fascism. In Germany it simply does not exist and cannot be directly called upon. It evolves only out of the sum of lives lived together."[66] In other words, "solidarity" as Jaspers conceived of it was largely a metaphysical concept (before God) but not political, at least not something that could be achieved among Germans.

Germans therefore seemed to be incapable of the political solidarity and active moral behavior that would qualify them to become citizens in Arendt's sense or even in Jaspers's more ecumenical sense. They are in a state of tutelage, one that requires a moral confrontation with their own guilt and, if possible, the metaphysical recognition that would allow them to surpass the narrower horizon of political and moral responsibility. But since they cannot yet achieve this, they must remain in some sense a pariah people.

VI.

A discussion between Jaspers and Arendt that had caused tensions between them more than fifteen years earlier (and which was still much on his mind, as Jaspers's letter of 1947 suggests) sheds more light on his ambivalent use of the term "pariah." Jaspers's answer to the threat that Germans be turned into a pariah nation by their occupiers was to return to the traditional ideal of Germany as a "cultural nation" (*Kulturnation*) bound by language and "spirit" as opposed to blood and geography. His vision of the German catastrophe as the event that permitted German redemption in the guise of the pariah was, as Jaspers's certainly knew, to identify with the historical image of the Jews in much the same terms that Arendt had spoken of in a 1930 lecture on Rahel Varnhagen. At that time Jaspers had objected to Arendt's assertion that the "Jewish essence" had undergone a decisive transformation in the negative circumstance of not belonging to a nation-state, a circumstance that had shaped the Jews' collective destiny. He vehemently protested against her conviction that a people's historical destiny could be the source of collective identity: existential concepts were not, he emphasized, determined by historical events.[67] Yet in *Die Schuldfrage* it is precisely this historical event of collective responsibility for crimes that binds Germans together. It is hardly incidental, then, that in his exchanges with Arendt over *Die Schuldfrage* in 1947, Jaspers returned to their earlier controversy, and with the rather surprising admission that he had not yet entirely divested himself of the thought that Germans and German Jews might still share the same identity.

It may be that for me the consciousness of being a German and the fact that from childhood on I have taken for granted that German Jews are Germans—both these things together have become a question to which I have a final answer on an emotional level but it is not one I can formulate in words. About 1932 [*sic*] (I'm not sure of the year anymore) you and I became aware of a difference between us that I did not perceive as a personal one even then, a difference that is not absolute in itself but is by no means trivial either. That it exists at all (it's the same between my wife and me, and we discuss it again every so often) is only a sign that we are working toward a state of the world in which such problems will cease to matter.[68]

The conundrum Jaspers faced in 1947 also confronts the reader of *Die Schuldfrage:* Are the Germans a nation, or have they become the new wanderers among nations? At this crucial point in the discussion Jaspers falls back on the traditional ideal of the Kulturnation as Jacob Burckhardt might have framed it. As we have seen, his concept of "Germanness" retains its cultural, not its political or territorial, definition. If he now conceded, as he did not in 1931, that Jews and Germans did not share the same fate, or belong to the same community in 1945, perhaps with the emergence of the German pariah and the simultaneous disappearance of both the Jewish parvenu and pariah (Rahel Varnhagen) a chance for Jewish-German symbiosis actually existed, perhaps for the first time. Jaspers revealed that the "foundationlessness" of the "destiny" of Germany (precisely Arendt's words in 1930) was a possibility. The negative "existence" that Jaspers had denied was possible when Arendt had proposed in 1930 her idea of the "foundationlessness" of the Jewish destiny was now—he insisted—Jaspers's own (and Germany's) fate. Arendt especially found his sentence, "Now that Germany is destroyed I feel at ease as a German for the first time," "devastating" because she recalled her husband, Heinrich Blücher, had said exactly the same thing a year earlier.[69] But she rejected Jaspers's suggestion that either then or now Jews and Germans were somehow in the same situation: "I recall our disagreement very well. In the course of it, you once said (or wrote) to me that we were all in the same boat. I can't remember now whether I answered you or only thought to myself that with Hitler as captain (this was before '33) we Jews would not be in the same boat. That was wrong, too, because under the circumstances you weren't in the boat much longer either or, if you were, then only as a prisoner."[70]

As Jaspers embraced the ideal of the pariah, Arendt seemed to abandon it with renewed conviction. In her essay "The Moral of History," published in January 1946, she wrote, "The events of recent years have proved that the 'excepted Jew' is more the Jew than the exception; no Jew feels quite happy any more about being assured that he is an exception. The extraordinary catastrophe has converted once again all those who fancied themselves extraordinarily favored beings into quite ordinary mortals."[71] More emphatically she defended her view that German Jews no longer want to be considered German: "If the German Jews don't want to be Germans anymore, that certainly can't be held against us, but it does of course look a little funny. What they really want to say by that gesture is that they have no intention of assuming any share of political responsibility for Germany; and in that they are right again. And that alone is the key point."[72]

VII.

Arendt was alert to the chief weaknesses of Jaspers's *Die Schuldfrage,* though she muted her criticisms, perhaps because, as she later admitted, Jaspers was always "better" than what he wrote.[73] According to her biographer, Elisabeth Young-Bruehl, Arendt was put off by what she perceived as strong residues of Jaspers's prewar Weberian nationalism, as well as by his Protestant emphasis on the atonement of the German people through acknowledgment of guilt.[74] In August 1946, Arendt wrote him of her reactions to *Die Schuldfrage,* in the course of which she also promised to help find a publisher for the book in the United States.[75] Blücher, who was also impatient with the book's religious language and tone, Arendt noted in her letter, was even more insistent than she that "assuming responsibility has to consist of more than an acceptance of defeat and of the consequences following on that."[76] More specifically, such an assumption of responsibility, which, she elaborated, was a precondition for the continuing existence of the German people (not the nation), had to be "accompanied by a positive political statement of intentions addressed to the victims."[77] Arendt also added some of her own proposals, including a constitutional guarantee that any Jew, regardless of birth or residence, could become an equal citizen of any future German Republic.

Most important, Arendt rejected Jaspers's definition of criminal guilt as inappropriate to encompass the kind of murder committed by the Nazi regime. For Arendt, the very inclusion of mass extermination as a crime was "questionable." "The Nazi crimes, it seems to me," she wrote, "explode the limits of the law; and that is precisely what constitutes their monstrousness. For these crimes, no punishment is severe enough. It may well be essential to hang Göring, but it is totally inadequate. That is, this guilt, in contrast to all criminal guilt, oversteps and shatters any and all legal systems. That is the reason why the Nazis in Nuremberg are so smug."[78] Arendt had already made the same point earlier in an article she published in *Jewish Frontier* in January 1945, and later republished in *Die Wandlung*: "Just as there is no political solution within human capacity for the crime of administrative mass murder, so the human need for justice can find no satisfactory reply to the total mobilization of a people for that purpose. Where all are guilty, nobody in the last analysis can be judged."[79] Arendt insisted on the incommensurability of crime and punishment: "We are simply not equipped to deal, on a human, political level, with a guilt that is beyond crime and an innocence that is beyond goodness or virtue."[80] She agreed with Jaspers that collective guilt could not be ascribed to all Germans because such a guilt would ironically mirror the absolute guilt ascribed to all Jews by the Nazi regime. But she underscored the disproportion between the genocide and ordinary punishment. As necessary as punishment of the guilty is, it is also necessary to remember that no punishment exists which would be commensurable with their crime.[81]

In his response, Jaspers pointed out the dangers of dismissing the guilt of the Nazis as so monstrous as to take on the dimension of the "demonic." "You say that what the Nazis did cannot be comprehended as 'crime'—I'm not altogether comfortable with your view, because a guilt that goes beyond all criminal guilt inevitably takes on a streak of 'greatness'—of satanic greatness. . . . It seems to me that we have to see these things in their total banality."[82] Ironically, Arendt may have forgotten the source of that phrase fifteen years later, when, in a striking turnabout, she made use of it to describe the Nazi bureaucrat Adolf Eichmann, and provoked the famous intellectual controversy over her "Report on the Banality of Evil."

Another touchstone of private controversy was Arendt's sense that Jaspers's concept of metaphysical guilt was excessively weighted with religious concepts or, to borrow Adorno's phrase, was "religiosity without religion."[83] For Jaspers, as we recall, metaphysical guilt occurred in the sphere of "the unconditional" where "no earthly judge" exists. By contrast, Arendt chose to emphasize the collective social aspect of "that solidarity which is the political basis of the republic (and which Clemenceau expressed in the words *'L'affaire d'un seul est l'affaire de tous*')."[84] This form of solidarity, which was almost completely absent in German society before and after 1933, is not simply the relative absence of civic courage, the courage to speak up for victims of injustice or ideas against overwhelming odds, it is also the absence of the positive ideal of a political community that is not restricted to one group or class and that would take up active engagement against threats to the heterogeneity of the social fabric, for pluralism, and for tolerance.[85] We can thus see Arendt's own far more political understanding of the catastrophe later elaborated in *The Origins of Totalitarianism*, in her two most pointed criticisms: that Jaspers understates the crimes of Nazism, which are not crimes in any normal legal sense any more than they are morally or metaphysically conventional crimes; and that Jaspers completely desocializes and depoliticizes the concept of human solidarity. For Arendt, it was the active engagement of citizens as moral actors that was missing in the tradition of the nation-state (and, by implication, in *Die Schuldfrage* as well).

VIII.

As early as 1946 Arendt compared Heidegger's philosophical "solitude" unfavorably to Jaspers's concern with "communication." She also valued Jaspers's notion of philosophy as opposed to Heidegger's insofar as it no longer claims for itself any privileged knowledge and "consequently gives up special prerogatives of any kind."[86] For Jaspers, the case of Heidegger was the ultimate proof of the dangers contained in the Platonic ideal of the incommunicative philosopher, whose distance from the public realm, and whose solitude, rendered him vulnerable to the seductions of dictatorship. In contrast to Heidegger, for whom other human beings are simply an element in the sphere of existence, for Jaspers, Arendt maintained, "communication is the preeminent form of philosophical participation" whose purpose is not to produce results but to " 'illuminate existence.' "[87] Here Heidegger's "Letter on Humanism," as we have seen, should properly be considered in counterpoint to Jaspers's call for a reckoning with the Nazi past issued at the same moment in *Die Schuldfrage*. Jaspers stood for the end of the German nation-state, for the embrace of the "West," and for the assumption of collective responsibility. Heidegger radicalized his identification with the "defeated" traditions of German culture, with the rejection of "Western" metaphysics, refused any public gesture of responsibility, and commended Germans to stolidly assume a state of "expectation."

Perhaps not surprisingly, Jaspers sent his book to his former friend with the recommendation that it might be useful for him to read it in connection "with your word about the 'shame.' "[88] The word "shame" refers to an extraordinary letter that Heidegger had sent to Jaspers on March 7, 1950, to my knowledge his only acknowledgment of any personal responsibility for his Nazi activities and sympathies (which took the form of a letter within a letter so as to emphasize that it had been written earlier):

> Dear Jaspers,
> Since 1933 I did not enter your house not because a Jewish woman lived there, *but simply because I was ashamed.* Since then, I neither set foot in your house, nor in the city of Heidelberg, since only through your friendship is it what it is for me. At the end of the 1930s, as the most violent persecutions inaugurated the greatest of evils, I thought immediately of your wife. At that time I received from Prof. Wilser, whom I know from here, and who had close relations to party circles there, that nothing would happen to your wife. But, the anxiety remained, the incapacity and the failure—and thus, I don't mention this in order to give even the slightest appearance of having tried to help.[89]

His letter arrived in response to Jaspers's hesitantly worded proposal that they begin a philosophical correspondence with the eventual aim of publication, as the resumption of their prewar plan to hold "a public debate between us."[90] That Jaspers saw such a debate as both risky and potentially significant is clear.

> If we risk the most extreme [*das Ausserste*], then it will be worth it. A document would then emerge, which could encourage and provide assistance. Especially if, at the end, it becomes clear, that a unified point of departure exists—which we do not know—something extraordinary would be achieved. It would answer the question: can philosophical human beings substantially speak with each other, or, even more, whether an inexpressible unanimity of ethos indubitably exists. We must demonstrate this.—Perhaps we should consider the plan.[91]

We should not be surprised that such a philosophical correspondence never took place. In fact, the private correspondence between Jaspers and Heidegger declined after this exchange, and their prewar relationship was never restored or repaired, though they continued to exchange brief letters and publications until Jaspers's death in 1963. Jaspers admitted to Arendt that he was not merely disappointed with Heidegger's response but that he saw it as symptomatic of the results of his own efforts to provoke a debate over German guilt: "As for what comes of discussions about 'guilt,' the private sphere throws some light on what would be possible in public. I've held back in my correspondence with Heidegger ever since his 'confession of guilt,' because it was not genuine and contained no real understanding. It was superfluous and without consequences." Heidegger's nonreaction, he said, paralleled that of "great numbers" of Germans. Yet, he noted, despite the "grave moral and intellectual consequences for us—one cannot constantly demand a reaction."[92]

Jaspers's belief that Heidegger's "confession" was inauthentic was soon confirmed by Arendt, who admitted that it was she who had elicited it when she visited him in Freiburg in the winter of 1949–1950. She was, she said, "the innocently guilty cause of his 'confession of guilt.' You're right with your phrase 'no real understanding,' but for that reason I think it is indeed 'genuine' this time. Explanations would not have been genuine because he really doesn't know and is hardly in a position to find out what devil drove him into what he did. He would be only too glad 'to let things fade out of sight.' I've obviously prevented him from doing that. [. . . .] As you can see, I have a guilty conscience."[93]

After that reunion, vividly described by Young-Bruehl and reprised by Elzbieta Ettinger, Arendt portrayed Heidegger's existence as the very antithesis of the *vita activa* she so admired: "This living in Todtnauberg, grumbling about civilization and writing Seyn with a "y," is really a kind of mouse hole he has crawled back into because he rightly assumes that the only people he'll have to see there are pilgrims who come full of admiration for him. Nobody is likely to climb 1,200 meters to make a scene."[94]

Yet, despite the fact that it was solicited and that Jaspers judged it to be "without understanding," it is not fully apparent why Jaspers considered the private occasion of Heidegger's confession to be insincere. Was it *because* it was merely private? Or was it because it was centered around the person of Gertrud Jaspers, so that only in the face of the fact of her Jewishness did there exist an implicit or "silent" source of judgment? Or was it because it was formulated in a way that was expressly "unphilosophical," and therefore for Jaspers "inessential," to use one of his most important words?

The story of "Heidegger's Confession" shifts the focus from the "Heidegger Question" to the far less frequently discussed "Jaspers Question," to the question of how the postwar German ideal of the representative public intellectual was formed in the aftermath of the event of Heidegger's Nazism, and in the mutual idealizations and disappointments that intellectual friendships frequently engender. This incident is just one among many that underscore the extraordinary reticence that Jaspers showed in regard to any discussion of Heidegger in public life. After 1945 Jaspers did not publicly write about Heidegger or even permit anyone to intimate that he was critical of his attitude or philosophy, though it was well known at the time. It was widely circulated information that Jaspers had written the devastating letter of evaluation to the Freiburg University commission deciding Heidegger's fate in December 1945, in which he condemned Heidegger's style of thinking as "unfree, dictatorial, lacking in communication," and which revealed hitherto unknown details of his anti-Semitism during the Rectorate.[95] Why, then, if Heidegger "had become the obvious and substantial adversary in the reality of [his] life and conduct," did Jaspers never permit these criticisms to come to light? Why did the philosopher of communication maintain his silence in regard to Heidegger, whose silence was the issue? Jaspers's reluctance to publicly air his dispute with Heidegger, a dispute that we now know he carried on monologically in his notes and drafts for planned but never published books and articles, is perhaps an important clue to the weakness in Jaspers's philosophy of communication and *Die Schuldfrage*. It illuminates Arendt's criticism that Jaspers's dialogic solution was more appropriate for face-to-face relations or friendship than for public life, which required a different order of reflection, which she later called "judgment."

Jaspers acknowledged that in postwar Germany he and Heidegger were constantly being played against each other, "as if the criticism of one, meant the affirmation of the other."[96] In his posthumously published autobiographical sketch, Jaspers confessed that to attempt such a critique "belongs merely to my plans, whose realization I cannot foresee." Jaspers also claimed, more disingenuously, "I did not arrive at a critique of Heidegger, essentially because I was particularly occupied with philosophy and because I lived in seclusion, having been excluded from the public."[97]

In fact, on at least three occasions, Jaspers suppressed his criticisms of Heidegger, and, in one case, he publicly disavowed them. First, Jaspers held back his autobiographical sketch of Heidegger, written in 1953, during either of their lifetimes, considering it "pejorative," fearing that it would result in a "final break," and considering it "fatally injurious" (N, 144, 145). Second, in a review of Jaspers's *Origin and Goal of History*, published in *Die Zeit* in December 1949, Paul Hühnerfeld accused him of indulging in an "enraged attack on Heidegger"

(without naming him) and judging his thinking "thought with impoverished content."[98] Jaspers was so concerned with removing any doubt
that he had intended to slight Heidegger that he replied in a long letter
to the editor entitled "Heidegger was not intended" (Heidegger war
nicht Gemeint), proclaiming, first, never to have spoken of Heidegger,
and second, to have merely created an "ideal type." The letter concluded with the words, "If I were to seek a public debate with Heidegger—which was not at all ever in question here—then I will do it
openly. My relationship to this important thinker, up to now and for a
long time has been essentially private, and cannot be confused by such
statements."[99]

Finally, in 1956, as a young student Jürgen Habermas publicly raised
the issue of Jaspers's relation to Heidegger in the *Deutsche Universitäts-
zeitung,* this time by wondering whether Jaspers had not in fact answered the question of why, again without naming him, he had attacked Heidegger (this time in his book on Bultmann): "Jaspers says: 'a
philosophical polemic, which is directed at a personality, means attraction, respect, honoring for that person, even when it becomes sharp divergence. Whereas a polemic directed against an author who is not
named, is either proper, insofar as it concerns an impersonal and widely
known matter, or it is an expression of contempt, which deprives the
object of the attack of any significance" (N, 308).

Jaspers noted defensively, "It is not true, that I attacked Heidegger
somewhere without naming him," and "that passage about polemic can
only be used against me maliciously—[to say] that it is an expression of
greater contempt not to name him here" (N, 134). But Jaspers was able
to admit the obvious reason for all the innuendo, at least to himself:
"that bringing Heidegger into this—in itself indecent and based on suspicions—still means: that I myself must once and for all take a stand
on Heidegger's philosophical reality. If I were to do so, it would be under Nietzsche's sentence: 'I honor whomever I attack. This cannot occur
casually or particularistically' " (N, 158).

Not surprisingly, the deleted remarks were filed away with the other
notes on Heidegger. There Jaspers conceded that "the question of the
possibilities of philosophical critique is one of the most disturbing problems for a philosophy aimed at communication" (N, 113). Also not surprisingly, we find a comment that confirms Hühnerfeld's suspicions as
well: "How he [Heidegger] influences the style of thought and mental
constitution, which today has reestablished itself in Germany: the same
ground, on which National Socialism grew up" (N, 104).

To attack or not to attack, is the question that dominates Jaspers's lengthy (and now published) notebooks on Heidegger. For more than twenty years Jaspers obsessively imagined such a polemic, for example, in a note marked "plan," in which the "Heideggerkritik" is conceived of as a long letter divided into individual ones (*N, 119*). At least a half-dozen titles were contemplated—for example, Martin Heidegger: Resistance and Appreciation (*Abwehr und Huldigung*); Karl Jaspers versus Martin Heidegger: Controversy and Honoring (*Auseindersetzung and Bekenntnis*). There are numerous reminiscences, commentaries, and notes, some of which did became components of the later published autobiographical sketch: "Against all my expectations, through his public advocacy as a National Socialist, he became my intellectual enemy. He seemed not to notice this, although he bore witness to it by the fact that he did not visit me again after 1933" (*N, 139*).[100]

Certainly Jaspers's reluctance to publicly engage with Heidegger can in part be explained by his mandarin suspicion of public controversy, which, he believed, shackles the critic to the object of his criticism, leaving him "caught in his web of thinking."[101] Privately, however, Jaspers returned again and again to the question of the nature of his philosophy as the source of his inhibition: "whether essential criticism and polemics are at all possible in actual philosophy, or whether there remains only the attitude of silent acceptance, as is the case with poetry." Philosophy, he affirmed, "lies in the thought process itself as an act of the thinker's nature," and with whose "Existenz" it is bound up. Whatever truth a philosophical doctrine contains, it must be mirrored in the mentality and lifestyle of the philosopher.[102] This implies that philosophical discourse cannot be part of public debate or discourse, insofar as it is the philosopher and not the philosophy that must be at the center of such a dialogue. Here is the conundrum that Jaspers could not untangle: a true polemic would presume communication in the public domain, whereas philosophical discourse can only take place where an authentic dialogue is possible, for example, in private. Jaspers writes to his fantasy partner Heidegger: "I implore you, when there was once something that leaped between us as philosophical impulses, then take responsibility for your one gift and put it in the service of reason and the reality of human dignity and capacity, instead of in the service of magic" (*N, 127*). But this, he adds, requires Heidegger's presence: "If Heidegger is not himself there, I cannot discuss with him" (*N, 129*). Yet since what led to all this occurred in a public space of political events, it could be repaired only in a public space of political events. "What occurred between us, is something public through your National Socialist actions; only publicly, it appears to me, can the conditions be restored, under which, then, what we cannot say to each other publicly would be possible" (*N, 130*).

Jaspers's decision not to "burden" Heidegger with a public debate over his moral failings and philosophical inadequacies was justified on the "dialogic" grounds that it would not be a genuine exchange unless Heidegger is present, while only a public statement by Heidegger would be a sign that some reparation was possible. This dilemma, the profound confusion between the public ideal of communication and the private, dialogical notion of philosophical communication, Arendt observed, pervades Jaspers's postwar writings. As she understood it: to insist on communication as the means of assuring truth "is to believe that the intimacy of the dialogue, the 'inner action' in which I appeal to myself or to the 'other self,' . . . can be extended and become paradigmatic for the political sphere."[103] One might conclude that the debate with Heidegger, though it never actually occurred, was the central theme of Jaspers's postwar philosophy.

There is perhaps another reason that Jaspers so tenaciously resisted the temptation to publish his critique of Heidegger that he considered so often and prepared for so assiduously (in more than 250 closely connected pages). Nietzsche's remark, which he always invoked in regard to the "polemic" (not correctly remembered), "Whomever I attack, I honor," is bound up with his own sense of a loss, not merely of their friendship, but of his idealization of Heidegger as a great philosopher. In Jaspers's ennobling philosophy, Heidegger is also ennobled, and this finally becomes another source of inhibition: "I hold him in too high esteem [*Er stehr mir zu hoch*], for merely to be able to speak about him, or to debate positions, as if it were a question of strangers" (*N, 129*).

This "impulse to reverence" harkens back to Jaspers's pre-1933 affinity to Heidegger's attempt to disentangle authentic experience from the ontic quotidian of "the They."[104] In 1931 Jaspers shared with Heidegger the conservative critique of modern life that bemoaned the cultural chaos and "the mass diffusion of knowledge and of its expression."[105] Their early exchange of letters during 1922 occurred under an intense and mutual consciousness of having become, even before their first meeting, a "Kampfgemeinschaft." When Jaspers first invited the younger Heidegger to Heidelberg, he wrote that "it would be nice, if we can for once spend a few days philosophizing at the appropriate hours, and try out and firm up the 'Kampfgemeinschaft.' I imagine that we would live together—each in his own room, my wife is traveling—each does what he wants to, apart from mealtimes, and that we meet and talk according to inclination, particularly evenings, or whenever, without any compulsion." To assure Heidegger's acceptance, Jaspers pinned a 1,000-mark note to the letter, "for the trip."[106] Jaspers also fantasized that they would found a journal, *Die Philosophie der Zeit: Kritische Hefte von Martin Heidegger and Karl Jaspers,* for which *only* they would write. When, in July 1923, a chance briefly appeared for Heidegger to move to Heidelberg, he spoke of an "invisible community" between the two philosophers.[107]

Even the notorious 1933 Rectorial Address was greeted by Jaspers with polite praise, with an only slightly critical edge: "My trust in your philosophizing, which has been newly strengthened since the Spring and our conversations at that time, has not been disturbed by the characteristics of this speech, which belong to the times [*Zeitgemäss*], or by something in it which seems to me to be a bit forced, and by sentences that appear to me to have a hollow ring. All in all I am only glad that someone can speak in this way, that he touches the authentic boundaries and origins."[108]

Thus the infidelity of 1933, which emerged during their last meeting when Jaspers saw how demonstrably enthusiastic Heidegger was about the euphoria surrounding the new regime, was felt all the more strongly. Twenty years later, Jaspers candidly recalled that "between 1920 and 1933, as Heidegger and I stood in a more frequent and deepening relationship, I still never called him a friend. And now, when I do this retrospectively, it is also true: he was the only one of my friends with whom I was not of one mind in 1933, the only one who betrayed me" (*N,* 96). Such idealizations do not easily dissolve, and words like "disappointment" and "betrayal" denote the sense of inadequacy, rivalry, and competition that never seem far from the surface. One motif that recurs often in Jaspers's notes is the juxtaposition of profundity and truth seeking: "Perhaps Heidegger's work is much more important than mine, but—it appears to me, I am more emphatically attempting to find truth" (*N,* 90). Or, "one can be completely unoriginal and also more fundamentally, completely uncreative, but also true" (*N,* 91).

It is hardly surprising, then, that when Jaspers records his only dream of Heidegger, it is these themes that appear in stark relief: "I never dream of Heidegger. But tonight I dreamt of him. I was together with some people who are attacking Heidegger in a way that made me indignant. Heidegger came over, we used the familiar form ('*wir dut-*

zen uns'), and I left with him" (*N*, 101). Jaspers is indignant at the attacks on Heidegger. He uses the familiar form and leaves with him: a dream of reconciliation and of protection, but also one in which Jaspers's own aggression is split off and projected onto others whose attacks disturb him. Jaspers's dream reflects his relation to Heidegger as melancholic identification with a lost ego ideal; it is a representation of the relation in which the need for identification and recognition triumphs over an externalized aggression and hostility, albeit one that is protectively split off. As Jessica Benjamin points out, the drama of ideal love involves the fantasy of surrender to a (more powerful) "rationally controlling and sadistic other" who is able to withstand destruction.[109] In the dream, Heidegger withstands the aggression, as he could not and did not survive Jaspers's real attack (in 1945), and this makes possible the reconciliation (*wir dutzen uns*) that leads ultimately to a more intense intimacy than even that of their prewar Kampfgemeinschaft and the two depart together. Jaspers's dream captures his ambivalence, the conflict between an admiring and idealizing identification and a split-off, envious, attacking component, which was further complicated by his sense of betrayal. The dream reveals yet another ambiguity, that Jaspers authentically believes in Heidegger's innocence, and it is his own guilt for attacking Heidegger (the fatal letter of 1945) that ultimately prevented their reconciliation.

Jaspers saw the test of his philosophy in the planned but never executed confrontation with Heidegger. Instead, Jaspers gave Heidegger his most convenient excuse, that he was—and this is also evident in some of Arendt's characterizations—*unmundig* (immature), a naif, an innocent, and therefore not responsible for his actions. In the letter responding to Heidegger's "confession," Jaspers offered this parable: "You will pardon me, if I say what I once thought: that you seem to have behaved in relation to the National Socialist events like a boy who is dreaming, who does not know what he is doing, and who blindly and absent-mindedly permits himself to get involved in an undertaking which appears to him wholly different than it is in reality, and then soon finds himself standing perplexed in front of a pile of ruins, and just goes on."[110] Heidegger found the analogy appealing: "With the image of the dreaming boy, you have hit the mark."[111] With the threat of further discussion lifted, Heidegger recalled how "from year to year, the more the evil emerged, the shame to have once participated in it here, grew both directly and indirectly."[112]

Heidegger once again reiterated that it was his "step into public discourse" that was at the root of his guilt, and he reaffirmed once again that the "matter of evil is not yet at its end." Heidegger thus returned to a litany of themes: that Germany's defeat is the greater catastrophe, that the evil "is now actually entering the global stage," that Stalin is winning "a battle every day," and finally, and most emphatically, that "all this is not taking place in the sphere of the political."[113] With that letter, Heidegger's confession, along with their fragile reconciliation, was added to the pile of ruin, and Jaspers admitted that it was the cause of his subsequent "inhibition," since he did write to him again for two years. It was above all the remark about "the sphere of the political" that enraged him, that would have resulted in a "storm of words," in "anger," "in an affirmation of reason." He asks, "Is this power of evil in Germany not that which has been constantly growing, and is in fact preparing Stalin's victory: the new so-called nationalism, the return of the old byways of thinking and the old ghosts?" And finally, "Is not a philosophy, which in such sentences as your letter imagines and poetizes that which produces the vision of the monstrous, once again the preparation for the victory of the totalitarian, insofar as it divorces itself from reality?"[114] Here Jaspers moved between the two familiar poles, between his sense that preserving the "human constitution" in a small circle of "educated men" (*gebildeter*) is no longer possible and his recognition that the sphere of the political cannnot disappear. Jaspers's insistence on guilt, on dialogue and communication, failed in the one instance that obviously mattered most, in his relationship to Heidegger, the one philosopher (apart from Max Weber) who, as he put it in an unsent seventieth birthday greeting, "was for me a man who knew what philosophy is."[115] That Heidegger, whose philosophical power was never in doubt, had failed to reestablish "communication" at the level of "human standards and human possibilities" was, for Jaspers, "the sign of the complete inadequacy of my philosophizing."[116]

IX.

Jaspers's private/public conundrum over Heidegger was paralleled by *Die Schuldfrage*'s division of German guilt into private moral/metaphysical and public criminal/political spheres, a distinction that gave considerable support to the so-called silent *Vergangenheitsbewältigung* (mastering the past) of the immediate postwar years. It encouraged the view that politics and morality belonged to separate spheres and that Nazism could be regarded simply as an inevitable consequence of the

German nation-state idea. The concept of metaphysical solidarity, with its manifest religiosity, was in no small part responsible for so much of the public language of the postwar era, which, as Adorno contemptuously remarked, "grasped at the banal, while elevating it and enshrining it in bronze at the very heights."[117] Jaspers's strict separation of political and moral responsibility also contributed to skepticism about denazification, and permitted the political culture of the early Federal Republic to substitute financial reparations and public declarations of responsibility for what might have been more effective and less ritualized attempts to reveal the truth of the Nazi past.[118] Its very sobriety, as Arendt recognized, was in no small part exculpation by understatement.

Jaspers registered Max Weber's impact on his thought in the sentence, "For my part, I can only refer to my continuity of opinion over fifty years, and to the fact that over all these years, I never philosophized without thinking of Max Weber." Jaspers argued that despite his wartime defense of the German "nation," after 1919 Weber recognized that a "sensible German politics" would be possible only through solidarity with the Western idea of political freedom and not through any assertion of German nationhood. But what might have happened had Max Weber lived to experience National Socialism? In 1961 Jaspers offered the following conjecture:

> His despair over things German certainly would have infinitely surpassed all previous despair. But what would he have thought and done politically? He could not have recognized as German a state that no longer commanded any fealty from the nation. For step by step that state annihilated the nation, and would inexorably bring about its end.[119]

This did not mean that Weber would have completely despaired of "what is German," since that concept no longer included the nation-state. In *Freiheit und Wiedervereinigung*, published just a year earlier, Jaspers elaborated: "The history of the German nation-state is at an end, not the history of the Germans. What we can achieve as a great nation for ourselves and for the world is insight into the current global situation: that the idea of the nation-state is the calamity [*Unheil*] of Europe, and of all continents."[120] The crimes of Hitler implicated not merely the German nation-state, but the very idea of the nation-state. In this way, by placing the largest burden of responsibility for Nazism on the German nation-state tradition, Jaspers often diminished the significance of Nazi ideology and its radicalism, its racial and aesthetic ideals. In so doing, Jaspers hoped to revive the tradition of the Kulturnation at the expense of the political nation. But he recognized, at least by 1960, that a "reversion from the nation-state to world citizen" was no longer an option.

In 1946–1947 and well into the cold war, the concept of the German pariah and German guilt and responsibility foreclosed any discussion of German unification. Despite Jaspers's rejection of collective guilt, the concept of the German as pariah implicitly attached a prohibition to the future existence of any German nation-state, which, in certain respects, approximated collective guilt. His juxtaposition of "freedom" to "reunification," the title of his 1960 pamphlet, *Freiheit und Wiedervereinigung*, underlined his emphasis on Germany's integration into the Western alliance and his belief that unification had been "played out" (*Verspielt*) by a state that Germans themselves had brought into being and loyally followed, and for whose acts they must now bear the consequences.[121]

After November 1989, however, Jaspers's taboo on any future political German nation-state became controversial. Nowhere was this more apparent than during the debates over German unification when politicians in both major parties dismissed the implied connection between Nazi crimes and the postwar geopolitical division of Germany. Jaspers's reservations about German unity were echoed in 1990 by prominent intellectuals like Günter Grass, who invoked Germany's "guilt-ridden past," and warned that "whomever today reflects on Germany and seeks an answer to the German Question, must also think about Auschwitz."[122] The intellectuals' Cassandra cries against German unity showed their now threadbare age, and they only fueled the truculence of a new generation of nationalist writers who denounced the continued obsession with guilt as "national masochism" (*Nationalmasochismus*).[123] As former Chancellor Willy Brandt remarked in his perceptive foreword to a new post-1990 edition of Jaspers's *Freiheit und Wiedervereinigung*, the claim that "knowledge of Auschwitz forbids German unity" contains a serious misjudgment, ignoring the expressly "antinational" character of National Socialism, which sacrificed Germans and Germany to its racial imperium.[124]

Despite those problematic aspects, *Die Schuldfrage* played an important role in the formation of postwar German political culture. In contrast to Heidegger's incontestable moral failure, after 1945 Jaspers was the first German philosopher who remained in Germany to identify the centrality of Auschwitz for postwar German political consciousness. His contribution above all else was to place the caesura at the center of philosophical reflection and to insist, in Habermas's words, that "Auschwitz has become the signature of an entire epoch—and it concerns all of us. Something happened there that no one could previously have thought even possible. It touched a deep layer of solidarity among all who have a human face."[125]

If Jaspers's notion of metaphysical guilt was still expressed in the language of German idealism and in the rhetoric of the "cultural nation," *Die Schuldfrage* recognized that in its nihilism and blindness, German philosophy had contributed its portion to the catastrophe. German veneration of the nation-state and rejection of Enlightenment modernity had been disastrous, elevating the state and the spiritual quest for transcendence above political responsibility and morality. The spiritualization of power politics, the solipsism of philosophical idealism, and the apocalyptic rejection of modernity and democracy (here Jaspers no doubt included his own prior thinking, especially *Die geistige Situation der Zeit*) could not be disentangled, at least not in 1946. In this regard Jaspers embodied the casting off of a certain type of German intellectual tradition still identified with pre-1933 German philosophy and still embodied in Heidegger's insular, antihumanist, and anti-Western stance. His embrace of the values of the Enlightenment—though mediated through a starkly Protestant and existentialist worldview—provided a point of orientation for Germany's intellectual confrontation with the Nazi past, affirming the place of the political responsibility in any postwar political constellation. Germany could henceforth belong to the community of nations only by rejecting the tradition of the nation-state. Finally, and most important, Jaspers gave intellectual support to the emergence of a minimum "national consensus" in German political life: that any future German state would become responsible for the crimes of the former, and that political responsibility—whatever form that might take, reparations, trials of criminals, education—would be an integral part of postwar Germany. Jaspers's legacy requires that the memory of Auschwitz continue to be part of German political consciousness: "to keep alive, without distortion, and not only in an intellectual form, the memory of the sufferings of those who were murdered by German hands."[126]

Jaspers chose a political ethic of communication as opposed to Heidegger's silence and evasion. He refused the fatal combination of intellectual arrogance and political naïveté that led to Heidegger's hubris in 1933, noting in his famous "evaluation" of December 1945 that Heidegger "embraced a National Socialism which bore no relationship to reality."[127] Despite that achievement, Jaspers's insistence on communication, a philosophical ideal that emerged from the ruin of his relationship with Heidegger, and from the catastrophe of 1945, the collapse of the German polity, was not capable of addressing the weaknesses of Heideggerian thought. In this respect Jaspers was incapable of finding a partner for his dialogic ideal, located as it was, midway between apocalypse and enlightenment.

The Cunning of Unreason

*Mimesis and the Construction of
Anti-Semitism in Horkheimer and
Adorno's* Dialectic of Enlightenment

I.

Dialectic of Enlightenment first appeared in 1944 in a limited mimeographed edition presented to Friedrich Pollock, the Institute for Social Research's economist, in honor of his fiftieth birthday. For that occasion the simple title *Philosophische Fragmente*—with its oblique allusion to Kierkegaard—sufficed. When an altered and expanded version of the text was published four years later by Querido Verlag, the German exile publishing house in Amsterdam, title became subtitle, and the title of the lead essay, "Dialectic of Enlightenment," became its permanent title. Stylistic improvement notwithstanding, the intense discussion of the authorship, composition, and place of *Dialectic of Enlightenment* in the ouevre of its coauthors that has unfolded over the past few years makes the rationale for the original title worth keeping in mind. Its mosaic of two main essays, two "excursus," seven "theses" on anti-Semitism, and aphoristic "notes and drafts," and its erratic mode of composition over several years, makes the presumption that a unified "critical theory" is embodied in this text, or in the work of the Frankfurt School as a whole, a dubious proposition.[1]

The publication of Rolf Wiggershaus's *Die Frankfurter Schule* and the Max Horkheimer *Gesammelte Schriften,* which includes correspondence, drafts, minutes of discussions, and internal institute debates that surrounded the composition of *Dialectic of Enlightenment,* has contributed a great deal to our understanding of the circumstances under which it emerged during the years between 1938 and 1944.[2] We can see the justification as well as the exaggeration of Horkheimer's assertion in the preface to the 1968 edition: "No outsider will find it easy to discern how far we are both responsible for every sentence. We jointly dictated lengthy sections; and the vital principle of the *Dialectic* is the tension between the two intellectual temperaments conjoined in it."[3] For all its ambiguity, Horkheimer stresses not merely the collaborative composition of the work, but the tensions out of which it was constructed. Gunzelin Schmid Noerr's caveat, in his otherwise indispensable essay, the "Place of *Dialectic of Enlightenment* in the Development of Critical Theory," that "it is nonetheless to be doubted that both theories represent, in the sense of this declaration, an unbroken unity," is slightly misplaced, since no such unity was implied.[4]

Work on a proposed book began in earnest in late 1941, after Adorno's decision, taken after much prodding, to leave New York and join Horkheimer (who provided detail descriptions of the local real estate) in Santa Monica, California. Much of the book was written before and during the early days of American involvement in World War II, when its outcome was still uncertain, and only the "Elements of Anti-Semitism" was drafted during the last two years of the war. Its seventh "thesis"—added in 1947—alone registers the authors' realization that Hitler's barbarism had exceeded even the most melancholy prognoses of the twentieth century's most melancholic thinkers.

Dialectic of Enlightenment was a collaborative work undertaken with no strict division of labor, or any superordinate effort to conceal its authors' distinctive sensibilities and voices. This makes any definitive mapping of their respective roles difficult, though the extant manuscripts do establish the rough main lines of responsibility for the book's distinct sections. According to Schmid Noerr, drafts found in either Horkheimer's or Adorno's papers make it reasonably certain that the introduction, "The Concept of Enlightenment," "Excursus II," and "Juliette or Enlightenment and Morality" were drafted by Horkheimer, while the Excursus I, "Odysseus or Myth and Enlightenment," and the chapter "The Culture Industry" were Adorno's responsibility. The "Notes and Drafts" are exclusively Horkheimer's, while the "Elements of Anti-Semitism" can be attributed to Adorno, with the collaboration of Leo Löwenthal; thesis "VII" was added to the 1947 edition by Horkheimer.[5]

Despite the relative certainty of the division of labor, there is still considerable controversy over the authorship of the first chapter. Robert

Hullot-Kentor, for example, casts doubt on Horkheimer's primacy in its composition, arguing that with few exceptions there are no comparable lines in Horkheimer's own works, where he did not "formulate such compelling ideas."[6] Though partisan to Adorno, this assertion is not entirely inconsistent with Rolf Tiedemann's account, attributed to Adorno, that both authors dictated "The Concept of Enlightenment."[7] Oral testimony and stylistic clues, as Schmid Noerr reminds us, must also be taken into account. Joint authorship is further attested by the fact that the recorded discussions between Horkheimer and Adorno in early 1939 bear most heavily on this chapter.[8] At the time, Horkheimer described his work habits to Paul Tillich as follows: "In the morning a short walk with Pollock, then directly after, based on rather methodical study, I write notes and drafts, and in the afternoon I see (at least) Teddie, in order to finalize the finished text."[9]

Horkheimer's sole authorship of the first chapter can also be disputed on the substantive grounds that its main theme of the self-destruction of reason through the domination of nature and the history of civilization as the "introversion of sacrifice" was already developed by Adorno in 1933 in his Habilitation on Kierkegaard and was reiterated in the draft of *Zur Philosophie der neuen Musik,* also written in 1941. Chapter 1, however, does contain many formulations, particularly its detours into intellectual history, that could only stem from Horkheimer. Sentences such as "The increasingly formalistic universality of reason, far from signifying an increasing consciousness of universal solidarity, expresses the skeptical separation of thought from its object" are typical of Horkheimer's other writings during this period, especially "The End of Reason," published in 1941.[10] Its general argument is characteristic of his early philosophical essays and set forth in the *Eclipse of Reason* (1946), that universally valid norms and the idea of a good society, once embodied in the tradition of "objective Reason" (Plato, Aristotle, German idealism), had given way to the calculating, self-preserving "subjective reason" of modern bourgeois society. However, in *Dialectic of Enlightenment* the categories of "objective" and "subjective" reason no longer appear, and the reconstruction of rationality as the "myth of omnipotence" is grounded not in the history of philosophy but in philosophical anthropology.

Even more difficult to disentangle than authorship, then, is the question of how to weigh the respective authors' contribution to the text's central philosophical themes. Jürgen Habermas has charged that *Dialectic of Enlightenment* was so Nietzschean a work that it remained "an aesthetic fragment," that its critique of reason took on an "affirmative twist," and that it succumbed to a theory of power that had itself become mythological: "Nietzsche's critique consumes the critical impulse itself."[11] *Dialectic of Enlightenment* marked a break with the program pursued in the *Zeitschrift für Sozialforschung,* while it "fits seamlessly into the continuity of a way of thinking later characterized as negative dialectics." Only in those chapters in which Horkheimer's "hand is visible" he asserts, can we find sentences that affirm that "Enlightenment must reflect on itself if humanity is not to be totally betrayed" (*DE,* 5). Habermas clearly holds Adorno responsible for the excesses of a book that became something of an embarrassment for Horkheimer, who identified with the "liberal heritage of the era of Enlightenment" and who "would rather entangle himself in contradictions than give up his identity as an enlightener and fall into Nietzscheanism."[12] This fateful turn in critical theory is only understandable, he asserts, against the background of "the darkest years of the Second World War," when it appeared to the authors "that the last sparks of reason were being extinguished from reality and had left the ruins of a civilization in collapse without any hope."[13] "It was not even Horkheimer's original intention that *Dialectic of Enlightenment* remain a collection of fragments. He had planned a systematic work and had previously made use of conventional forms of presentation. By contrast, Adorno was convinced from early on that fragmentary representation was the only suitable form for philosophical thought."[14] It should at least be pointed out here that Horkheimer's own ambivalences regarding Nietzsche are more complex, a point that can be made by simply referring to Horkheimer's earlier collections of aphorisms, which even bore the Nietzschean title *Dämmerung* (Daybreak). Habermas's view makes Horkheimer and Adorno's close collaboration in the late 1930s and early 1940s something of a *pactum diaboli,* and its most important result, *Dialectic of Enlightenment,* if not anathema, certainly an anomaly in the history of critical theory.

II.

A reading of the text of *Dialectic of Enlightenment,* as well as the supporting documentation, published and unpublished correspondence in the Max Horkheimer-Archiv, suggests that this account is too polemical to fully illuminate the conditions under which it emerged. A rather different, perhaps even opposing, interpretation in which Horkheimer's often undialectical pessimism is consistently challenged by Adorno's more acutely "desperate hope" is more plausible.[15] No doubt in the 1940s both authors shared a sense of civilizational breakdown—hardly illegitimate in light of the events of that era. But even their specific prognoses, for example, differences over the probable outcome of the war, show that Adorno often registers far more optimism than does Horkheimer. For example, in a May 1945 letter to Horkheimer, lamenting the fact that they could not be together at the moment that the Hitler regime collapsed, Adorno could not resist commenting that his "bourgeois thesis, that Hitler could not hold on, had, with a belatedness that renders it ironic, been confirmed."[16] Habermas's interpretation ignores, as Alfred Schmidt notes, "the fact that Horkheimer appropriates historical materialism from a Schopenhauerian point of view from the very beginning."[17] Horkheimer regarded the rejection of all rationalistic systems and the "move from Kant to Schopenhauer" as "an advance in the self-enlightenment of reason, not a relapse into irrationality," a view that underscores the many references to Schopenhauer throughout his early work, particularly in his belief that the blind contingency of history and the suffering of individuals could not be redeemed by an abstract, objective Reason.[18]

Adorno never "slipped into irrationalism" as Habermas's interpretation implies, while Horkheimer's prognoses and philosophical reflections frequently take on the contours of a truly apocalyptic pessimism. Nor is there any firm evidence, as Hullot-Kentor rightly points out, that the passages arguing for the weak power of reason are "from Horkheimer's hand," and many other passages from Adorno's work attest to the fact that "he is pursuing a critique of reason by way of reason."[19] In fact, Rolf Wiggershaus cites examples from Adorno's draft of *Zur Philosophie der neuen Musik* (published 1949), written shortly after his arrival in California at the end of 1941, which closely correspond to certain passages in the first chapter, though restricted to the development of modern music: "Conscious control over natural musical material is both the emancipation of humanity from the musical compulsion of nature and the subordination of nature to human aims."[20]

Moreover, even an adequate summary of their distinct philosophical positions would not exhaust the ambivalences and "tensions" between the authors alluded to by Horkheimer in his preface. For example, in a letter to Adorno, written just before the latter's arrival in California and the beginning of the period of close collaboration on *Dialectic of En-*

lightenment, Horkheimer remarked, "That I myself feel, comically enough, that we are being pressed against our will into a front with rationalism, which no longer exists, and as the main content of my essay I am thinking about the delimitation from rationalism. But I confess that at the moment, I do this with difficulty."[21] To be sure, both before and after writing *Dialectic of Enlightenment* Horkheimer placed greater emphasis than Adorno on "rescuing the enlightenment" (a title he proposed for the never written sequel to *Dialectic of Enlightenment*), but it was, as I will argue, Horkheimer's and not Adorno's pessimism that precluded further collaboration on the planned volume in the post–World War II era. Perhaps we can conclude that it is more in reaction to the perceived threat of an "irrationalist" postmodernism that Adorno's negative influence has so readily been emphasized to restore the rationalist roots of an authentic critical theory.[22]

III.

To understand the philosophical divergence between Horkheimer and Adorno when *Dialectic of Enlightenment* was composed, it is illuminating to briefly consult some of the conversations they recorded in the 1930s. During the fall of 1931 a series of internal discussions were held at the Institut für Sozialforschung in Frankfurt on the general theme of the "crisis of science." Their point of departure was Horkheimer's recently published article, "The Present Situation of Social Philosophy," where Horkheimer maintained that a reconstruction of social philosophy was no longer possible and that the interdisciplinary research program that he had proposed for the institute—guided by theoretical reflection on "the essential"—was the only reasonable way to confront the impasse: "The current situation of social philosophy can be understood in principle in terms of its dissolution, and of the impossibility of reconstructing it in thought without falling behind the current state of knowledge."[23] At that juncture Horkheimer defended his conclusions against Adorno's criticism that such an interdisciplinary social theory was "too primitively formulated" and conceded far too much to analytical empirical research. Adorno objected to what he called Horkheimer's "two world theory," in which subjective reason was confronted with the impossibility of objective knowledge, and objective knowledge with the limits of subjectivity. Theoretical reflection could, Adorno noted, be pursued only by "the singular moment of nonidentity," in which dia-

lectical thought gives itself over to the object as "merely concrete phe-
nomenality."[24] It was, Adorno said, more preferable to completely ab-
jure any "total dialectic" than risk, as did Horkheimer, becoming both
"a theoretical positivist and a practical materialist."[25]

When the institute moved to New York in 1936, these discussions
resumed, and by 1939, they began to touch on some of the central
themes of *Dialectic of Enlightenment*. Horkheimer retained his conviction that an interdisciplinary research program, as he hoped the institute in exile would conduct, could bring sensual empirical reality into
the domain of theory without abandoning the achievements either of
the scientific understanding of the world or of Hegel's critique of Kant.
These conversations often go to the core of the distinct understandings
of "theory" that coexisted in critical theory at that time. When Horkheimer expressed his conception of theory in conventional Hegelian
terms "as the tension between you yourself and reality," or as "a means
to come to terms with the world," Adorno reacted caustically: "Theory
is, god knows, not the holy Spirit. Nor can Theory be reduced to spon-
taneity or to thought, it has the facts within itself."[26] Though he reassured Horkheimer: "I believe that our conceptions are much more similar here than it may at first appear. I always say that theory does very
little, almost nothing, it can solve only the questions that are put to it
from the material world."[27] Horkheimer, by contrast, asserted that "the
whole is our entire theoretical edifice," a statement that appeared to
Adorno as confirmation of his fixation on the concept of totality:

HORKHEIMER: "For me it is a matter of more strongly highlighting the
positive importance of the moment of the factual for dialectical theory. Even we have to work with substantial relations [*Sachverhalte*], which can be controlled, or else we no
longer have any criteria to distinguish sense from nonsense."

ADORNO: "One must be very subtle here. We must determine the distinctions between the positivist concept of facts and our
concept of substantial relations."[28]

Here Adorno alluded to his unpublished manuscript on the philosophy of Edmund Husserl, which was concerned with establishing the nature of *Sachverhalte,* or substantial relations, without falling, as he believed Husserl had, into assuming the existence of a transcendental ego.
"Facts," Adorno claimed, "are always that which as *caput mortuum*
[dead physical existence] is left over from the historical process. The
substantial relations of which we speak are actually never a first, but

always a last: they are the *Residua*, that which remains indissoluble against a fully developed state of theory."[29] Recalling Benjamin's epistemological prologue to the "Baroque book" (*The Origin of the German Play of Mourning*), Adorno admitted that "the kind of gaze that I have, is such that it finds in things the refraction [*Widerschein*] of that light source, which can never be the object of intention and thought."[30] Adorno's recourse to what he called "the great Jewish theology" remained incomprehensible to Horkheimer, who ironically suggested that Adorno might have an "omniscient wink of the eye." That Adorno took the joke seriously is not untypical: "All that remains of theology is the wink of the eye."[31] Unlike Horkheimer, Adorno remained skeptical of any statement in which truth was positively expressed: "I cannot conceal my opinion that a formulation of the concept of truth without a particular conception of negative theology is impossible."[32] Instead he affirmed the credo he had expressed in his Kierkegaard study in 1933: "The supreme paradox of all thought is the attempt to discover something that thought cannot think."[33]

If these conversations demonstrate different styles and very distinct philosophical "sensibilities," they also point to broad areas of consensus. Adorno did not entirely reject Horkheimer's insistence on facticity, or his implication that theory was linked to experience, remarking that he too had to "follow the facts." While Horkheimer's mistrust of any closed theory presupposed the identity of "each insight" and the whole of the theory, Adorno asserted, "I instead require the thicket of experience."[34]

These exchanges also often acknowledged their differences in style and depth with a brutal frankness. Horkheimer's prose, Adorno says, "is below the experience which you would like to communicate, while mine is far above that, which I can communicate."[35] But he reassured Horkheimer that, despite their differences, they still shared a "hope for utopia." Adorno the metaphysician who distrusted metaphysics, and Horkheimer the materialist who distrusted positivism had, Adorno observed, arrived at a similar point from two different perspectives:[36] "The fact that I was influenced by certain metaphysical thoughts, and that you liquidated the entire positivistic heritage of Marxism is not accidental. It comes from a certain feeling of impoverishment in that kind of knowledge, where there is cognizance of the traces." This, he said, contained "my core philosophical experience, and your critical motor."[37]

IV.

In June 1941 Hannah Arendt provided Adorno with a copy of Benjamin's last text, the now famous "On the Concept of History." Though Benjamin had explicitly instructed Gretel Adorno, "Nothing was further from me than the thought of publishing these sketches (not to mention, in the form that they are now before you)," Adorno urged Horkheimer to publish his theses as a testament.[38] More important, he emphasized that "no other work of Benjamin shows him to be closer to our intentions." Its major themes—history as a permanent catastrophe, the critique of progress, the domination of nature, and the attitude toward culture—were indicative of his, and their, intellectual preoccupations. But Adorno also expressed his reservations that "a certain naïveté in the passages that speak of Marxism and politics cannot be overlooked." In a postscript he added that thesis XIII with its notion of "progression through a homogenous empty time" troubled him, since it appeared to reduce the "conformist conception of history" to the "appearance of time" as something "sui generis." And finally, Adorno questioned whether Benjamin's explicitly messianic emphasis on "the presence of the now" would not "entirely liquidate the image of the future from utopia," adding parenthetically and underlining the word *ratio* in handwriting, "By the way, we would have difficulty *speaking* of the 'whore' *ratio*."[39]

V.

The death of Benjamin and the arrival of his philosophical testament provided Horkheimer and Adorno, as Wiggershaus notes, with a kind of "guiding star" around which the constellation of themes—the fate of the exile, the fate of the Jews, and the catastrophe of civilization—that ultimately make up *Dialectic of Enlightenment* could be organized. In a work of exile that makes Homer's ancient exile its "hero," the narrative of Odysseus provides a kind of allegory of the theory elaborated in the first chapter. Odysseus embodies the "homesickness" that is the source of the adventure through which subjectivity is first constituted in the epic narrative and the hero who "by his cunning and reason escapes prehistory" (O, 139). As Odysseus resists regression into the world of magic and matriarchy, the modern epic of the homelessness, exile, and diaspora of reason is self-consciously counterposed to the fascist glorification of rootedness and the mythology of *Heimat*. In the

Odysseus chapter, any "phantasm of a lost golden age" is explicitly re-jected. Rather, Heimat "is the state of having escaped" (O, 139).[40] To Nietzsche's adage "It is even part of my good fortune not to be a home-owner," Adorno once commented, "Today, we should have to add: it is part of morality not to be at home in one's home."[41] Yet the price of this "escape" in Adorno's theory is always sacrifice, the subordination of the individual consciousness that takes place in the *imitatio* of the power of the gods over nature in reason. Here the theme of the domi-nation of external nature is introjected as the domination of inner na-ture is directly linked to the "introversion of sacrifice." Reason outwits myth only if it becomes mythological. Rational thought, the intellect, binds itself to its object to the degree that it attempts to undo its power over thought. Reason thus sacrifices itself to myth in its effort to outwit myth by replicating nature. By its very dependency on the object, it is robbed of its autonomy and freedom, so that, as Adorno explained in his study of Kierkegaard, "all sacrifice in the domain of consciousness assumes the form of the paradoxical" (K, 119).

Adorno's 1933 *Habilitationsschrift* on Kierkegaard's theology of sac-rifice is also a study of the "innermost model of every sacrifice that oc-curs in philosophy," a sacrifice that is always bound up with any system of idealism and is replicated in Hegel, in Marx, and in Kierkegaard. At the same time, the intellectual sacrifice that occurs when the individual idea or moment is drawn into the "whirlpools" of the system is, for Adorno, an "unalloyed replica" of the sacrifice that occurs in mythical thought: "The two meet on the stage of spirit and carry out the dia-logue of idealism as mythical thought's own play of lamentation" (K, 108). In that passage Adorno elaborates on the connection between philosophical idealism as the intellectual sacrifice and mythical sacrifice as one in the same tragic event—with reference to Benjamin's 1928 *Trauerspiel* book. "Lamentation" here refers to the parallel between lit-eral death and the aesthetic character of sacrifice, the submission to the gods, to fate, and to the idea that is always the way out or escape that necessarily takes the form of annihilation. As Claude Lévi-Strauss once noted, sacrificial destruction "is meaningful only in the form of a holo-caust."[42] Adorno expresses a similar idea succinctly: "Thus power over natural life remains dedicated to its annihilation in spirit rather than to reconciliation" (K, 109).

For Horkheimer and Adorno, therefore, enlightenment does not con-sist of drawing boundaries against myth. Rather, their enterprise was both less and more ambitious, to demonstrate the ways that consciousness is bound up with annihilation and domination in the conceptual realm. However complex are the ways that sacrifice pervades the culture of enlightenment, its paradoxical character remains the same: "The sacrifice of consciousness is carried out according to its own categories, rationally" (K, 114). The attempt to annihilate nature by myth, theology, art, reason, and ultimately science cannot escape what Adorno called the "impulse toward self-destruction and annihilation," which he had already demonstrated in Kierkegaard's theology of " 'consciousness at its apex'—in absolute spirituality" (K, 114). Kierkegaard's theology is preoccupied with how man's divinity rules over "sinful creation" through a demonic sacrifice of consciousness in which "the name of the divinity succumbs to his demonic nature" (K, 118). In *Dialectic of Enlightenment*, a similar paradox is at work in "the mythical sacrifice of Reason" (K, 119). Consequently, "just as the myths realize enlightenment, so enlightenment with every step becomes more entwined in mythology" (DE, 16). Exile from myth and nature brings speech, discourse, and the depersonalized "cold distance of narration" (O, 140).

The first chapter of *Dialectic of Enlightenment* is an attempt to reconstruct the genealogy of this sacrifice through an analysis of the fate of mimesis: first in the order of animistic identification, then in magic, subsequently in myth, and finally in Reason: "The categories by which Western philosophy defined its everlasting natural order marked the spots once occupied by Oncus and Persephone, Ariadne and Nereus" (DE, 5). At all these stages the concept of mimesis is not understood as mere imitation, but as a form of mimicry or semblance that appropriates rather than replicates its object in a nonidentical similitude. Mimesis is not the suppression of difference but an act of substitution that intervenes between the helpless subject and the overpowering object: it appears in the terror with which all living creatures react to fear, in the magician's impersonation of demons, in his gestures of appeasement to the gods, or in the wearing of masks that guarantee that the identity of self "cannot disappear through identification with another" (DE, 10).[43] In this way semblance preserves the possibility of freedom, of a resistance to the assimilation of the concept in much the same way that in Kierkegaard's theology "enciphered images oppose the existential sacrifice" (K, 133). Adorno's concept of mimesis is close to Benjamin's insofar as it is both the remembrance of a "nonsensuous similarity" between image and thing and an attempt to conceptually capture the survival of mimesis in language, as "a gap between the words and the things they conjure."[44]

Following Freud's *Totem and Taboo* (1924), Horkheimer and Adorno regard mimesis as directly connected to the substitution that occurs in ritual sacrifice, the appeasement of the gods with an animal that is both representative and surrogate; the "nonspecificity of the example" already "marks a step toward discursive logic" (*DE*, 10). Yet, at the same time, mimesis is a step away from discursive logic in its preservation of the concrete, sensual, and thinglike substance that is the very opposite of the liquidation of subjectivity in the symbol or concept that Adorno saw in his analysis of intellectual sacrifice. Mimesis therefore represents both the prefiguration of and the "other" of reason: in *Dialectic of Enlightenment* the modern principle of calculability and equivalence is already prefigured by a growing abstraction and distance from nature that occurs first in the "specific" duplication of anthropomorphism, in the "nonspecific" sacrifice, and ultimately in the unification of myth as the sovereignty of the human subject over nature. Yet mimesis too undergoes repression in the act of subjugating nature to instrumental reason: The *ratio,* which represses mimesis, is not simply its opposite. It too is mimesis: "mimesis of death." The domination of nature is adaptation, renunciation, calculation. It "renders unto nature what is nature's and precisely thereby deceives it" (O, 122). Mimesis in the modern world only retains its former status "weakly" in works of art that self-consciously refuse to "imitate" or "authentically" replicate reality, that refuse, as Martin Jay notes, "to imitate or be assimilated entirely to a bad external reality. . . . [B]y paradoxically honoring, one might say, the Jewish taboo on graven images . . . works of art hold out the hope for the return of a more benign version of mimesis in a future world beyond domination and reification."[45]

The taboo on pictoriality in the modern world is explicitly identified by Horkheimer and Adorno as beginning with Jewish monotheism, which proscribed imitation by converting ritual substitution and sacrifice into law. The prohibition on the graven image extends far beyond the representation of nature in animism or sacrificial substitution: "Just as hieroglyphs bear witness, so the word too originally had a pictorial function" (*DE*, 17). The Jews, they maintained, crossed the threshold from mythology to symbolism not by eliminating adaptation to nature but by converting the image into a series of duties in the form of ritual: the Jews "transformed taboos into civilizing maxims when others still clung to magic" (*DE*, 186). Over thousands of years the Jews carried forward the process of enlightenment by enacting and transforming the prohibition on images: "The Jews seemed to have succeeded where

Christianity failed: they defused magic by its own power—turned against itself as ritual service of God. They have retained the aspect of expiation but have avoided the reversion to mythology which symbolism implies" (DE, 186). However, even in the "disenchanted world of Judaism," Horkheimer and Adorno wrote, mimesis is still expressed in the "bond between name and being" that is recognized in "the ban on pronouncing the name of God" (DE, 23).

Horkheimer and Adorno's account of the prohibition on mimesis closely parallels Freud's discussion of the origins of the prohibition on uttering the name of the dead in Totem and Taboo. As is well known, Freud claimed that "totemic religion arose from the filial sense of guilt, in an attempt to allay that feeling and to appease the father by deferred obedience to him."[46] Fear of the dead is the result of a hostile projection of evil impulses into demons, the substitution of animal names for the name of the dead, extending through a series of displacements designed both to outwit the evil spirits and to efface the hostile feelings. In the fully developed totemic system, the prohibition on the image of the father gives way to religion. The prohibition on representing the dead is thus "probably the earliest form in which the phenomenon of conscience is met with."[47] Freud placed great emphasis on how "identification with the totem is carried into effect" by various forms of mimicry, "dressing in the skin of the animal, by incising a picture of the totem upon his own body, and so on." In the ascent from *mana,* the originary mysterious power of the taboo, to the "ancient covenant with the totem, and the elevation of the father to a God, imitation plays a role, no matter how "impious" it may appear "to us moderns."[48] Freud also remarks on how the mimetic impulse takes the form of the "symptom" in hysteria and how neurotic behavior parallels the growing process of abstraction from totem animal to God and ultimately to scientific rationality: "It might be maintained that a case of hysteria is a caricature of a work of art, that of an obsessional neurosis is a caricature of a religion, and that of a paranoic delusion is a caricature of a philosophical system."[49]

In Horkheimer and Adorno's account, this impiety is the very definition of Enlightenment: "Ultimately the Enlightenment consumed not just the symbols but their successors, universal concepts" (DE, 23). Enlightenment occurs at the intersection of two decisive processes: the prohibition of the image and its displacement into the abstract system and the need to differentiate self from nature. The Jewish proscription on images, the *Bildverbot,* is the origin of enlightenment and at the same time provides its redemptive moment:

> The disenchanted world of Judaism is reconciled with magical thought through its negation in the idea of God. The Jewish religion does not tolerate any word that offers solace to despair in the face of mortality. It associates hope only with the prohibition against calling what is false God, against invoking the finite as the infinite, lies as truth. The guarantee of redemption lies in the rejection of any belief that would subscribe to this; it is knowledge obtained in the denunciation of madness. [. . . .] The rectitude [*Recht*] of the image is salvaged [*Gerettet*] in the faithful carrying out of this prohibition.[50]

The theological paradox underpinning this argument is unmistakable: redemption can only be salvaged by a thinking that radically refuses any compromise with magical practices, myth, or the transposition of worldly events into symbols. In short, only disenchantment, carried out to its logical conclusion, can bring about salvation. Horkheimer and Adorno clearly believed that Judaism in this regard represented a superior form of religion to Christianity, with its cultic regression to a world of images.[51] As Gertrud Koch points out, Adorno did not simply consider this prohibition in terms of a historical moment of cultural anthropology, but also conceived of aesthetics as a "particular variant of the Jewish prohibition on images." The prohibition leads, on the one side, to the liquidation of the image and the traces of animism in magical cult and ritual but also, on the other, to the autonomy of the artistic representation.[52]

Mythic mimesis, as Andrew Hewitt has argued, is already a step beyond archaic images, a step toward the symbolic, to the point where "mimesis feeds into rationality."[53] To fall back into the premythic world is to enter a matriarchal, magical world populated by "ancient heroines" and by Odysseus' own mother; to fall back into the "nondifferentiation of nature." Fascism, too, is characterized by its attempt to restore an archaic world of inauthenticity and terror masking as authenticity, heroism, and "being-in-the-world."[54] The "language of images" of mass cultural hieroglyphics is equally regarded as a "medium of regression" that "displays the archaic images of modernity."[55]

For Adorno and Horkheimer, there is no "outside" of enlightenment once image and knowledge are completely severed. No "authentic experience" can artificially restore the lost unity. Similarly, as Miriam Hansen shows, mimesis in the realm of art does not claim authenticity but "assumes a critical and corrective function vis-à-vis instrumental rationality and the identifying logic of conceptual language which distances subject from object and represses the non-identity of the latter."[56] Art can never substitute for concepts, nor can a world of images be restored. If enlightenment is a "universal taboo" on images, dialectic counters the taboo by interpreting every "image as writing," disclosing its false claims to authenticity. The "sacrifice" required of consciousness here is understood by Horkheimer and Adorno in Hegel's sense, not as positivistic reason, but as the negation of false mythology.

Rationality is thus both equated with and marked off from other historical forms of mimesis, as mimesis's realization, overcoming, and prohibition. Reason "asserted the power of repetition over reality, long after men had renounced the illusion that by repetition they could identify themselves with the repeated reality and thus escape its power" (DE, 12). However, in enlightenment, the word as sign abandons the claim to be like nature and is distributed among the different art forms, further separating mimesis or "imitation" from substitution as the abstract equivalence of the concept: "as a system of signs, language is required to resign itself to calculation in order to know nature and must discard the claim to be like it" (DE, 18). Self-conscious "inauthenticity," not merely imitatio, is the all-important element in mimesis. Inauthenticity is a ruse, for example, in the ritual sacrifice, and in the amalgamation of sacrifice and totemism that dispenses with the need for actual murder: the "stupidity of the ritual" serves "the cleverness of the weaker." Art contains the utopian remembrance of the world before the prohibition and the illusion of its overcoming: "the capacity of representation is the vehicle of progress and regression at one and the same time" (DE, 35). In Minima Moralia Adorno chides Nietzsche for having famously reproached Wagner with playacting since "all art, and music first of all is related to drama" and, more important, because his reproach betrays his own inability to penetrate the fetishism of authenticity. Despite Nietzsche's radical approach to truth, "the word genuine stands unquestioned, exempt from conceptual development."[57]

If, as Adorno asserts, all that is human is "indissolubly linked to imitation," any claim to genuineness is ultimately disingenuous. Theology adopts the "likeness" of self to God but never assumes its identity. As opposed to the idea of genuineness and authenticity, the "self should not be spoken of as the ontological ground, but at most theologically, in the name of its likeness to God."[58] Mimesis, for Adorno, thus stands in the same relation to authenticity, as theology stands in relation to ontology. Ontology refers here to the claim to totally encompass being by its concept, which is the essence of any claim to authenticity: "Indeed, not only an inauthenticity that poses as veridical ought to be convicted of lying: authenticity itself becomes a lie the moment it becomes authentic, that is in reflecting on itself, in postulating itself as genuine, in which it already oversteps the identity that it lays claim to in the same breath."[59] By its repression of mimesis—which is the prohibition on the name and likeness of God—the self-sacrifice of enlightenment, as Adorno had written in the Kierkegaard study, "is carried out with its own categories, rationally" (K, 114).

VI.

During their initial conversations about myth and enlightenment during the winter of 1939, the idea for an *Urgeschichte,* or primal history, of subjectivity first makes an appearance in Horkheimer's question: "Where does the experience of the individual appear decisively for the first time?" Significantly, it is Oedipus and not, as is later the case, Odysseus who immediately comes to mind as the figure who embodies the identity of selfhood with property and power. A passage retained only in altered form in *Dialectic of Enlightenment* offers this account: "Oedipus' answer to the riddle of the mythical sphinx, which he makes disappear, constitutes the identity of the human being against the disparity of his stage of life. In the same moment as the word 'the human being' drives the sphinx into the abyss, both the vagabond wife and the imperium fall into his possession."[60] The real crime of Oedipus is perhaps "nothing less than the fact that he became an individual and possessed something." Here they drew a tentative connection between the incest taboo and the dissolution of communal property. The site of the tragedy is the boundary line between "myth and maturity" (Adorno) or what Horkheimer calls "the announcement of the power of humanity through thought: the beginning of 'humanism.'"[61] Not surprisingly, it is also in the course of this discussion of the mythical stage of history that a direct parallel is drawn between "regression to the collective body" (Adorno) and the fascist concept of the "mass."[62]

Horkheimer and Adorno's decision to shift the focus from Oedipus to Odysseus can therefore only be partially explained as a shift from psychoanalytic theory to philosophical anthropology. Freud, as the authors were aware, invested Oedipus' fate with the originary tale of maturity against myth, individual against multiplicity, identical subject against the chthonic forces of nature that conspire to tear the ego asunder. The Oedipal narrative is at once a prohibition against regression to the maternal body, to a descent into undifferentiated nature, and an assertion of the struggle to acquire the autonomous ego of the father to internalize the paternal prohibition. However, since the ego "knows nothing" of the id, the latter remains "the perennial element of that which is not absorbed into identity." In the course of their discussions of myth, both Adorno and Horkheimer retreated from the Freudian concept of the individual. Freud, they claimed, resisted the conclusion that there are no parallels between totemic mimesis and the scientific description of nature. Instead Freud restricted the absolute identity of thought and reality to magic, ignoring the way that sovereignty reappears in the autonomy of ideas achieved by the rational ego. The problem with Freud's Oedipal story is that it already assumes as a goal what it purports to explain, whereas "the individual is only a theater." Since the outcome of the struggle presumes authentic selfhood, Horkheimer and Adorno regarded Freud's account as the "inadequate attempt to do justice to the historical transformations which the individual undergoes."[63]

In their initial conversations Adorno and Horkheimer often equated Odysseus with Oedipus, perhaps following a passage in *Beyond Good and Evil* where Nietzsche anticipates the dialectic of enlightenment: "hardened in the discipline of science, he [man] stands before the *rest* of nature, with intrepid Oedipus eyes and sealed Odysseus ears, deaf to the siren songs of old metaphysical bird catchers who have been piping at him all too long, 'you are more, you are higher, you are of a different origin.' "[64] The equation of Odysseus with Oedipus here concerns their respective blindness and deafness to nature, while for Adorno and Horkheimer the capacity for speech divides humanity from nature. In the Freudian account, the story of Oedipus presents the differentiation from mother and myth as tragedy. However, in Horkheimer and Adorno's, Oedipus' blindness to his fate cannot compare with the more powerful theme of the Homeric hero's successful evasion of the presymbolic and premythical world of identity through cunning and reason. In the published text Oedipus is not the clever man who solves the riddle of the sphinx but one who also, by dint of a trick, "evades" it. The element of deception, which occurs in the very act of substituting the "mask" for the name or image, is even more central to the story of Odysseus, and thus to the central theme of the prohibition on mimesis that emerges in the first chapter.

The fundamental paradox of enlightenment, that its rectitude derives from radical disenchantment, drew them even more strongly to the conclusion of the Homeric epic: "Myth bears witness equally to the enslavement of humanity to nature, and to the possibility of escape."[65] In their conversations, Adorno made frequent reference to his book on Kierkegaard, where he wrote that in the act of annihilating nature, spirit becomes subordinate to nature by its very act of mimesis: "originating in nature itself, hope is only able to truly overcome it by maintaining the trace of nature" (*K, 112*).

Mythical narratives, like the Homeric epic, are for Adorno "replicas of prelinguistic experience in a world from which prelinguistic experience has already disappeared."[66] His interest in the destructive aspect of mimetic identification with nature was reinforced by a curious text that played an important if peripheral role in the discussions out of which *Dialectic of Enlightenment* emerged, *La mante religieuse: Recherche sur la nature et la signification du mythe*, by the French anthropologist Roger Caillois. Caillois was a leading figure of the Collège de Sociologie (with which Benjamin was briefly associated) who also wrote two significant articles on the problem of mimesis in nature.[67] Adorno reviewed his 1937 book on the mantis for the *Zeitschrift für Sozialforschung*.[68] He was, he admitted to Benjamin, "positively moved" ("Es hat mich positiv berührt") by this strange book because of its emphasis on the mimetic impulse in nature, an impulse that was all the more "strange" because Caillois demonstrated that the female mantis devours the male during intercourse. It is this element of mimesis, the eradication of the vital difference between life and matter, or the organic and inorganic in the sexual act, that suggests the theme of annihilation in Adorno's own reflections. For Caillois, the mimetic impulse in nature was an allegory of the cultural compulsion to "de-virilization," to death in the modern "apocalypse of entropy."[69] Clearly his entirely negative account of mimesis does not distinguish between playing and being dead. But in a letter to Benjamin, Adorno explained that he admired the fact that Caillois had not dissolved myths into some immanent theory of consciousness, or elevated them into a growing capacity for conscious symbols (a reference to Ernst Cassirer's account of myth, which he and Horkheimer explicitly rejected in their discussions), a fact that ironically resulted from the "materialism that he has in common with Jung and certainly with Klages," and with a "cryptofascist belief in nature."[70] But whereas Caillois focused on the residues of a kind of primal biological "memory" of "psychasthenia" in human behavior, Adorno was fascinated by the ways in which mimesis could lead to a "fatal attraction" that annihilates the object of its desire. The sacrifice of the mate, he implied, was not unlike the analysis of theological sacrifice we have already discussed. His analysis of anti-Semitism in *Dialectic of Enlightenment,* as we shall see, adopts the same strategy, locating in modern Jew hatred the return of the archaic impulse to mimesis, which in its paranoid fear, imitates and therefore liquidates the Jew all the more consequentially.

VII.

Dialectic of Enlightenment initially arose from two distinct projects, a book on "dialectical logic" that Horkheimer planned to write as early as 1934, with the assistance of Herbert Marcuse and Karl Korsch, and the so-called anti-Semitism project that was initially financed by the American Jewish Committee (on which Horkheimer and several other members of the institute worked intensively during 1943). By then, however, it was already evident that Horkheimer and Adorno's joint enterprise conformed to neither of these projects but would consist of a separate work, one in which, as Horkheimer noted, the "fragments contain the principles of philosophy to which we can stand and which is really original."[71] At that time, several theses on the psychology of anti-Semitism, originally destined to become part of the larger empirical research project on anti-Semitism, ended up as material to be included in the volume of "fragments."[72] Thus it is understandable that in the first months of collaborative work on the *Dialectic of Enlightenment,* during the winter of 1941–1942, anti-Semitism did not manifest itself as a central concern. Nor was it mentioned in the internal institute "memorandum" of 1942 that outlined the institute's future projects in terms of a conventionally Marxian program of political and economic analyses. "It appeared," Wiggershaus comments, "as if Horkheimer and Adorno were still afraid of this theme, or they allowed it to perform its function as a 'hidden center' of the book."[73] No doubt a decision to shift the focus of critical theory from the traditional Marxist questions of monopoly capitalism or class conflict to the fate of the Jews would have produced dismay and skepticism among the institute's more orthodox Marxist contributors. Franz Neumann, for example, wrote Adorno in 1940, "I can imagine, and I have done this in my book [*Behemoth*], that one can represent National Socialism without attributing to the Jewish problem a central role."[74]

Wiggershaus suggests that Benjamin's death played an important part in Adorno and Horkheimer's decision to seriously propose a joint book on anti-Semitism. Indeed, only a few months later, Adorno wrote to Horkheimer: "For me it is gradually becoming the case, also because of impressions from the latest news from Germany, that I cannot detach my thoughts any longer from the fate of the Jews. It often seems to me as if all that which we were used to seeing in terms of the proletariat has today shifted with a terrible intensity on to the Jews. I ask myself, though it is not completely consistent with the project, if the things which we actually want to say should not be said in connection with the Jews who represent the counterpoint to power."[75] In the fall of 1940, Horkheimer wrote, "I remain committed to our joint conviction that grant [from the American Jewish Committee] or none we will go ahead with anti-Semitism."[76]

In September 1940 Adorno sent Horkheimer "a couple of—completely unformulated—thoughts on the theory of anti-Semitism." However "provisional" these thoughts were, and however much "they might be in need of modification, we have arrived at a really important place," Adorno wrote, "namely, at a unified and non-rationalistic explanation for anti-Semitism."[77] Adorno began with the inadequacy of all rational economic and social explanations of anti-Semitism since anti-Semitism predates both liberalism and capitalism. The deep and stubborn resistance of anti-Semitism to rational argument seems to point toward the fact "that very old motifs that have long since become second nature must be in play, motifs that have nothing to do either with the relationship between Jews and Christians, or with the money economy, or directly with enlightenment, although the last presumably stands in a deep relation to those archaic motifs."[78] Adorno's analysis is something of an imaginary prehistory of the Jews, with its emphasis on their persistence in a nomadic existence long after the world consisted of permanent settlements. As "the secret gypsies of history," the Jews are a "prematriarchal" peoples whose lack of ties to the earth and to a fixed locale always threatened to subvert the ideals of civilized life: home, family, labor. From the standpoint of other peoples, "the image of the Jew represented a stage of humanity which did not yet know labor, and all later attacks on the parasitic, thieving character of the Jews were mere rationalizations."[79]

Here the Jews represent, not the imperative to civilization, or the purveyors of a universal enlightenment, but the very refusal to be "civilized" and submit to the primacy of labor. The Jews' collective remembrance of a "land of milk and honey" is the "Jewish utopia." Adorno suggests that the Jewish refusal to accept "local and partial Gods" is connected to their refusal to be tied to a spatially delimited "Heimat." The *Bildverbot,* with its taboo on mimesis, was intimately linked to the nomadic character of the Jews, abstraction to the condition of exile. At the same time, however, the *Bildverbot* also inaugurates the taboo on utopia, on the remembrance of the nomadic condition when labor and homeland did not exist. As such, the expulsion of the Jews from Israel reproduces the expulsion from Paradise, and the condition of exile, its imitation. According to Adorno it is this taboo, the taboo on the image of utopia, and on the image per se "that is the origin of anti-Semitism."[80]

In a letter sent only two weeks earlier, Adorno alluded to the broader significance of the theses for the conception of the Jews as representatives of the principle of nonidentity in the modern world: "There are by the way the closest connections between the theory of the Jews as 'fools' and our conception of modern art and that of Jews as nomads, since the absence of a settled existence and the failure to bind to the reified character of an object of action stem from the same source."[81]

In October 1941, Adorno, anticipating his impending move to Los Angeles, hoped that the planned joint book on anti-Semitism would soon "crystallize" with the justification that anti-Semitism "signifies today really the focal point of injustice, and our sort of physiognomy must return to the world, where it shows its most terrible face."[82] In the Odysseus essay, which was finished one year later (1942), we find clues to the suspicion that the figure of Odysseus is not merely the primordial "subject," the bourgeois in *nuce,* but also the Hellenic prototype of Ahasverus, the wandering Jew. In a letter to Pollock, Horkheimer explained that "the Odyssey is the first document on the anthropology of man in the modern sense, that means, in the sense of a rational enlightened being." But he also noted that the study "will also be of some value for the [anti-Semitism] project since the idea of ritual sacrifice which Odysseus tries to overcome will probably play a dominant role in the psychology of anti-Semitism."[83] Odysseus reveals "the fate that the language of the cunning man, the middleman brings down on himself." He is described in terms that suggest the stereotype of the Jewish tradesman: he is a rootless wanderer, a Greek Ahasverus, physically weak, deceitful, and babbles incessantly. In his excessive attachment to speech, to language, Homer embodies in his hero, as does the eternal Jew, "the disaster that the enlightened word brings down on itself" (O, 132). The "semitic element" of the Odyssey is also suggested in a footnote that echoes the theme that Odysseus, "the feudal lord, bears the trace of the oriental merchant" (O, 125). If this is indeed the case, the figure of Odysseus is directly linked to the nomadic, prematriarchal character of the figure of the Jew outlined in Adorno's theory of anti-Semitism in 1940.

By the middle of 1943, the chapter on the culture industry as well as the first, second, and third essays had been completed and work was focusing on what was still thought of in terms of the theoretical part of the anti-Semitism project. It is apparent, however, that by then little remained of the central argument of Horkheimer's "The Jews and Europe" (1939), which interpreted the persecution of the Jews as a direct consequence of monopoly capitalism's systematic elimination of the "sphere of circulation," on which the Jews, as personifications of market "rationality," were dependent.[84] In 1941, Leo Löwenthal joined Adorno in formulating what became the "Elements of Anti-Semitism," which unequivocally announced that National Socialist anti-Semitism was "a turning point in history" (DE, 200).

"Whereas there is no longer any need for economic domination," the first thesis maintains, the Jews are "marked out as the absolute object of domination pure and simple" (though, as a concession to Marxism, the workers are still considered "the ultimate target"). For the fascists, the Jews are "an opposing race," "the embodiment of the negative principle," and, as such, their extermination is necessary "to secure the happiness of the world" (DE, 168). For Adorno and Horkheimer, modern anti-Semitism is no longer a diversionary tactic, a "luxury for the masses," but rather a manifestation of its deep roots in civilization that still remain obscure.

The relationship between the reappearance of a false, mythologizing mimesis in fascism and the project of the extermination of the Jews is also boldly stated at the beginning of the "Elements": "The portrait of the Jews that the nationalists offer to the world is in fact their own self-portrait" (DE, 168). Paradoxically, the anti-Semitic goal of ridding the world of the stigma of difference led to the Jewish desire to assimilate, just as the "barbaric collective" singled them out as different. But such rational explanations ignore the fact that both "persecutor and victim belong to the same circle of evil." Anti-Semitism is "a deeply imprinted schema, a ritual of civilization" (DE, 171).

Though the argument that commerce is the "fate of the Jews" is still mentioned, the "Elements of Anti-Semitism" is in fact a series of interpretations of the "ritual" of anti-Semitism, of the sacrifice of the Jews

in which theological, psychological, and anthropological motifs are in-
tertwined. All of these suggest a connection both to the Odysseus chapter and to Adorno's provisional 1940 theses: that the Jews are sacrificed
as the ultimate victims of the taboo on mimesis. As I have indicated, the
origins of the thesis that the prohibition against making an image of
God was the specific form of a more generalized renunciation of mimesis can, of course, be attributed to Freud, who noted in *Moses and
Monotheism* that "it meant that a sensory perception was given second
place to what may be called an abstract idea."[85] For Horkheimer and
Adorno, anti-Semitism is identified with the proscription on mimesis:
"Civilization has replaced the organic adaptation to others and mimetic
behavior proper, by organized control of mimesis" (*DE*, 180). Uncon-
trolled mimesis is expunged first in the religious prohibition on idolatry,
on images of God, subsequently in the general contempt for all image-
bound wanderers—nomads, actors, gypsies—and finally, in rationalized production, "the indelible mimetic heritage of all practical experience is consigned to oblivion" (*DE*, 181). The murder of the Jews is a
form of revenge for civilization's triumph over nature; those who first
turned ritual sacrifice into rationality by carrying out the prohibition
are themselves sacrificed as the expression of "repressed mimesis" (*DE*,
187). The secret gypsies of history "are abandoned by domination
when its progressive alienation from nature makes it revert to mere nature" (*DE*, 184).

The Jews represent not only the carriers of the taboo on mimesis but
also those who have not entirely succumbed to its logic: "those blinded
by civilization experience their own tabooed mimetic features only in
certain gestures and behavior patterns which they encounter in others"
(*DE*, 181). As Horkheimer and Adorno point out, it is of little consequence whether the Jews really do have the "mimetic features" attributed to them: "When all the horror of prehistory which has been over-
laid with civilization is rehabilitated as rational interest by projection
onto the Jews, there is no restriction" (*DE*, 186). The very attempt to
rid civilization of them reenacts the taboo as it enforces it.

The most archaic form of anti-Semitic mimesis is designated as
"idiosyncrasy," the fear of and obsession with the "alien" quality of
certain gestures, or psychological techniques, like flattery, "passed on
by a process of unconscious imitation." Mimesis also reappears in the
fascist refusal of a "homeland" to the Jews, who are forced to imitate
their nomadic past, and finally in the very physiognomy of terror in the
faces of the victims: in "the convulsive gestures of the martyred, we see

the mimetic impulse which can never be completely destroyed" (*DE*, 183).

The prohibition on mimesis thus brings all of its past history to bear on the persecution of the Jews: the ritual discipline, the uniforms, the marches, the "monotonous repetition of words and gestures are simply the organized imitation of magic practices." This fact explains the peculiar synthesis of rational and irrational practice—the "rationalized idiosyncrasy"—that fascism employs: the violence of speech, the gesticulating of the fascist leaders, the abrogation of law, the replication of mythical practices, and the rationality of destructive violence all partake in a "surrender to the mimetic attraction" (*DE*, 183). Even the nature that fascism claims to resurrect is not authentic nature but a copy of its copy, a "mimesis of mimesis" (*DE*, 185).

The taboo is evoked first in nationalist hatred of cosmopolitanism, but also in deep-seated religious hostility at the Jewish responsibility for Christianity's "interdiction on natural religion." The fact that Christianity cannot sustain the taboo and is forced to resort to mimesis, first in the "spiritualized idolatry" of Christ as spirit become flesh and second in the reversion to pagan and magical practices in the church (lighting candles, the cult of the saints), compensates for the unfulfilled promise of salvation, for which the Jews are also sacrificed. In a lecture given at Temple Israel in Los Angeles in April 1943, Horkheimer quoted Freud's *Moses and Monotheism* that Christian rage against the Jews derived not from the Jews themselves but from a deeper core of pagan resentment against Christianity: "They have not got over a grudge against the new religion which was imposed on them; but they have displaced the grudge on to the source from which Christianity reached them."[86]

Jews represent, at once, power and abjection, property and impotence, which evokes fear and "attracts the enemy of impotence" (*DE*, 169). The very torment that the Jews experience as a result of their lack of security and membership in the community, the image of the Jew as powerful, intellectual, wealthy, but also as suffering and powerless, evokes the unfulfilled promises of civilization, whose "image is then used by domination to perpetuate itself" (*DE*, 172). The fascist transgression against the prohibition on mimicry, imitation, and archaicism is endemic to fascism's sanctioning of the visual image over the written word, and more specifically evident in the anti-Semitic obsession with the physiognomic and corporal marks of Jewishness.

The "Elements of Anti-Semitism," it might be argued, ultimately holds the Jews accountable for their own fate. In contrast to the image of the Jews in the first chapter, where, in Freud's words, they secure "a triumph of intellectuality over sensuality," the Jews appear here in a more ambivalent light, both as those who impose the taboo on mimesis and as the carriers of a "premythological," "prematriarchal" residue of mimesis.[87] Adorno's thesis that anti-Semitism preserves the image of Jews as "nomadic" explicitly identifies them, not merely with the perpetration of the taboo, but with the refusal to adapt to it. Even assimilation is a deception: for the Jews, a self-deception; for the anti-Semites, a magical ruse. The Jews appear here as they are sometimes portrayed in the Nazi racial propaganda, as in the film portrayal of "Jüd Süss," for example, who cleverly masks the gestures of the "Ostjude" and transmogrifies his physiognomy in order to "pass" as an enlightened man of Western culture. In the "Elements," this image is turned against the Nazis in the form of a paradox. Insofar as the Jews are at one level responsible for the renunciation on mimicry, they at the same time evoke the taboo in their enemies, who employ the techniques of mimesis to destroy them. From the standpoint of the anti-Semites, even the desire to assimilate is mere imitation. Both the Jewish experience of modernity and modernity's refusal of the Jew can be seen as mutually constitutive facts of their historical experience.

Mimesis returns in anti-Semitism, not merely in its fetishism of physiognomy but in its "false projection." Anti-Semitism "is the counterpart of true mimesis, and fundamentally related to the repressed form; in fact it is probably the morbid expression of repressed mimesis" (*DE*, 187). In the confusion of inner world and outer world, fascism reenacts the mimetic impulse of "animal prehistory" by turning the world into its own image. Thus the sacrifice of the Jews to the paranoid pathology of "archaic nondifferentiation" is the extreme example of the logic of sacrifice: "hatred leads to the unification with the object—in destruction" (*DE*, 199). If Judaism regards reconciliation as the highest ideal, and expectation is in the service of that ideal, anti-Semitism is the attempt to realize the "negative absolute" (*DE*, 199). What is never expressed in the "Elements" is the implicit connection between the defamed Jews and "degenerate" modernist art (which are considered identical by the Nazis), which are both subject to execration and repugnance because of their "mimetic attraction." Both are condemned to be obliterated by the practitioners of the cult of false mimesis because they alone still bear traces of a dangerous "true mimesis," the shared refusal of complete absorption in the object as "picture," representation, and symbol.[88]

VIII.

It is difficult to find fault with Habermas's argument that *Dialectic of Enlightenment* "owes more to Nietzsche than just the strategy of an ideology critique turned against itself."[89] Nietzsche, Adorno remarks, "was one of the few since Hegel who recognized the dialectic of enlightenment. He formulated its ambiguous relation to domination" (O, 110). Yet Habermas's assertion that "Nietzsche radicalizes the counter-Enlightenment" could hardly be further from Adorno's own evaluation, when he described Nietzsche in 1947 as "one of the most advanced enlighteners of all."[90] Nietzsche, he claimed, "sensed in the 'system' and what it entailed the same apologetic desire he sensed in the religion of redemption or, for that matter, in the truly systematic totality of the Wagnerian music drama. When he turned against the accepted values of civilization, love and pity, ultimately reaffirmed by Wagner, his motive was not complicity with the dawning relapse into barbarism, but just the opposite; he realized the barbarian momentum inherent in official cultural values."[91]

This judgment aligns Adorno with a Nietzsche who is the radicalizer of enlightenment, who "recognized in enlightenment just as much the universal movement of sovereign spirit." The question of whether or not *Dialectic of Enlightenment* stands firmly within the Enlightenment's own tradition, or threatens to undermine it, can only be answered if the place of Nietzsche is established. In a letter to Horkheimer, Adorno remarked that Nietzsche's "misconception" was only that he failed to see that the will to power was nothing more than the anxiety of losing power, of becoming caught in the compulsion of nature. Nietzsche's will to power became his own ideology, insofar as he did not recognize that what he regarded as a "pure drive," or instinct, was already undergoing rationalization: "Had Nietzsche really grasped the will to power as anxiety and entrapment in nature, and he often comes close enough, then his philosophy would have coincided with the truth."[92] Adorno's sparse comments on the fascist appropriation of Nietzsche could be expanded on, but it is clear that, unlike Horkheimer, Adorno considered "the liquidation of enlightenment" and the ideological glorification of naked force in the name of an archaic mythology as entirely inconsistent with Nietzsche's philosophy. Nietzsche's "error" was not his failure to take the victim into account, as Horkheimer had once said, but rather his "amor fati," his willingness to sanction as fate the "infinity of such sacrifice."[93] As we have already seen, it is the infinity of sacrifice that defines the "fate" of the concept, and turns Nietzsche into the accomplice of the rationality he otherwise despises. One can, without stretching the analogy too much, also see an act of mimesis in the relationship between *Dialectic of Enlightenment* and *On the Genealogy of Morals:* through similitude and appropriation, the genealogy of morals becomes the genealogy of domination.

Adorno, more than any other figure in the Frankfurt School's inner circle, was attracted to Nietzsche. This is clearly evident from the revealing transcript of a lecture and discussion led by Ludwig Marcuse, the biographer and historian, in Los Angeles on July 14, 1942. Though Marcuse's lecture is not preserved apart from a brief summary, it focused on three distinct concepts of culture in Nietzsche: the cult of the genius artist; the antiaestheticism of the "free spirit"—the breaker of idols; and the Übermensch as the "distillation of all historical utopias." Marcuse's conclusion, which amounted to a defense of Nietzsche's "radical work of destruction" and his transcendence of the material through "desire," provoked a strong reaction by most of the institute members present, most prominently Herbert Marcuse (no relation). Marcuse questioned whether the Übermensch could ever be equated with "utopia" and refused to accept Horkheimer's more conciliatory proposition that, with the abolition of material human want, our thinking, as well as Nietzsche's, "will appear radically different."[94] "If Marx is right, then Nietzsche is wrong," Marcuse replied. By contrast, Adorno saw advantages in Nietzsche's thinking that did not merely supplement but went beyond the insights of Marxism: "Despite its categories, Nietzsche's cultural criticism reveals certain aspects of the social problematic, which are not immediately evident through the Critique of Political Economy. We have to decode Nietzsche and to see what sort of weighty experience lies behind it. I believe, that one then arrives at things, which are not so distant from the interests of most human beings." For example, Adorno saw in Nietzsche's phrase "no shepherd but a herd" the intimation that domination can survive the eclipse of direct forms of control, that control can "migrate into human beings themselves."[95]

In this intimate circle Adorno could only hint at his debt to *On the Genealogy of Morals,* but he readily acknowledged that he shared with

Nietzsche the view that sacrifice was the key to the "prehistory" of man.[96] Both Marx and Nietzsche understood history as sacrifice incurred through exchange. Where Marx sees the price of labor's transformation of nature as self-alienation and abstraction, Nietzsche sees the history of exchange as a spiral of sacrifice: spiritualization of cruelty, the internalization of instinctual renunciation, religious self-denial, and the asceticism of modern science.[97] The sources of *Dialectic of Enlightenment*'s Nietzscheanism are also apparent in his version of the taboo on mimesis in *The Birth of Tragedy.* "Theoretical man" substitutes for Dionysian "wisdom and art," and for myth, "a metaphysical comfort and earthly consonance, in fact a *deus ex machina* of its own, the god of machines and crucibles, that is the powers of the forces of nature, recognized and employed in the service of a higher egoism."[98]

Elsewhere in *Dialectic of Enlightenment,* especially in Horkheimer's excursus II, "Juliette or Enlightenment and Morality," this positive view of Nietzsche is nowhere to be found. Instead, Horkheimer asserts that critical theory ultimately prefers "the formalism of reason" to Nietzsche's remythologization of power and preference for the "predators" over the weak (*DE,* 99). Horkheimer considers the "will to power" as the ultimate incarnation of Kantian morality, insofar as the self-legislating subject ultimately leads to the "abrogation of the law." Here there is little trace of Nietzsche the "enlightener." Instead, there appears the figure who maliciously celebrates the powerful and their cruelty: "The fact that Sade and Nietzsche insist on the *ratio* more decisively than even logical positivism implicitly liberates from its hiding-place the utopia contained in the Kantian notion of reason" (*DE,* 119). Here there is little hint of the arguments about sacrifice, cunning, and mimesis that redeem enlightenment in its moment of self-preservation. If enlightenment can be rescued from these "dark" but "true" thinkers, Horkheimer implies, it is only by the vaguest homilies about "the Law," the "ten commandments," "spiritual love," and other pieties. Yet, ironically, it is also in this chapter, the weakest of all, where we can take the full measure of Horkheimer's pessimism. "Hope," wrote Horkheimer, in "The End of Reason," "has been overshadowed by the consciousness of universal doom."[99]

IX.

In late 1944 both Horkheimer's and Adorno's preoccupation with anti-Semitism grew in intensity and conviction. That concern was motivated in part by Horkheimer's hope to secure sponsorship for the study of anti-Semitism from the American Jewish Committee. But even at that late stage both thinkers still regarded the assault on the Jews as symptomatic of a much broader social transformation that fascism had initiated only by its more radical and paranoid stance. On November 3 Adorno wrote that in totalitarian anti-Semitism "the Jews are even in their most inconspicuous functions victims of the elimination of competition."[100] Horkheimer concurred, remarking that the Jews were at best victims of a revenge for the sins of liberal capitalism and that "fascism was the distorted image (*Zerrbild*) of a social revolution."[101] In a letter addressed to Isaac Rosengarten, editor of the American-Jewish journal *Jewish Forum,* Horkheimer underscored the centrality of anti-Semitism in this new configuration: "Whoever accuses the Jews today aims straight at humanity itself. The antisemites have invested the Jews with the reality of that democracy which they wish to destroy. Wittingly or unwittingly, the Jews have become the martyrs of civilization. To protect them is no longer an issue involving any particular group interests. To protect the Jews has come to be a symbol of everything mankind stands for. Antisemitic persecution is the stigma of the present world whose injustice enters all its weight upon the Jews. Thus the Jews have been made what the Nazis always pretended that they were,—the focal point of world history. Their survival is inseparable from the survival of culture itself."[102]

If the survival of the Jews was now a paramount theme in the thinking of Horkheimer and Adorno, so the psychology of anti-Semitic mimesis—that the temptation to traduce the norms of enlightenment by the enemies of the Jews was to no small degree elicited by the Jews themselves—increased Horkheimer's anxiety. In July he posed the question to Löwenthal: "Should antisemitism, even in this point, be an unconscious imitation of Jewish structures, and what is the precise meaning of these structures in Jewish life?"[103] Though no direct answer was forthcoming, the humor of the Frankfurt School in exile should not be ignored as an important clue. Consider, for example, the perhaps not so tongue-in-cheek 1944 memorandum from Adorno to Horkheimer, suggesting that since "not all the recurring objections against the Jews are of an entirely spurious, projective, paranoid character," a "manual for distribution among Jews" be prepared which lists these objectionable traits and "contains suggestions how to overcome them." For example, "the disproportionate concern with one's own bodily comfort or with health."[104] Adorno further remarked that the "manual" should "appeal to the inexhaustible source of Jewish self-criticism, irony." It should "encourage Jews to draw the consequences out of the critical insight into their own deficiencies instead of simply laughing at them." Among the jokes suggested is this one: "if a gentile is thirsty he drinks a glass of water, whereas the Jew sees a Doctor and gets a test for diabetes."[105] "Dr." Adorno received from "Dr." Horkheimer a response suggesting that he take this idea up with the "section on business ethics of the Anti-Defamation League in Chicago."[106] Did Adorno slip here from a description of the paranoid projection of the anti-Semite, of the Jew as the physical embodiment of the tabooed gestures and repressed emotions, to the belief that it is the Jews themselves who unconsciously provoke the anti-Semitic reaction? This ironic text, which should be taken just so seriously, echoes the ambivalence toward the Jews that is expressed in the "Elements of Anti-Semitism." Just as the Jews themselves participate unconsciously in eliciting the "mimetic attraction" of the anti-Semites, so too American Jews must be warned against evoking anti-Semitism through their unconscious behavior.

In the concluding pages of the Odysseus essay, Adorno proposes yet another reading of the mimetic impulse in enlightenment, one that emphasizes the element of wit in the act of substitution. If the gods are appeased with human objects and animal sacrifices, their stupidity in the face of the ruse is the object of Homeric laughter. Laughter not only outwits external nature, it confounds the gods, and makes escape possible: "Laughter is bound to the guilt of subjectivity, but in the suspension of law, which it announces, it also points beyond entrapment. It promises the way home" (O, 139). This sentence also helps to explain why Adorno, who wrote with such seriousness, could also at times, as his contemporaries knew, be so silly (*Albern*).[107] He composed parodies of Hasidic folktales à la Martin Buber and collected clippings of "Nancy," "Steve Canyon," and other comics of the day. Anyone who reads the correspondence between Max Horkheimer and Theodor Adorno is immediately struck by the pet names with which they frequently addressed each other. Horkheimer was the wooly "mammoth"; Adorno, "Archibald" and "Hippopotamus" (*Nilpferd*); Gretel Adorno, "Giraffe" and "Gazelle." Awaiting word on his decision to emigrate to California, Adorno reminded Horkheimer that "for a hippopotamus the most important thing is peace and quiet."[108] These "cute" terms of endearment are so unnerving perhaps because they partake of the animism that lives on, not least in the culture industry, whose most prominent stars are animals endowed with human speech and countenances.

Such figures belong to the mythology of childhood, and their continued use by the philosophers of the Frankfurt School attests to the intimacy of relationships begun in adolescence and early adulthood. But under the conditions of exile, their persistence can also be seen in a more biblical light. The institute was Horkheimer's Ark, and Adorno's Odysseus essay, which pays homage to another heroic voyager, offers a more profoundly theological interpretation of these nicknames as the echo of a primordial laughter that is "the irruption of blind and obdurate nature," as Adorno writes. Such names also represent triumph over natural force: "In laughter blind nature gives up its destructive force. This duality of laughter is close to that of the name and perhaps names are nothing but frozen laughter, as is still evident today in nicknames, the only names in which something of the original act of naming survives" (O, 139). As Benjamin showed in his famous 1916 essay, "On Language as Such and the Language of Man," the naming of the animals occurred before language "fell into the abyss of the mediateness of all communication."[109] Nicknames thus contain a weak totemic power insofar as they evoke the memory of solidarity with nature before it had become mute.

For the theorists of the Frankfurt School, the catastrophe of the Jews was inextricably bound up with the prohibition on mimesis and its return in the form of anti-Semitism and "false" politicized mimicry. The loss of the capacity to imitate nature (Horkheimer's notorious ability to imitate birdcalls might be mentioned here) and the taboo on "reverting to mimetic modes of existence" were the price of civilization. But if the "pitiless prohibition of regression becomes mere fate," the tabooed mimesis was most manifestly preserved in the fear of the victims. The persistence of mimesis in art or in the nicknames or jokes that parry terror retains the remembrance of the nature that is obliterated by the taboo.[110] As Odysseus replaced Oedipus because his wit permitted him to evade the fate to which Oedipus blindly succumbed, Horkheimer and Adorno's *Dialectic of Enlightenment* was an effort to philosophically outwit myth and to create "the possibility of escape" through enlightenment sensitized to the power of mimesis.

X.

In December 1946, in a lecture at the American Philosophical Association meeting in Eugene, Oregon, Horkheimer defended critical theory against the often-repeated criticism that "since neither the revival of the

old nor the discovery of new mythologies can bring the process of Enlightenment to a halt, they had been pressed into a pessimistic attitude,
a condition of despair and nihilism." Far from falling into "romantic
wish-dreams," as so many critics of Enlightenment had done, he concluded, "the hope of reason lies in emancipation from its own fear of
despair."[111] Only a few months earlier, Horkheimer elaborated on his
idea to Adorno, proposing that they collaborate on a sequel to *Dialectic
of Enlightenment,* which Horkheimer suggested calling "Rescuing Enlightenment" (*Rettung der Aufklärung*). In contrast to existentialism,
which hypostatized the moment of existence, Horkheimer suggested a
"solution to our opposition in relation to Schopenhauer." Our theme,
he continued, is "to positively embrace truth in the determination of
meaninglessness, and by this measure, to save thought."[112] It was not
any "irrationalism" on Adorno's part, or the "Nietzscheanism" of critical theory, that divided the authors. The issue that divided the authors
was Horkheimer's Schopenhauerian embrace of the senselessness of
the world and his refusal of any reconciliation with it. From Adorno's
perspective, Horkheimer's solution, to turn "senselessness into sense,"
brought him into too close proximity to Heidegger, for whom the
"transcendence of being realizes itself through the consciousness of its
nothingness." Schopenhauer, Adorno responded, was, in fact, the "an-
cestor" of existentialism.[113]

For Adorno, Horkheimer's insistence on the "consciousness of nega-
tivity" still seemed anchored in the philosophy of totality: "If for you
I am a positivist, you are an idealist," Adorno wrote. "Bad enlightenment dispenses with the concept of difference through absolute totality,
the correct one holds on to the concept of difference [*Differenz*] against
its flattening."[114] It is perhaps less important here that Adorno once
again reiterated his critique of all philosophical reconciliation and his
insistence on the "experience of difference" than the more important
fact that these exchanges bear witness to Horkheimer and Adorno's
inability to work through all of the consequences of their critique of
reason. "As theoreticians of reason," Adorno remarked, "we cannot
simply leap with one jump into the categories of politics and society."[115]
Evoking Benjamin, in *Minima Moralia,* Adorno expressed his notion of
theory as addressing itself to those things that were not embraced by
the dynamics of victory and defeat, "which fall by the wayside—what
might be called the waste products and blind spots that have escaped
the dialectic."[116]

Unlike Heidegger's ontological difference, which, in Adorno's terms, sacrifices the experience of being to the logic of Being, or Jaspers's pariah, which sacrifices the German for the Jew, *Dialectic of Enlightenment* did not repress the suffering of mortal beings while grasping at the apocalypse as a transformative event. In this regard the text holds true to its most important, and most theological, assertion, that the most valid legacy of the taboo on mimesis is the injunction against continuing the sacrifice of the particular to the universal, the finite to the infinite, truth to lies. Only in the faithful carrying out of that prohibition can the "rectitude of the image be salvaged." What might still be salvaged from Enlightenment in the aftermath of catastrophe was enlightenment itself, conceived as a refusal of the "*Intellectus sacrificium intellectus*" and, in terms that accord with the Odysseus chapter, as a ruse of reason: "Theory must needs deal with cross-grained, opaque, unassimilated material, which as such admittedly has from the start an anachronistic quality, but is not wholly obsolete since it has outwitted the historical dynamic."[117]

Conclusion

The shadow cast by the title of this book is far longer than these five essays could ever hope to encompass. In the seventy-five years of what historians now like to call the "short century," two world wars, the Jewish genocide, and untold other cataclysmic events have made the figure of catastrophe ubiquitous in art, literature, philosophy, and public discourse. Indeed, the terms that have become the common coin of debates on memory and memorialization, for example, "coming to terms with the past" or the philosophical categories of "caesura" and "rupture" that thinkers like Jean-François Lyotard and Hannah Arendt have invoked, are attempts to fix the long shadow that has now become a permanent accompaniment to our modernity.

With characteristic irony and breathtaking brevity, the Hungarian critic George Konrad once summed up the century: Had there been no Franco-Prussian rivalry there would have been no World War I; if there had been no World War I there would have been no Hitler, and without Hitler there would have been no World War II, no Yalta, and no cold war.[1] His economy notwithstanding, no single book could do justice to the long shadow, and for that reason I have chosen to address only what might be called the short shadow of catastrophe as it appeared in the immediate postwar eras. My strategy has been to capture that shadow as it appeared fleetingly in a few key philosophical texts and essays written either during or immediately after the two world wars. That conceit would not alone have merited a book if it were not also the case that the authors and texts I have chosen have become justly famous. These works are now emblematic of the conditions of their origin, and they cast their own intellectual shadows. That all three texts in Part 2 were published at almost the same juncture is hardly coincidental. If I have singled out those works that are closest to catastrophe in both theme and date of inception, it has been an equally important aspect of this study to reread and reconsider them in terms of their broader philosophical influences, and for the political consequences that have frequently radiated from them.

Nor is it coincidental that these texts seem to speak directly to each other. Their authors were closely and intimately linked, though sometimes as much through deep antipathy as through strong friendship. That these intense male friendships and equally intense animosities often infused their complex personal relations is significant, not merely for purposes of biographical or anecdotal color, but because these connections often make explicit the agonistic elements that only appear as veiled or cloaked in the texts themselves.

Bloch and Benjamin were first introduced by Hugo Ball in Interlaken in 1919 where they immediately recognized in each other intellects already touched by the messianic currents that in Max Weber's term seemed to "pulsate" among small intellectual coteries in wartime exile communities. Yet profound differences as much as elective affinities soon appeared in the different emotional textures, political choices, and philosophical resonances that created new divisions after the war. Chapter 2 details the highly strained relations that eventually arose between Hugo Ball and Bloch, whose friendship had been solidified in Bern several years earlier when the two collaborated on the antiwar paper *Die Freie Zeitung*. So close were these two men at that time that Ball recorded in his diary that he was often "seen in the company of his utopian friend, Ernst Bloch."[2] Likewise, Bloch's praise for Ball's anarchist and pacifist ideas in the concluding pages of his 1919 article, "On Some Political Programs and Utopias in Switzerland," was so effusive that Marianne Weber opposed its publication on the grounds of its excessively "positive portrayal" of Ball.[3] Their friendship dissolved, however, when Ball's anti-Semitism revealed a side of his messianism that, despite his antiwar and anti-Kaiser political stance, had far more in common with the nationalism he despised than Bloch could tolerate.

Hugo Ball and Martin Heidegger almost certainly never met. But Heidegger's biographer, Rüdiger Safranski, has rightly pointed to the remarkable affinity between Heidegger's early philosophical concerns and Ball's Dadaist metaphysics, especially his insistence that Dada represented a new reality that would inaugurate a radical questioning of the origins of Being.[4] It was that questioning that also drew Karl Jaspers to the much younger Heidegger when they first met in 1920, and it explains Jaspers's comment, "[I became] bound to him in the consciousness of a rare and uniquely framed *Kampfgemeinschaft* that I have otherwise, even today, found nowhere else."[5] In 1933 Jaspers's *Kampfgemeinschaft* with Heidegger was suddenly shattered by his friend's seemingly inexplicable enthusiasm for a regime that Jaspers abhorred and which he ultimately endured only at great risk to himself and to his Jewish wife.

In contrast to Heidegger, whose stoical silence is legendary, after the war Jaspers expressed in *Die Schuldfrage* his deep conviction that an authentic guilt had to be *assumed* by future German generations lest it be *imposed*. For Jaspers, Heidegger's guilt was not merely the "moral" and "metaphysical" guilt of every German but the guilt of a mode of philosophizing that in its irresponsibility was as much culpable in Heidegger's political choices as it was incapable of confronting them in retrospect. If Jaspers did not, as I have argued, air his dispute with Heidegger, it was because of that earlier commitment, as well as his ambivalence about public political controversy that helps explains that silence which also marks the philosophical weaknesses of *Die Schuldfrage*.

Theodor Adorno recalled that he was drawn to Walter Benjamin "with an enormous fascination" after they were introduced by their mutual friend Siegfried Kracauer in the Frankfurt Café Westend in 1923.[6] Their published correspondence attests to their growing mutual recognition and intimacy during the 1920s, as well as to the later flashpoints of tension between them.[7] It also reveals Adorno's deep animus against Heidegger. From his inaugural lecture "On the Actuality of Philosophy" in May 1931 to his posthumously published *Ästhetische Theorie* (1970), Adorno regarded Heidegger's philosophy—allusion intended—as the mythology "of the twentieth century."[8] Though Adorno explicitly recognized that Heidegger's philosophy, not unlike his own, judged the history of thought as "a dialectic of enlightenment," he accused Heidegger of taking a "plunge into the abyss of archaism."[9] During the well-publicized episode when Adorno's compromising 1934 review of a collection of poems by the Nazi youth leader Baldur von Schirach was revealed by a German student magazine in the

1960s, Adorno regretfully admitted his brief error of judgment, but he was deeply offended by any comparison "with Heidegger, whose philosophy is fascist right down to its innermost components."[10]

The influence of the texts discussed in this book hardly need to be documented. Both Heidegger's authoritative "Letter on Humanism" and Horkheimer and Adorno's *Dialectic of Enlightenment* have been the subject of book-length monographs and extensive bibliographies. After decades of relative obscurity, *Dialectic of Enlightenment* enjoyed a phenomenal revival during the 1960s, along with the works of Benjamin and Bloch, in which the Western left found the afterglow of the theoretical and utopian currents of the 1920s extinguished by the Soviet dogma of domination. The revival of "critical theory" by a generation in search of its own theoretical traditions merits its own history, but it also deserves credit for unearthing the forgotten works of a creative and heterodox Marxism whose image of redemption was not yet constricted by the doctrinal precepts of those whom Arthur Koestler called "neo-Machiavellians in the name of universal reason."[11]

Similarly, Heidegger's postwar influence can hardly be underestimated. Apart from Sartre's indebtedness to his earlier philosophy, the core of post-1968 French philosophy from Foucault to Derrida has frequently been described as a movement among philosophers who had become more Heideggerian than Heidegger himself.[12] If Jaspers is now largely forgotten, in postwar Europe he enjoyed an extraordinary esteem, not only because his *Die Schuldfrage* was the sole and single most important statement by a German to assume responsibility for the crimes of the Nazi era but also in part because of Jaspers's memorable confrontation with Georg Lukács on the eve of the cold war at the 1946 symposium "L'Espirit Européen" in Geneva. From that time on it was Jaspers who called German intellectuals to account for their past commitments and to demonstrate their future devotion to moral responsibility.[13] Unlike Heidegger's "Letter," Jaspers's *Die Schuldfrage* demanded the transfiguration of the German nation-state into the stateless nation and the German citizen into the "pariah" who, in an astonishing parallel to the Jewish pariah described by Max Weber, would henceforth assume the burden of moral responsibility and political diaspora as the consequences of the collapse of the nation-state. However, after November 1989, when Germany was again on the verge of unification, another liability of Jaspers's originary statement surfaced as the now obsolete prohibition on German unity, which for three decades had dominated the discourse of the German nation. During the acrimonious debates on

German unification, Jaspers's legacy, rearticulated by a new generation of German intellectuals, left them, as Andreas Huyssen observed, "out of step with events."[14]

These personal connections and political disseminations only scratch the surface of the complex philosophical trajectories I have tried to examine. But they help ring these texts with a vital personal as well as an intellectual dimension. The sometimes odd trajectories of these authors form yet another important theme of this book. Ball's odyssey from Munich's Bohemian avant-garde to the passionate politics of the antiwar left and ultimately to his rejection of the West for a spiritualized "Bakuninist" anarchism with strong overtones of anti-Semitism reminds us that in the century of catastrophe political itineraries are often erratic and unpredictable. In the chapter on Heidegger's "Letter on Humanism" I have focused on Heidegger's postwar emergence as a figure whose philosophical authority was secured by a text that strategically placed the history of humanism in the context of his, and Germany's, moral and political catastrophe. Heidegger's postwar self-exonerations may have emphasized the errors or miscalculations that led to his commitment, but the "Letter" indirectly reveals what he otherwise did not acknowledge, that he saw in the Nazi revolution the potential for realizing his deepest philosophical hope, the new beginning for the West that would in essence replicate the fateful moment in human history when the West emerged in the words of Parmenides and Heraclitus. Read from Heidegger's perspective in 1946, the "Letter" is a politically polysemic text with possibilities for Heidegger's own exoneration and for the recuperation of his philosophy in the face of Germany's defeat, the defeat of the movement he had once regarded as "the total transformation of our German existence."[15] Nor did those possibilities exhaust the significance of the "Letter" in initiating a renewal of Heidegger's influence among a generation of younger French philosophers on the left. The French assimilation of Heidegger's postwar antihumanism inherited the philosopher's attunement to the metaphysical character of the philosophy of the subject, and along with it, his failure to distinguish among the doctrines it encompassed. Heidegger's text, I have also demonstrated, did not emerge sui generis, but also echoed his extensive attempts to negotiate the complex debates on "humanism" under the Nazi regime during the early 1940s, at a time when his own affiliation to Nazism had become precarious.

Though they are often paired in discussions of postwar German philosophy, Jaspers and Heidegger represented two starkly opposing intellectual trajectories in postwar Germany. As Arendt recognized, Heidegger's postwar philosophy averted any confrontation with its own earlier political transgression, a defect that in her view indicted not merely his own antimetaphysical thinking but an entire tradition of German philosophy. Jaspers, by contrast, conceived of his postwar philosophy in an imaginary dialogue with his silent partner Heidegger, and his immediate postwar writing, most prominently *Die Schuldfrage,* was intended as a counterpoint to the absence of a public reckoning by the man Jaspers had once considered the greatest of German philosophers. Still, even if Jaspers's text was the beginning of a new, post-Nazi German reckoning with catastrophe, his own failure to speak publicly condemned his reflections on Heidegger to the silence that he himself had found so burdensome in the postwar generation, and which contributed to the intellectual inhibition to confronting the past in postwar Germany.

The concluding chapter on Horkheimer and Adorno's *Dialectic of Enlightenment* charts these groundbreaking philosophers' attempt to reflect on the catastrophe in ways that departed substantially from those of both Heidegger and Jaspers. For the latter two the catastrophe was essentially a German event—whether in the collapse of Heidegger's project for a renewal of the Western *archē* or the end of the Weberian nation-state. For Horkheimer and Adorno, it is the catastrophe of the Jews that now occupied center stage as the primary purpose of the genocidal regime that had forced them into U.S. exile. *Dialectic of Enlightenment* therefore offers a very different reading of the catastrophe, one that centers on the role of the Jewish *Bildverbot* and the prohibition on mimesis in eliciting the civilizational urge to destroy the world of disenchantment and restore a lost mimetic world through violence and anti-Semitic remythologization. Combining theology and anthropology, Horkheimer and Adorno's text is both a "philosophical fragment" and an attempt to read the dialectic of enlightenment as a history of what Benjamin called "the mimetic faculty," of the capacity to read nature as an image-text whose prohibition through enlightenment also obliterated the image of utopia. One important conclusion drawn here is that in contrast to customary readings of *Dialectic of Enlightenment,* which place the onus of interpretation on its first chapter, "The Concept of Enlightenment," it may be more illuminating to focus on "Odysseus or Myth and Enlightenment" and on the "Elements of Anti-Semitism" for understanding how and why, as Horkheimer wrote at the time, the Jews had become "the martyrs of civilization."[16] In *Dialectic of Enlightenment* the catastrophe of the Jews is bound up with their own role in perpetuating the taboo on mimesis and with their historical status as those who most emphatically insist on radicalizing rather than repudiating Enlightenment. That insight has led me to adduce the reasons for regarding this text not, as it is often portrayed, as a diatribe against modernity and enlightenment but as a desperate attempt at rescue, under conditions when such a rescue seemed at best a risky undertaking. Rather than fall prey to "irrationalism," Horkheimer and Adorno's notion of critique in fact reveals a concept of enlightenment that is itself an act of mimesis, an attempt to outwit the rationality of identificatory reason by its openness to experience and its capacity to explode with concepts what concepts cannot assimilate.

If, as Adorno once observed, the melancholy of Baroque imagery "broke down before the reality of judgment," the reality of the modern apocalyse seems to elude judgment (*K,* 124). As this book has shown, the specter of the apocalypse haunts all of the German intellectuals treated in this study. In Part 1, Bloch, Benjamin, and Hugo Ball represented a mode of messianic thought in which avant-garde aesthetics, philosophy, politics, and prophecy conspired to exalt the redemptive and tranfigurative possibilities that could still be detected in the ruins of tradition. These figures embody a particularly acute version of that modernist critique of modernity that binds philosophy to radical politics and seeks to reverse or bring to a standstill a once progressive history betrayed by the event of conflagration. In the years during and after World War I the apocalyptic and messianic imagination was still oriented toward a radically different future. After World War II and certainly after Auschwitz, however, the image of "rupture" or "caesura" becomes inseparable from the *telos* of modernity. The texts treated in Part 1 are still concerned with the unfulfilled promises of modernity (though in highly esoteric linguistic, aesthetic, and utopian ways). After World War II the figure of catastrophe undergoes a profound and subtle transformation. It is no longer the harmonious world that is interrupted and redeemed *in* and *by* the historical-political catastrophe but the catastrophe itself that is brought into the center of thinking, as the permanent sign of an unredeemed history.

Indeed, after World War II it is the figure of a no longer redemptive history marked by the immutable caesura that defined the "postapocalyptic" writings of Heidegger, Jaspers, Horkheimer, and Adorno. Here there is little trace of the messianic and melancholic pathos of utopia and renewal that might be said to have constituted the tradition of modernity in Bloch, Benjamin, and Ball. On the contrary, in Heidegger, Jaspers, and in Horkheimer and Adorno's *Dialectic of Enlightenment* it is modernity itself that is now held culpable for the catastrophe. As Lyotard has argued, the very fact of Auschwitz represents a historical trauma that not only forecloses the project of redemption but also acts as an imperative to resist closure, to question representation, and is a sign of that which has not yet, and cannot be, determined.[17] In the immediate postwar era, the texts I have discussed and the preoccupations of their authors with the burdens and limits of "humanisms," "guilt," and "enlightenment" attest to the distinctly different dimensions of modernity that are indicted not so much for their failure to prevent the catastrophe as for having made it possible.

It would, however, be shortsighted to conclude by affirming the prevalent view that postmodernism is modernism without redemption and without apocalypse.[18] Rather, if I have found the distinction between the two postcatastrophic epochs revealing in this regard, I have tried to remain aware of both the apparent elective affinities among these thinkers and their distinctive characteristics. In other words, despite many overt similarities, the reactions of each of these thinkers to what he considered to be the apocalyptic apotheosis of the "West" should not be prematurely fused. Rather, as I hope to have shown, there is no consensus even as to the specificity of the catastrophe among these writers. Heidegger's "Letter on Humanism," Jaspers's *Die Schuldfrage,* and Horkheimer and Adorno's *Dialectic of Enlightenment* can all be described as "rubble texts," but they are also reflections on the collapse of three entirely distinct "projects of modernity." Heidegger's catastrophe is the collapse of his own project of overcoming metaphysics in the historical and resolute authentic action that would bring about the end of the epoch of the fallen, corrupt, routinized quotidian inhabited by what Heidegger called "Das man" (the they). After the war, Heidegger envisioned the end of not merely that German project but of all existential projects of transcendence, and he instead extolled the humility that accompanied living in the "light of Being." Yet it is precisely this pretense of humility that was the source of Jaspers's suspicion of Heidegger's stance, especially of his postwar silence, that permanently interrupted their friendship.

Since World War II and the Holocaust, the apocalypse has become suspect as a source of redemption. Yet, there can be little doubt that even Heidegger's flight from the conflicts of a radically demystified modernity into the purported purity of a politicized philosophy of regeneration does not wholly undermine his postwar suspicion of projects of transcendence, any more than does the collapse of communism and Marxism completely remove the sting from Marx's discoveries of alienation and reification in capitalism. The postapocalyptic mood in contemporary philosophy is not merely antiutopian or posttraumatic. Rather, Jaspers's *Die Schuldfrage* and Adorno and Horkheimer's *Dialectic of Enlightenment* have in part endured because they appeared at a particular conjuncture of catastrophe and lucidity, and because they testify to the fact that the most sober philosophies of modernity can never be entirely freed from responsibility for accounting for the crimes that arose from this century's projections of redeemed humanity. The texts I have analyzed have persisted because they serve as a warning that contemporary thought can continue to exist only in the awareness of how the burdened traditions of modernity remain stranded between apocalypse and enlightenment.

Notes

INTRODUCTION

1. Eric Hobsbawm, *The Age of Extremes: A History of the World, 1914–1991* (New York: Pantheon, 1994), 6, 7.

2. Agnes Heller, "Requiem für ein Jahrhundert: Auf der Ruinen der menschenverschuldeten Apokalypsen," *Frankfurter Rundschau* 29 (April 1995): 2.

3. Michael Löwy, *Redemption and Utopia: Jewish Libertarian Thought in Central Europe: A Study in Elective Affinity*, trans. Hope Heaney (Stanford: Stanford University Press, 1992). For an analysis of other strands of German mystical and messianic anarchism at the same time, see Christine Holste, *Der Forte-Kreis (1910–1915): Rekonstruktion eines utopischen Versuchs* (Stuttgart: M&P Verlag für Wissenschaft und Forschung, 1992).

4. Walter Benjamin, "Critique of Violence," in Benjamin, *Reflections,* ed. Peter Demetz, trans. Edmund Jephcott (New York: Harcourt Brace Jovanovich, 1978), 289.

5. Norbert Bolz, *Auszug aus der entzauberten Welt: Philosophischer Extremismus zwischen den Weltkriegen* (Munich: Wilhelm Fink Verlag, 1989), 80.

6. Karl Jaspers, *Die Schuldfrage: Von der politischen Haftung Deutschlands* (Munich: R. Piper Verlag, 1987), 69.

7. Saul Friedländer, "Trauma, Transference and 'Working through' in Writing the History of the *Shoah,*" *History and Memory* 4, no. 1 (Spring/Summer 1992): 43, 44.

8. Dominick LaCapra, *Representing the Holocaust: History, Theory, Trauma* (Ithaca: Cornell University Press, 1994), 192.

9. Philippe Lacoue-Labarthe, "The Caesura of the Speculative," *Glyph: Johns Hopkins Textual Studies* 4 (1978): 58.

10. Jay Winter, *Sites of Memory, Sites of Mourning: The Great War in European Cultural History* (Cambridge: Cambridge University Press, 1995), 157, 164.

11. On this point, see Richard Wolin, "Introduction to the Revised Edition," in Wolin, *Walter Benjamin: An Aesthetic of Redemption* (Berkeley, Los Angeles, and London: University of California Press, 1994), xxix–xxxv. Also see George L. Mosse, "Fascism and the Avant-Garde," in Mosse, *Masses and Man: Nationalist and Fascist Perceptions of Reality* (New York: Howard Fertig, 1980), 229–245.

12. See Ivo Frenzel, "Utopia and Apocalypse in German Literature," *Social Research* 39, no. 2 (Summer 1972): 314.

13. Klaus Vondung, *Die Apokalypse in Deutschland* (Munich: DTV, 1988).

14. Friedrich Gogarten, "Between the Times" (1920), *The Beginnings of Dialectic Theology*, ed. James McConkey Robinson (Richmond, Va.: John Knox Press, 1968), 279.

15. Carl Schmitt, *Political Theology: Four Chapters on the Concept of Sovereignty*, trans. George Schwab (Cambridge, Mass.: MIT Press, 1988), 36.

16. Max Weber, "Science as a Vocation," in *From Max Weber: Essays in Sociology*, trans. and ed. Hans H. Gerth and C. Wright Mills (New York: Oxford University Press, 1946), 155.

17. Cited in Peter Zudeick, *Der Hintern des Teufels: Ernst Bloch—Leben und Werk* (Moos: Elster Verlag, 1988), 94.

18. Gershom Scholem, *On Jews and Judaism in Crisis* (New York: Schocken Books, 1976), 187.

19. Bolz, *Auszug aus der entzauberten Welt*, 11.

20. Frank Kermode, "Apocalypse and the Modern," in *Visions of Apocalypse: End or Rebirth?* ed. Saul Friedländer, Gerald Holton, Leo Marx, and Eugene Skolnikoff (New York: Holmes & Meier, 1985), 87.

21. Ibid.

22. Vondung, *Apokalypse in Deutschland*, 151.

23. On this definition of secularization, see Hans Blumenberg, *The Legitimacy of the Modern Age*, trans. Robert M. Wallace (Cambridge, Mass.: MIT Press, 1983), 30.

24. Walter Benjamin, "Theses on the Philosophy of History," in *Illuminations*, ed. Hannah Arendt, trans. Harry Zohn (New York: Schocken Books, 1969), 257.

25. Scholem, *On Jews and Judaism*, 196. On Benjamin's philosophy of history, see the excellent account by Stéphane Moses, *L'ange de l'histoire: Rosenzweig, Benjamin, Scholem* (Paris: Editions du Seuil, 1992).

26. Gershom Scholem, "Toward an Understanding of the Messianic Idea in Judaism," in Scholem, *The Messianic Idea in Judaism and Other Essays on Jewish Spirituality* (New York: Schocken Books, 1971), 35.

27. Martin Jay, "The Apocalyptic Imagination and the Inability to Mourn," in Jay, *Force Fields: Between Intellectual History and Cultural Critique* (London: Routledge, 1993), 97.

28. Ibid.

29. Ernst Jünger, *Strahlungen* II (Munich: DTV, 1988), 113.

30. See Elliot Neaman, "History, Metaphysics, and Wit," Session "Ernst Jünger One Hundred and Counting: Ernst Jünger and Visions of the Twenty-first Century," German Studies Association, Chicago, September 22, 1995.

31. Hannah Arendt, "Nightmare and Flight," in *Hannah Arendt: Essays in Understanding, 1930–1954,* ed. Jerome Kohn (New York: Harcourt, Brace & Co., 1993), 134.

32. Max Horkheimer and Theodor W. Adorno, *Dialectic of Enlightenment,* trans. John Cumming (New York: Seabury, 1972), 169.

33. Löwy's discussion of this problem is somewhat at cross-purposes with his argument that Kafka was at the same time a rather conventional anti-authoritarian anarchist and that "for Kafka messianic redemption will be the work of human beings themselves." See Löwy, *Redemption and Utopia,* 77.

34. Thomas Mann, *Die Entstehung des Doktor Faustus* (Amsterdam, 1949). Cited in Vondung, *Apokalypse in Deutschland,* 10.

35. Walter Benjamin, "Theses on the Philosophy of History," 257, 258.

36. Theodor W. Adorno, *Negative Dialectics,* trans. E. B. Ashton (New York: Seabury, 1973), 361.

37. Dan Diner, *Zivilisationsbruch: Denken nach Auschwitz* (Frankfurt am Main: Fischer Verlag, 1988), 9.

38. Berel Lang, *Act and Idea in the Nazi Genocide* (Chicago: University of Chicago Press, 1990), 8. Lang usefully distinguishes between the term "unprecedented," which admits to the possibility of future genocides, and "unique," which does not allow for such a possibility and therefore remains metaphysical rather than historical.

39. W. H. Lawrence, "Nazi Mass Killing Laid Bare in Camp," *New York Times,* August 30, 1944, 1.

40. On the history of the term "civilization," see the early essay (1930) by Lucien Febvre, "*Civilisation:* Evolution of a Word and a Group of Ideas," in *A New Kind of History and Other Essays,* ed. Peter Burke, trans. K. Folca (New York: Harper & Row, 1971), 219–257.

41. Hannah Arendt, "We Refugees," in *The Jew as Pariah: Jewish Identity and Politics in the Modern Age,* ed. Ron H. Feldman (New York: Grove Press, 1978), 66.

42. This "postapocalyptic" view is associated with postmodernism in Matei Calinescu, *Five Faces of Modernity: Modernism, Avant-Garde, Decadence, Kitsch Postmodernism* (Durham: Duke University Press, 1987), 277. Umberto Eco has offered an alternative view that identifies "apocalyptic intellectuals" as naysayers of modern mass culture who offer pseudoconsolation and compensation for the presumed decadence and destructiveness of the "reigning banality." See Umberto Eco, "Apocalyptic and Integrated Intellectuals" (1964), in *Apocalypse Postponed,* ed. Robert Lumley (Bloomington: Indiana University Press, 1994), 18.

43. Klaus R. Scherpe, "Dramatisierung und Entdramatisierung des Untergangs—Zum ästhetischen Bewußtseins von Moderne und Postmoderne," in *Postmoderne: Zeichen eines kulturellen Wandels,* ed. Andreas Huyssen and Klaus R. Scherpe (Reinbek bei Hamburg: Rowohlt, 1986), 270–301. This article appeared in English as Klaus R. Scherpe, "Dramatization and De-dramatization of 'the End': The Apocalyptic Consciousness of Modernity and Post-Modernity," *Cultural Critique* 5 (Winter 1986–1987): 101. All translations are from the English-language version.

44. Ibid.

45. Ibid., 122.

46. Ibid., 117.

47. Michael Ignatieff, "The Rise and Fall of Vienna's Jews," *New York Review of Books* 36, no. 11 (June 29, 1989): 22–24. Cited in Michael André Bernstein, *Foregone Conclusions: Against Apocalyptic History* (Berkeley, Los Angeles, and London: University of California Press, 1994), 17.

48. "Jacques Derrida," in *Französische Philosophen im Gespräch,* ed. Florian Rötzer (Munich: Klaus Boer, 1986), 78.

49. Jean-François Lyotard, *The Postmodern Condition: A Report on Knowledge,* trans. Geoff Bennington and Brian Massumi (Minneapolis: University of Minnesota Press, 1984), 82.

50. Maurice Blanchot, *The Writing of the Disaster,* trans. Ann Smock (Lincoln: New Bison Books, 1995), 3, 5.

51. See, for example, Zygmunt Bauman, *Modernity and the Holocaust* (Ithaca: Cornell University Press, 1991). For a critical assessment of Bauman, see Anson Rabinbach, "Nationalsozialismus und Moderne: Zur Technik-Interpretation im Dritten Reich," in *Der Technikdiskurs in der Hitler-Stalin-Ära,* ed. Wolfgang Emmerich and Carl Wege (Stuttgart-Weimar: J. B. Metzler, 1995), 94–113.

52. Zygmunt Bauman, *Modernity and Ambivalence* (Ithaca: Cornell University Press, 1991), 233.

53. Eric L. Santner, *Stranded Objects: Mourning, Memory, and Film in Postwar Germany* (Ithaca: Cornell University Press, 1990), 13.

54. LaCapra, *Representing the Holocaust,* 188.

55. On this question, see the important introduction by James Schmidt to his edited volume, *What Is Enlightenment? Eighteenth-Century Answers and Twentieth-Century Questions* (Berkeley and Los Angeles: University of California Press, 1996).

56. Philippe Lacoue-Labarthe, "Transcendence Ends in Politics," *Social Research: An International Quarterly of the Social Sciences* 49, no. 2 (Summer 1982): 436.

57. Philippe Lacoue-Labarthe, "Neither an Accident nor a Mistake," *Critical Inquiry* 15, no. 2 (Winter 1989): 484.

58. Philippe Lacoue-Labarthe, *Heidegger, Art, and Politics,* trans. Chris Turner (Oxford: Basil Blackwell, 1990), 95.

59. Most recently in Tom Rockmore, *Heidegger and French Philosophy: Humanism, Antihumanism and Being* (London: Routledge, 1995).

60. For a discussion of this theme in the work of Karl Löwith, see Richard Wolin, "Löwith and Heidegger: An Introduction," in Karl Löwith, *Martin Heidegger: European Nihilism,* ed. Richard Wolin (New York: Columbia University Press, 1995), 16.

61. For a polemical approach to Heideggerian antihumanism in France, see Luc Ferry and Alain Renaut, *Heidegger and Modernity,* trans. Franklin Philip (Chicago: University of Chicago Press, 1990), 16.

62. On Heidegger and Nazism, see Victor Farias, *Heidegger and Nazism,* trans. Gabriel R. Ricci (Philadelphia: Temple University Press, 1989), and the

more sophisticated accounts by Hugo Ott, *Martin Heidegger: Unterwegs zu Seiner Biographie* (Frankfurt: Campus, 1988); Richard Wolin, *The Politics of Being: The Political Thought of Martin Heidegger* (New York: Columbia University Press, 1990); and Tom Rockmore, *On Heidegger's Nazism and Philosophy* (Berkeley and Los Angeles: University of California Press, 1992).

63. Karl Jaspers, *Notizen zu Martin Heidegger*, ed. Hans Saner (Munich: R. Piper Verlag, 1989), 201.

64. Hannah Arendt, "Concern with Politics in Recent European Philosophical Thought," in *Hannah Arendt: Essays in Understanding*, 444, 445.

65. On this distinction, see Dominick LaCapra, "Rethinking Intellectual History and Reading Texts," in *Modern European Intellectual History: Reappraisals and New Perspectives*, ed. Dominick LaCapra and Steven L. Kaplan (Ithaca: Cornell University Press, 1982), 67, 68.

66. Martin Jay, "Should Intellectual History Take a Linguistic Turn," in *Modern European Intellectual History*, 97.

67. On the concept of caesura, see Lacoue-Labarthe, *Heidegger, Art, and Politics*, 41–46.

68. Fernand Braudel, "Personal Testimony," *Journal of Modern History* 44 (1972): 453, 454.

69. Fernand Braudel, *On History*, trans. Sarah Mathews (Chicago: University of Chicago Press, 1980), 77.

70. Cited in Jacques Le Goff, *History and Memory*, trans. Steven Rendall and Elizabeth Claman (New York: Columbia University Press, 1992), 186.

71. This is the theme of Andreas Huyssen, *Twilight Memories: Marking Time in a Culture of Amnesia* (London: Routledge, 1995).

72. Bernstein, *Foregone Conclusions*, 7.

73. Ibid., 9.

74. Bernstein is not unaware of these controversies, as his notes amply indicate. See, for example, his acknowledgment of a similar argument in Amos Funkenstein, "History, Counter-History, and Narrative," in *Probing the Limits of Representation: Nazism and the "Final Solution,"* ed. Saul Friedländer (Cambridge, Mass.: Harvard University Press, 1992), 69.

75. Martin Broszat, "A Plea for the Historicization of National Socialism," in *Reworking the Past: Hitler, the Holocaust, and the Historians' Debate,* ed. Peter Baldwin (Boston: Beacon Press, 1990), 87.

76. Peter Gay, *Freud, Jews and Other Germans: Masters and Victims in Modernist Culture* (Oxford: Oxford University Press, 1978), 8.

77. Saul Friedländer, "Some Reflections on the Historicization of National Socialism," in *Reworking the Past*, 94.

78. Ibid., 100.

CHAPTER 1

The original version of this chapter was written before the explosion of Benjamin and Bloch scholarship in the late 1980s and 1990s. Since then a number of essay collections and indispensable documents have appeared, including Ernst Bloch's *Briefe 1903–1975* (Frankfurt: Suhrkamp, 1985) and *Theodor W.*

Adorno und Walter Benjamin. Briefwechsel, 1928–1940 (Frankfurt: Suhr-kamp, 1994). New English-language translations of Benjamin's works and cor-respondence have appeared as well. Because this essay played a small role in provoking scholarly interest in Benjamin's early career and messianism and be-cause it is a first formulation of many of the themes in this book, I have chosen to include it. In view of the subsequent discussion, I have tried to acknowledge some of the recent scholarship in the notes.

1. On the German-Jewish culture of Bildung, see George L. Mosse, *German Jews beyond Judaism* (Bloomington: Indiana University Press, 1985), 10; David Sorkin, *The Transformation of German Jewry, 1780–1840* (New York: Oxford University Press, 1987); Shulamit Volkov, *Jüdisches Leben und Anti-semitismus im 19. und 20. Jahrhundert* (Munich: C. H. Beck, 1990). The rela-tionship between the messianic revival and the appropriation of *Bildung* in Ger-man-Jewish culture is explored by Steven Aschheim, "German Jews Beyond Bildung and Liberalism: The Radical Jewish Revival in the Weimar Republic," in *The German-Jewish Dialogue Reconsidered: A Symposium in Honor of George L. Mosse*, ed. Klaus L. Berghahn (New York: Peter Lang, 1996), 125–140.

2. For detailed studies of the decline of self-confidence among German Jews of the fin-de-siècle, see Uriel Tal, *Christians and Jews in Germany: Religion, Politics and Ideology in the Second Reich, 1870–1914*, trans. Noah Jonathan Jacobs (Ith-aca: Cornell University Press, 1975); Jehuda Reinharz, *Fatherland or Promised Land: The Dilemma of the German Jew, 1893–1914* (Ann Arbor: University of Michigan Press, 1975); and Ismar Schorsch, *Jewish Reactions to German Anti-Semitism, 1870–1914* (New York: Columbia University Press, 1972).

3. Leo Baeck, *The Essence of Judaism* (New York: Schocken Books, 1961). On Baeck's rationalism, see Leonard Baker, *Days of Sorrow and Pain: Leo Baeck and the Berlin Jews* (New York: Oxford University Press, 1978), 46. The rationalism of Wilhelmine Jewish intellectuals is epitomized by Hermann Co-hen, *Die Religion der Vernunft aus den Quellen des Judentums* (Berlin: Bruno Cassirer, 1959 [1929 ed.]), and his essays, especially "Deutschtum und Juden-tum," in *Hermann Cohen's Jüdische Schriften*, 2 vols., ed. Bruno Strauss (Berlin: C. A. Schwetschke & Sohn, 1924). See Hans Liebeschütz, "Hermann Cohen and His Historical Background," *Leo Baeck Institute Yearbook* 12 (1968): 3–33. Useful collections are Hans Liebeschütz, *Von Georg Simmel zu Franz Rosenzweig: Studien zum jüdischen Denken im deutschen Kulturbereich* (Tübingen: J. C. B. Mohr, 1970); Peter Gay, *Freud, Jews and Other Germans: Masters and Victims in Modernist Culture* (New York: Oxford University Press, 1978); also see Werner E. Mosse, ed., *Juden in Wilhelminischen Deutschland 1890–1914: Ein Sammelband* (Tübingen: J. C. B. Mohr, 1976); Werner E. Mosse, ed., *Deutsches Judentum in Krieg und Revolution 1916–1923: Ein Sam-melband* (Tübingen: J. C. B. Mohr, 1971); George L. Mosse, *Germans and Jews: The Right, the Left, and the Search for a "Third Force" in Pre-Nazi Ger-many* (New York: Howard Fertig, 1970); Sidney M. Bolkosky, *The Distorted Image: German Jewish Perceptions of Germans and Germany, 1918–1935* (New York: Elsevier, 1975); Gershom Scholem, "Jews and Germans," in Scho-lem, *On Jews and Judaism in Crisis* (New York: Schocken Books, 1976), 71–92.

4. Central to any study of modern socialism and the Jewish question is Julius Carlebach, *Karl Marx and the Radical Critique of Judaism* (London: Routledge and Kegan Paul, 1978); also see Robert S. Wistrich, *Socialism and the Jews* (Rutherford, N.J.: Fairleigh Dickinson University Press, 1982); Robert S. Wistrich, *Revolutionary Jews from Marx to Trotsky* (London: Harrap, 1976); Donald S. Niewyk, *Socialist, Anti-Semite, and Jews: German Social Democracy Confronts the Problem of Anti-Semitism, 1918–1933* (Baton Rouge: Louisiana State University Press, 1971); Isaac Deutscher, *The Non-Jewish Jew and Other Essays* (Boston: Alyson, 1968). A reinterpretation of Kautsky, which shows him to be an exceptional case, is Jack Jacobs, "Kautsky on the Jewish Question" (Ph.D. dissertation, Columbia University, 1983).

5. Ludwig Quessel, "Die jüdische Neukolonisation Palästinas," *Sozialistisches Monatshefte*, Bd. II, Heft 11 (June 4, 1914): 673.

6. Stephen M. Poppel, *Zionism in Germany, 1897–1933: The Shaping of a Jewish Identity* (Philadelphia: Jewish Publication Society of America, 1977); Walter Laqueur, *A History of Zionism* (New York: Holt, Rinehart, & Winston, 1972); David Vital, *The Origins of Zionism* (Oxford: Oxford University Press, 1975).

7. There is no adequate study of the Jewish generation of 1914. The memoir literature is, however, voluminous. Good introductions are provided by Eva Reichmann, "Der Bewusstseinswandel der deutschen Juden," in *Deutsches Judentum in Krieg und Revolution*, 511–613; Robert Weltsch, "Die schleichende Krise der jüdischen Identität—Ein Nachwort," in *Juden im Wilhelminischen Deutschland*, 689–704.

8. Béla Bálazs, "Notes from a Diary (1911–1921)," *New Hungarian Quarterly* 13, no. 47 (Autumn 1972): 125, 126. On the assimilated milieu of Lukács and Balázs, see Mary Gluck, *Georg Lukács and His Generation, 1900–1918* (Cambridge, Mass.: Harvard University Press, 1985), 48.

9. In an interview with István Eörsi, Lukács said of his Jewishness, "I always realized that I was a Jew, but it never had a significant influence on my development." See István Eörsi, ed., *Georg Lukács Record of a Life: An Autobiographical Sketch*, trans. Rodney Livingstone (London: Verso, 1983), 29.

10. Robert Wohl, *The Generation of 1914* (Cambridge, Mass.: Harvard University Press, 1979); Jeffrey Herf, *Reactionary Modernism: Technology, Culture, and Politics in Weimar and the Third Reich* (Cambridge: Cambridge University Press, 1984) (esp. chap. 1); Michael Löwy, *Georg Lukács: From Romanticism to Bolshevism*, trans. Patrick Camiller (London: New Left Books, 1979); Michael Löwy, "Jewish Messianism and Libertarian Utopia in Central Europe," *New German Critique* 20 (Spring/Summer 1980): 105–115; Ferenc Féher, "Am Scheideweg des romantischen Antikapitalismus: Typologie und Beitrag zur deutschen Ideologiegeschichte gelegentlich des Briefwechsels zwischen Paul Ernst und Georg Lukács," in *Die Seele und das Leben: Studien zum frühen Lukács*, ed. Agnes Heller (Frankfurt am Main: Suhrkamp Verlag, 1972), 241–327; Robert Sayre and Michael Löwy, "Figures of Romantic Anti-Capitalism," *New German Critique* 32 (Spring/Summer 1984): 42–92.

11. The term "normative Judaism" comes from the work of George Foot Moore, *Judaism in the First Centuries of the Christian Era*, 3 vols. (Cambridge:

Cambridge University Press, 1927), also a major source for the origins of messianism. Harold Bloom has used the term in regard to Freud, Kafka, and Scholem, all of whom stand outside of that tradition, and whose work shares "something of the strong light of the canonical, of that perfection which destroys," as Scholem said of Kafka. Cited in Harold Bloom, "Introduction," in *Sigmund Freud,* ed. Harold Bloom (New York: Chelsea House, 1985), 3. The most important work on the tradition of messianism is Gershom Scholem's *The Messianic Idea in Judaism and Other Essays on Jewish Spirituality* (New York: Schocken Books, 1972); also see the early work by Joseph Klausner, *The Messianic Idea in Israel from Its Beginnings to the Completion of the Mishnah* (New York: Schocken Books, 1955), and more recently, Moshe Idel, *Kabbalah: New Perspectives* (New Haven: Yale University Press, 1988).

12. Balázs, "Notes from a Diary," 124.

13. There is a growing literature on both Benjamin's and Bloch's messianic thought, too extensive to list here with any completeness. On Benjamin, see Richard Wolin, *Walter Benjamin: An Aesthetic of Redemption* (New York: Columbia University Press, 1982 [2d ed., Berkeley and Los Angeles: University of California Press, 1995]); Bernd Witte, *Der Intellektuelle als Kritiker: Untersuchungen zu seinem Frühwerk* (Stuttgart: J. B. Metzlerische Verlagsbuchhandlung, 1976); Winfried Menninghaus, *Walter Benjamins Theorie der Sprachmagie* (Frankfurt am Main: Suhrkamp Verlag, 1980); Gershom Scholem, "Walter Benjamin and His Angel," in *On Jews and Judaism,* 198–236; Irving Wohlfarth, "On the Messianic Structure of Walter Benjamin's Last Reflections," *Glyph* 3 (1978): 148–212; Jürgen Habermas, "Consciousness-raising or Redemptive Criticism," *New German Critique* 17 (Spring 1979): 30–59; Rolf Tiedemann, "Historical Materialism or Political Messianism? An Interpretation of the Theses 'On the Concept of History,'" *The Philosophical Forum* 15, nos. 1–2 (Fall/Winter 1983–1984): 71–104. On Bloch, see Jürgen Habermas, "Ernst Bloch: A Marxist Romantic," *Salmagundi,* nos. 10–11 (Fall 1969/Winter 1970): 633–654; Jürgen Moltmann, "Messianismus und Marxismus," in *Über Ernst Bloch* (Frankfurt am Main: Suhrkamp Verlag, 1968), 42–60; Ferenc Fehér, "Am Scheideweg des romantischen Anti-Kapitalismus," unpublished ms. (Budapest, 1976); Gerald Raulet, "Critique of Religion and Religion as Critique," *New German Critique* 9 (Fall 1976): 71–87; Sándor Rádnoti, "Lukács and Bloch," in *Lukács Reappraised,* ed. Agnes Heller (New York: Columbia University Press, 1983), 63–75.

14. Gershom Scholem, "With Gershom Scholem: An Interview," in *On Jews and Judaism,* 2.

15. For Löwy, there exists "a remarkable structural homology, an undeniable spiritual isomorphism between these two cultural universes situated in these apparently completely distinct spheres: the Jewish messianic tradition and libertarian revolutionary utopia." During the years 1900–1933 among a certain number of Jewish intellectuals of German culture, he argues, this homology became "dynamic" and took the form of a *"veritable elective affinity."* Michael Löwy, "Jewish Messianism and Libertarian Utopia," 105–115. Also see Michael Löwy, *Redemption and Utopia: Jewish Libertarian Thought in Central Europe,*

a Study in Elective Affinity, trans. Hope Heaney (Stanford: Stanford University Press, 1988), 24, 25.

16. Max Brod, *Der Prager Kreis* (Stuttgart: W. Kohlhammer Verlag, 1966), 48.

17. See David Biale, *Gershom Scholem: Kabbalah and Counter-History* (Cambridge, Mass.: Harvard University Press, 1979), 52–60; Scholem, "With Gershom Scholem: An Interview," 1–26.

18. On Rosenzweig, see Nahum N. Glatzer, *Franz Rosenzweig: His Life and Thought* (New York: Schocken Books, 1953); Hans Liebeschütz, *Von Georg Simmel zu Franz Rosenzweig: Studien zum Jüdischen Denken im deutschen Kulturbereich* (Tübingen: J. C. B. Mohr, 1970); and *The Philosophy of Franz Rosenzweig,* ed. Paul Mendes-Flohr (Hanover and London: Brandeis University Press, 1988). On the Buber-Rosenzweig translation of the Bible, see Martin Jay, "Politics of Translation: Siegfried Kracauer and Walter Benjamin on the Buber-Rosenzweig Bible," *Leo Baeck Yearbook* 21 (1976): 3–24.

19. The best introduction to these groups is Gershom Scholem, *From Berlin to Jerusalem* (New York: Schocken Books, 1980).

20. Seth Taylor, *Left-Wing Nietzscheans: The Politics of German Expressionism, 1910–1920* (Berlin: Walter de Gruyter, 1990), 60–88, 117–141. Also see George L. Mosse, "Left-Wing Intellectuals in the Weimar Republic," in *Germans and Jews,* 186–190. Friedländer is portrayed by Alfred Kubin, "S. Friedländer, Schöpferische Indifferenz," *Ziel: Jahrbücher für geistige Politik* 4 (1919): 118–121. Interesting biographical information on Theodor Lessing can be found in the preface to his strongly Nietzschean *Geschichte als Sinngebung des Sinnlosen: Oder die Geburt der Geschichte aus dem Mythos,* 4th ed. (Leipzig: Verlag Emmanuel Reinicke, 1927), 1–32. The Goldberg circle is humorously caricatured in Scholem, *From Berlin to Jerusalem,* 146–149. For a summary of the philosophy of the Goldberg circle, see Erich Unger, *Wirklichkeit, Mythos, Erkenntnis* (Munich and Berlin: Verlag von Oldenbourg, 1930). On Landauer's philosophy of language, see Charles B. Maurer, *Call to Revolution: The Mystical Anarchism of Gustav Landauer* (Detroit: Wayne State University Press, 1971). For more general studies, see Ruth Link-Salinger (Hyman), *Gustav Landauer: Philosopher of Utopia* (Indianapolis: Hackett, 1977); Paul Breines, "The Jew as Revolutionary: The Case of Gustav Landauer," *Leo Baeck Institute Yearbook* 12 (1967): 75–84; Eugene Lunn, *Prophet of Community* (Berkeley and Los Angeles: University of California Press, 1973). On the Prague scene, see Max Brod, *Der Prager Kreis;* and Ernst Pavel, *The Nightmare of Reason: A Life of Franz Kafka* (New York: Schocken Books, 1984).

21. Scholem, "The Messianic Idea in Judaism," 4.

22. See Richard Wolin's discussion of this theme in his *Walter Benjamin,* 36–44; also see my comments on Benjamin's theory of origins in "Critique and Commentary/Alchemy and Chemistry," *New German Critique* 17 (Spring 1979): 7–9.

23. Scholem, "The Messianic Idea in Judaism," 6. This idea is most strongly represented in Christian tradition in the theology of Joachim of Floris. In this view, "at the end of time there is a secret unfolding, a revelation of that which

was hidden in the historical process: that the oppressed, the humble, the anonymous are those who carry history. At the end of time the absurd dark, obscure
passages of Scripture will be revealed as the great mysteries." Cited in Franklin
H. Littell, *The Origins of Sectarian Protestantism* (New York: Macmillan,
1964), 52. Bloch also notes Joachim of Floris's "heretical" eschatology in his
Erbschaft dieser Zeit (1935) (Frankfurt am Main: Suhrkamp Verlag, 1962),
132–140. Also see the classic work on this tradition: Jakob Taubes, *Abend-
ländische Eschatologie* (Berlin: A. Francke, 1947).

24. Ernst Bloch, *Geist der Utopie* (Frankfurt am Main: Suhrkamp Verlag,
1964), 347. *Geist der Utopie* appeared in two editions, in 1918 (Munich and
Leipzig: Duncker & Humblot) and in fully revised form in 1923. Since some of
the crucial texts for this essay are in the earlier version, I will refer to the original 1918 edition unless otherwise specified. The modern editions are cited as
Frankfurt am Main, 1964, or Frankfurt am Main, 1973 (both based on the
1923 edition).

25. On the young Lukács, see Paul Breines and Andrew Arato, *The Young
Lukács and the Origins of Western Marxism* (New York: Seabury Press, 1979);
Löwy, *Georg Lukács: From Romanticism to Bolshevism*; Agnes Heller, ed., *Die
Seele und das Leben*; Lee Congdon, *The Young Lukács* (Chapel Hill: University
of North Carolina Press, 1983).

26. Scholem points out that this notion of Redemption is diametrically opposed to the Christian idea of Salvation, which is always private, personal, and
spiritual. Scholem, "The Messianic Idea in Judaism," 16.

27. Cited in Habermas, "Consciousness-raising or Redemptive Critique,"
38, 39. From "Das Leben der Studenten," in *Walter Benjamin: Gesammelte
Schriften*, ed. Rolf Tiedemann and Hermann Schweppenhäuser, II:1, 75 (hereafter referred to as *W.B., GS*).

28. Scholem, "The Messianic Idea in Judaism," 7.

29. Ibid., 10.

30. Hans Blumenberg, *The Legitimacy of the Modern Age,* trans. Robert M.
Wallace (Cambridge, Mass.: MIT Press, 1985), 41.

31. Baeck, *The Essence of Judaism,* 232.

32. Scholem, "The Messianic Idea in Judaism," 10.

33. See Sándor Rádnoti, "Benjamin's Politics," *Telos,* no. 37 (Fall 1978):
64–66.

34. On the political context of Weber's *Ancient Judaism,* see Hans Liebeschütz, "Max Weber's Historical Interpretation of Judaism," *Leo Baeck Institute Yearbook* 9 (1964): 41–68. Also see Gary Abraham, *Max Weber and the
Jewish Question* (Champaign: University of Illinois Press, 1992).

35. Max Weber, *Ancient Judaism,* trans. Hans H. Gerth and Don Martindale (New York: Free Press, 1952), 326. Weber once remarked that "Judaism
and especially Zionism rests on the presupposition of a highly concrete 'promise.'" Ibid., xv.

36. Martin Buber, *Drei Reden über das Judentum* (Frankfurt am Main,
1911); a second collection appeared as *Vom Geist des Judentums* (Leipzig,
1916); a collection including these and other essays was published as *Reden
über das Judentum* (Frankfurt am Main, 1923). The English edition, based on

the heavily revised 1963 German edition, appeared as Nahum N. Glatzer, ed., *On Judaism* (New York: Schocken Books, 1972). On Martin Buber's early career, see Paul Mendes-Flohr, *From Mysticism to Dialogue: Martin Buber's Transformation of German Social Thought* (Detroit: Wayne State University Press, 1989); Gershom Scholem, "Martin Buber's Conception of Judaism," in *On Jews and Judaism,* 126–171.

37. On Buber and Nietzsche, see Biale, *Gershom Scholem,* 37–39, 43–47.

38. *Vom Judentum: Ein Sammelbuch,* ed. Verein Jüdischer Hochschüler Bar Kochba in Prag (Leipzig: Kurt Wolff Verlag, 1913). Max Brod notes that the Bar Kochba included, in addition to himself and Kafka, Robert and Felix Weltsch and above all Hugo Bergmann, who was its leading light. The contributors to the anthology included Gustav Landauer, Moritz Heimann, Erich Kahler, Margarethe Susman, Karl Wolfskehl, Arnold Zweig, Hugo Bergmann, Hans Kohn, Ludwig Strauss, Oskar Epstein, Robert Weltsch, and Brod. See Max Brod, *Der Prager Kreis,* 57.

39. Hans Kohn, "Geleitwort," in *Vom Judentum,* viii.

40. Bloch, *Geist der Utopie,* 319. This section bears the date 1912–1913 and was not included in the 1923 edition of *Geist der Utopie* but appeared that year in an essay collection entitled *Durch die Wüste,* republished as "Symbol: Die Juden (1912/3)," in Ernst Bloch, *Durch die Wüste: Frühe kritische Aufsätze* (Frankfurt am Main: Suhrkamp Verlag, 1964), 122–140.

41. Bloch, *Geist der Utopie,* 319.

42. Ibid.

43. Gershom Scholem, "Martin Buber's Conception of Judaism," in *On Jews and Judaism,* 138.

44. Walter Benjamin, Letter to Herbert Belmore, August 12, 1912, in Walter Benjamin, *Briefe,* 2 vols., ed. Gershom Scholem and Theodor W. Adorno (Frankfurt am Main: Suhrkamp, 1966; 2d ed. 1979), 1:44 (hereafter cited as W.B., *Briefe*).

45. For a discussion of Wyneken's influence on Benjamin, see Wolin, *Walter Benjamin,* 4–13; Witte, *Der Intellektuelle als Kritiker,* 15–22.

46. Scholem notes that according to a letter from Tuchler (February 26, 1963), the "exchange of ideas was continued with great intensity in letter form." W.B., *Briefe,* 1:44n.

47. This correspondence is in the Ludwig Strauss collection of the Jewish National and University Library, Jerusalem. Of the four letters in the archive, three (October 10, 1912; November 21, 1912; and January 7, 1913) are partially published in W.B., *GS,* II:3, 836–844. The subsequent citations and page numbers are from photocopies of the originals and not from the published versions (cited as Letter, W.B./L.S.).

48. In 1913 Strauss wrote to Buber of the influence of his *Speeches:* "The hours in which I doubt myself and my Judaism turn into an embittered doubt of your strength and your work. And the hours in which I am firm before my goal are full of an overflowing thankfulness to you." Cited in Maurice Friedman, *Martin Buber's Life and Work: The Early Years 1878–1923* (New York: Dutton, 1981), 140.

49. Gershom Scholem, *Walter Benjamin: Die Geschichte einer Freundschaft*

(Frankfurt am Main: Suhrkamp Verlag, 1975), 10; English: *Walter Benjamin: The Story of a Friendship*, trans. Harry Zohn (Philadelphia: Jewish Publication Society of America, 1981), 3. Subsequent references are to the English edition.

50. Scholem, *The Story of a Friendship*, 3.

51. Neither Susan Buck-Morss nor Bernd Witte refer to this earlier confrontation with the problem of Jewishness. See Susan Buck-Morss, *The Origin of Negative Dialectics: Theodor W. Adorno, Walter Benjamin, and the Frankfurt Institute* (New York: Free Press, 1977), 6; and Witte, *Der Intellektuelle als Kritiker*, 9. Martin Jay, in his history of the Frankfurt School, goes so far as to argue inaccurately that "Zionism became the dominant passion in his life" during the war, "crowding out the Youth Movement." Martin Jay, *The Dialectical Imagination: A History of the Frankfurt School and the Institute of Social Research 1923–1950* (Boston: Little, Brown, 1973), 199. Richard Wolin refers to the published correspondence with Strauss but only to affirm that by 1912 Benjamin distanced himself from the Zionist movement. This is also the view of the editors of the *Gesammelte Schriften* who offer only the following meager commentary on the correspondence: "In numerous letters, which Benjamin wrote to Ludwig Strauss in 1912 and 1913, he justified his decision for Wyneken in detail." *W.B., GS*, II:3, 836.

52. Moritz Goldstein, "Deutsch-jüdischer Parnass," *Der Kunstwart und Kulturwart: Halbmonatsschrift für Ausdruckskultur auf allen Lebensgebieten* 24, no. 11 (March 1912): 283. Also see Goldstein's later reflections on the *Kunstwart* debate and the notorious *misuse* made of his article by the Nazis in "German Jewry's Dilemma: The Story of a Provocative Essay," *Leo Baeck Institute Yearbook* 2 (1957): 236–254.

53. Goldstein, "Deutsch-jüdischer Parnass," 284.

54. Ibid., 292.

55. Goldstein, "German Jewry's Dilemma," 246.

56. For a detailed discussion of the impact of the *Kunstwart* debate on the Jewish community in Germany, see Reinharz, *Fatherland or Promised Land*, 193–206.

57. Franz Quentin (Ludwig Strauss), contribution to "Aussprachen mit Juden," *Der Kunstwart*, Jg. 25, Heft 22 (August 1912): 238–244.

58. Ibid., 244.

59. Goldstein, "Deutsch-jüdischer Parnass," 292.

60. Quentin (Strauss), "Aussprachen mit Juden," 243.

61. On this point Benjamin is remarkably prescient since he apparently did not know that Goldstein had originally submitted his article to the *Berliner Tageblatt*, which promptly rejected it. See Goldstein, "German Jewry's Dilemma," 245.

62. Letter, W.B./L.S., September 11, 1912.

63. Ibid.

64. Ibid.

65. Ibid.

66. Ibid.

67. Letter, W.B./L.S., October 10, 1912.

68. Ibid.

69. Word obliterated in the original document. "Speak" seems to be the missing word.

70. Letter, W.B./L.S., October 10, 1912.

71. Actually entitled "Dialog über der Religiosität der Gegenwart," *W.B., GS,* II:1, 16–35.

72. Ibid., 22.

73. Ibid., 34.

74. Letter, W.B./L.S., November 21, 1912.

75. Ibid.

76. Ibid.

77. Letter, W.B./L.S., January 7, 1913.

78. Ibid.

79. Walter Benjamin, *The Origin of German Tragic Drama,* trans. John Osborne (London: New Left Books, 1977), 36.

80. Letter, W.B./L.S., January 7, 1913.

81. Ibid.

82. In his memoirs Scholem recalls that he first saw Benjamin in a debate with Zionists at the forum (founded by Benjamin) called the Sprechsaal der Jugend in Berlin where he represented the Wyneken position but "did not reject Zionism outright but somehow relegated it to a secondary position." See Scholem, *The Story of a Friendship,* 3.

83. Walter Benjamin, "Die Schulreform, eine Kulturbewegung," *W.B., GS,* II:1, 13.

84. Letter, W.B./L.S., January 7, 1913.

85. Ibid. There is one more letter, dated February 6, 1913, attesting to Strauss's decision to end the discussion by not responding and to Benjamin's desire to continue it:

> Ich verstehe Ihr Schweigen aus der Peinlichkeit des Abiturs. Nur eine Anfrage: studieren Sie im nächsten Semester bestimmt hier? Ich werde wider mein Erwarten wahrscheinlich hier sein und ein Semester der freien Studentschaft als erster Vorsitzender opfern. Mein Entschluss würde mich leichter, wenn ich wüsste, dass Sie hier sind. Bitte antworten Sie mir sogleich, da in einigen Tagen die Entscheidung fällt.
> (I comprehend your silence to be a result of the embarrassment of the *Abitur* [German high school exam]. Just one question: are you planning to definitely study here next semester? Against my expectations I will in all likelihood be here and sacrifice a semester as the first chairman of the Free Student Organization. My decision will be easier were I to know that you will be here. Please answer immediately, as in a few days the decision must fall.)

86. Bloch, *Geist der Utopie,* 140.

87. Ernst Bloch, *Kritischer Erörterungen über Rickert und das Problem der modernen Erkenntnistheorie: Inaugural-Dissertation . . . vorgelegt am 7. Juli 1908* (Ludwigshafen am Rhein, 1909). A copy of this dissertation, printed in a limited edition, is in the Hermann Cohen Archive, the Jewish National and University Library, Jerusalem (Var. COH 121/B62). Cited in Paul Mendes-Flohr, " 'To Brush History Against the Grain': The Eschatology of the Frankfurt School and Ernst Bloch," in *Divided Passions: Jewish Intellectuals and the Experience of Modernity* (Detroit: Wayne State University Press, 1991), 370–389.

88. Margarethe Susman, *Ich habe viele Leben Gelebt: Erinnerungen* (Stuttgart: W. Kohlhammer, 1966), 78–81.

89. Cited in Friedman, *Martin Buber's Life and Work,* 134.

90. Bloch, *Geist der Utopie,* 321, 322.

91. Ibid., 13.

92. Ibid., 322.

93. Ibid., 321. For a different view of Kraus, see Harry Zohn, "Jüdischer Selbsthasser oder 'Erzjude,'" *Modern Austrian Literature* 8, no. 1–2 (1975): 1–18.

94. Bloch, *Geist der Utopie,* 329.

95. Ibid., 330.

96. Wolin, *Walter Benjamin,* 49.

97. "Program of the Coming Philosophy," trans. Mark Ritter, *The Philosophical Forum,* Special Issue on Walter Benjamin, 4: 1,2 (Fall/Winter 1983–1984): 42.

98. For a detailed discussion of this text, see Wolin, *Walter Benjamin,* 31–37.

99. Friedrich Nietzsche, *Die fröhliche Wissenschaft,* in Nietzsche, *Sämtliche Werke: Kritische Studienausgabe,* Bd. 3 (Munich: DTV, 1980), 633.

100. Susman, *Erinnerungen,* 87.

101. Ibid., 80.

102. Cited in Silvia Markus, *Ernst Bloch in Selbstbildnisse und Bilddokumenten* (Hamburg: Rowohlt, 1977), 24.

103. Cited in Paul Honigsheim, *On Max Weber,* trans. Joan Rhytra (New York: Free Press, 1968), 29.

104. On the impact of the war, see George L. Mosse, "War and the Appropriation of Nature," in *Germany in the Age of Total War,* ed. Volker R. Berghahn and Martin Kitchen (London: Croom Helm, 1982); Paul Fussel, *The Great War and Modern Memory* (Oxford: Oxford University Press, 1977); Wohl, *The Generation of 1914;* Herf, *Reactionary Modernism.*

105. Letter, W.B. to Gustav Wyneken, March 9, 1915, in W.B., *Briefe,* I, 120, 121. Also see Wolin, *Walter Benjamin,* 13.

106. Walter Benjamin, *A Berlin Chronicle,* in Walter Benjamin, *Reflections,* ed. Peter Demetz, trans. Edmund Jephcott (New York: Harcourt Brace Jovanovich, 1978), 21.

107. Letter, W.B. to Gustav Wyneken, March 9, 1915, in W.B., *Briefe,* I, 121.

108. Ibid.

109. Here I take issue with other commentators on this crucial essay who have chosen to neglect its political dimension: see Menninghaus, *Walter Benjamins Theorie der Sprachmagie,* 9–50; Wolin, *Walter Benjamin,* 41–43. Witte acknowledges Bloch's, Lukács's, and Benjamin's positions as a general protest against the war, but this point is not developed; see *Der Intellektuelle als Kritiker,* 8–10.

110. Letter to Gershom Scholem, November 11, 1916, in W.B., *Briefe,* I, 128.

111. Letter to Martin Buber, July 1916, in W.B., *Briefe,* I, 125–128. This

letter, along with its impact on Scholem, who also found the first issue of *Der Jude* repugnant, is discussed in David Biale, *Gershom Scholem, Kabbalah and Counter-History*, 104. To my knowledge Biale is the first to correctly identify the significance of the language essay in Benjamin's confrontation with Buber over the war issue. The phrase "die Krisis in das Herz der Sprache verlegt" is from a letter to Herbert Belmore, also dated 1916; W.B., *Briefe*, I, 131. The same letter also appears in *Martin Buber: Briefwechsel aus sieben Jahrzehnten*, ed. Grete Schaeder, Bd. I, 1897–1918 (Heidelberg: Verlag Lambert Schneider, 1972), 448–450.

112. Cited in Walter Laqueur, *A History of Zionism*, 172.

113. Letter to Martin Buber, July 1916, in W.B., *Briefe*, I, 126.

114. Ibid.

115. Ibid.

116. Ibid., 126, 127.

117. Ibid., 127.

118. Benjamin, *The Origin of German Tragic Drama*, 108. Ironically, although the idea for the *Trauerspiel* book dates from the precise period of the essay on language and the probe entitled "Die Bedeutung der Sprache in Trauerspiel und Tragödie" (1916), Benjamin did not actually read Rosenzweig's work—composed in the trenches between the fall of 1918 and the spring of 1919—until sometime in 1922. The quotation is from Franz Rosenzweig, *Stern der Erlösung* (Frankfurt am Main: J. Kaufmann Verlag, 1921), 98, 99. On the relationship between Benjamin and Rosenzweig, see Stéphane Moses, "Walter Benjamin and Franz Rosenzweig," *Philosophical Forum* 15, no. 1–2 (Fall/Winter 1983–1984): 188–206. There is another important parallel between Benjamin's and Rosenzweig's conceptions of language. For Rosenzweig, like Benjamin, the only true language of the All is the Word of God. With the loss of transparency, language also loses the confidence to reestablish the authentic identity of words and things. Idealism, the philosophy of identity, confronts the inability of reason to achieve self-identity by constructing an aesthetic prototype of the ego. As a result the individual finds "a surrogate for the lost garden that God himself had granted." This garden, which is the aesthetic apotheosis, imitates the cosmos insofar as it bears all the earmarks of purposive labor (perfection), even though it is originally aimless. For Rosenzweig, however, a return to a more basic faith overcomes this dilemma, while for Benjamin no such return is possible and art remains the sphere of intellectual activity. On Rosenzweig and Benjamin, see Jay, "Politics of Translation."

119. Letter to Martin Buber, July 1916, in W.B., *Briefe*, I, 127.

120. Rosenzweig, *Stern der Erlösung*, 98, 99. Cited in Benjamin, *The Origin of German Tragic Drama*, 108.

121. Benjamin, *The Origin of German Tragic Drama*, 108.

122. Walter Benjamin, "Über Sprache überhaupt und über die Sprache des Menschen," in *W.B., GS*, II:1, 149; "On Language as Such and on the Language of Man," in Benjamin, *Reflections*, 323 (subsequent citations from the English edition).

123. Ibid., 326, 327.

124. Ibid., 328.

125. *W.B., GS,* I:3, 1235.

126. Benjamin does not seem to have become aware of Saussure until much later, although several passages are strikingly close to Saussure's idea of the arbitrary nature of signs ("Signs must be confused where things are entangled") though of course with very different implications. See Benjamin, "On Language as Such and on the Language of Man," 329. Benjamin makes some critical remarks on Saussurean linguistics in the course of his résumé of the modern literature on language written in 1934, "Probleme der Sprachsoziologie," *W.B., GS,* III:9, 468.

127. Letter to Herbert Belmore, end of 1916, *W.B., Briefe,* I, 130, 131. Paul Fussel also has addressed the relationship between the war and the crisis of language in his magnificent study of the displacement of innocence with cynicism and irony in the poetry of the war, *The Great War in Modern Memory.* Benjamin takes up this theme again in his later reflections on the "mystical fascist" Ernst Jünger's poetics of war. See Walter Benjamin, "Theorien über deutschen Faschismus," *W.B., GS,* III:8, 238–250; English: "Theories of German Fascism: On the Collection of Essays *War and Warrior,*" *New German Critique* 17 (Spring 1979): 120–128.

128. Letter to Herbert Belmore, end of 1916, W.B., *Briefe,* I, 130, 131.

129. "Die Welt bis zur Kenntlichkeit verändern." Interview with Ernst Bloch, May 1974, in Arno Muenster, ed., *Tagträume vom aufrechten Gang: Sechs Interviews mit Ernst Bloch* (Frankfurt am Main: Suhrkamp Verlag, 1977), 34.

130. Ibid., 35.

131. Ibid.

132. Ernst Bloch, "Über einige politische Programme und Utopien in der Schweiz," *Archiv für Sozialwissenschaft und Sozialpolitik* 46, no. 1 (1918): 140–162.

133. "Bis zur Kenntlichkeit," 42. Hugo Ball notes, in his diary, that in those years Bern, "with all its rationalists, is a dry milieu" and that he was often "seen in the company of his utopian friend, Ernst Bloch." Hugo Ball, *Flight out of Time: A Dada Diary,* ed. John Elderfield, trans. Ann Raimes (New York: Viking, 1974), 143, 145. Their relationship is discussed in chapter 2.

134. Martin Korol, "Über die Entwicklung des politischen Denkens Ernst Bloch im Schweizer Exil des Ersten Weltkriegs, Dargestellt an Drei Texten aus den Jahren 1917, 1918, 1919," in *Bloch-Almanach* 1, ed. Karlheinz Weigand (Ludwigshafen: Ernst-Bloch-Archiv der Stadtbibliothek Ludwigshafen, 1981), 27. Korol discovered the key to Bloch's numerous pseudonyms in the archive of Johann Wilhelm Muehlon, the former Krupp director and diplomat who supported the Blochs in exile.

135. Bloch's relationship with Muehlon is documented in a few published letters: Ernst Bloch, *Briefe 1903–1975,* ed. Karola Bloch and Jan Robert Bloch et al. (Frankfurt am Main: Suhrkamp Verlag, 1985), 1:209–248. Also see Martin Korol, ed., *Kampf nicht Krieg: Politische Schriften 1917–1919* (Frankfurt am Main: Suhrkamp Verlag, 1984). Bloch's exile is described in Peter Zudeick, *Der Hintern des Teufels: Ernst Bloch—Leben und Werk* (Moos: Elster Verlag, 1985), 50–95.

136. Ernst Bloch, *Schadet oder Nützt Deutschland eine Niederlage seines Militärs?* (Bern: Freie Verlag, 1918), 22.

137. On Simmel's and other early evaluations, see Zudeick, *Der Hintern des Teufels*, 64, 65.

138. Bloch, *Geist der Utopie*, 433.

139. Ibid., 411, 412.

140. Ibid., 439, 445.

141. Scholem, *The Story of a Friendship*, 78.

142. Ibid., 79.

143. Bloch, "Bis zur Kenntlichkeit," 44.

144. Ernst Bloch, "Wie ist Sozialismus Möglich?" *Die weissen Blätter: Eine Monatsschrift* 5, no. 6 (May 1919): 193–201. René Schickele added the following introduction to Bloch's article: "Rather than Ernst Bloch's 'France' and 'Entente' I would prefer to say 'Western cultural circles' because this concept better signifies the new man and his history that we are talking about than a geographic, national or even historical delimitation."

145. Scholem, "The Messianic Idea in Judaism," 35.

146. Letter to Gershom Scholem, January 31, 1918, in W.B., *Briefe*, I, 171.

147. Michael Löwy, "Interview with Ernst Bloch," *New German Critique* 9 (Fall 1976): 41.

148. Letter to Ernst Schoen, September 19, 1919, in W.B., *Briefe*, I, 219.

149. Letter to Gershom Scholem, September 15, 1919, in W.B., *Briefe*, I, 217.

150. According to a letter to Scholem, the review was finished in January 1920. Benjamin describes it as "a thorough review" in which the "good things and advantageous aspects speak for themselves," while "the errors and weaknesses are diagnosed in a thoroughly esoteric language." Letter to Gershom Scholem, January 13, 1920, in W.B., *Briefe*, I, 229. The significance Benjamin attributed to it can be seen in the many subsequent references to the piece in his letters, not to mention his disappointment when it failed to find a publisher. Letter to Gershom Scholem, January 1, 1921, in W.B., *Briefe*, I, 255.

151. Letter to Gershom Scholem, February 13, 1920, in W.B., *Briefe*, I, 234, 235.

152. Letter to Ernst Schoen, February 2, 1920, in W.B., *Briefe*, I, 233.

153. Letter to Walter Benjamin, February 5, 1920, in Scholem, *The Story of a Friendship*, 88.

154. Scholem, *The Story of a Friendship*, 80.

155. Ibid., 88.

156. Letter to Gershom Scholem, February 13, 1920, in W.B., *Briefe*, I, 234.

157. Letter to Gershom Scholem, December 1, 1920, in W.B., *Briefe* I, 247.

158. Letter to Gershom Scholem, February 13, 1920, in W.B., *Briefe*, I, 234.

159. Salomo Friedländer, "Der Antichrist und Ernst Bloch," *Ziel: Jahrbücher für geistige Politik* 4 (1919): 103–116. Kurt Hiller, the editor, in a "Nachwort" declared his hatred for Bloch, "a man I never saw," for his religiosity, his "Catholic salad," and his "arrogant-ecstatic style." Hiller further derided Bloch as "a would-be utopist," "a pretend believer," "a profundity dervish," "yes, a spirit ahead of his time, but an unholy gaseous toad (with the

countenance of a superior European teacher)—in short, not a Christ, but a vomitive." Ibid., 117. Gustav Landauer also joined the chorus of critics, calling Bloch a "fascinating competitor of Rudolf Steiner" and complaining bitterly about the "unabashed charlatanry of the 'system of theoretical messianism.'" See Gustav Landauer, Letter to Margarethe Susman, January 31, 1919, in *Gustav Landauer, Sein Lebensgang in Briefen,* ed. Martin Buber (Frankfurt am Main: Rütten, 1929), 2:371, 372.

160. Friedländer, "Der Antichrist," 107.

161. Ibid., 106.

162. Zudeick, *Der Hintern des Teufels,* 69.

163. Ernst Bloch, "A Jubilee for Renegades," *New German Critique* 4 (Winter 1975): 18. This article first appeared in *Die neue Weltbühne* in December 1937 as Bloch's infamous apologia for his defense of Stalinism and the Moscow trials in those years. Read as a document of his political psychology, it offers an unparalleled insight into his reasons for his eventually adopting an uncritical position vis-à-vis the Soviet Union. Also See Oskar Negt, "Ernst Bloch: The German Philosopher of the October Revolution," *New German Critique* 4 (Winter 1975): 3–16.

164. Letter to Ernst Schoen, September 19, 1919, in W.B., *Briefe,* I, 218, 219.

165. See Rádnoti, "Benjamin's Politics," 66; and Richard Wolin, "From Messianism to Materialism: The Later Aesthetics of Walter Benjamin," *New German Critique* 22 (Winter 1981): 83–91; Wolin, *Walter Benjamin,* 110.

166. Scholem, *The Story of a Friendship,* 84.

167. Letter to Ernst Schoen, September 19, 1919, W.B., *Briefe,* I, 218.

168. Letter to Gershom Scholem, April 17, 1920, in W.B., *Briefe* I, 237.

169. Letter to Gershom Scholem, December 1, 1920, in W.B., *Briefe,* I, 247.

170. Scholem, *The Story of a Friendship,* 85.

171. Letter to Gershom Scholem, January 1921, in W.B., *Briefe,* I, 252.

172. Scholem, *The Story of a Friendship,* 91.

173. Walter Benjamin, "Theologisch-Politisches Fragment," in *W.B., GS,* II:1, 203–204. Citations are from the English version "Theologico-Political Fragment," in Benjamin, *Reflections,* 312.

174. Ibid., 313.

175. Scholem, *The Story of a Friendship,* 78.

176. Walter Benjamin, "Zur Kritik der Gewalt," in *W.B., GS,* II:1, 199; and "Critique of Violence," in Benjamin, *Reflections,* 295.

177. "Critique of Violence," 292.

178. Benjamin, "Theologico-Political Fragment," 313.

179. F. M. Dostojewski, *Politische Schriften, Sämtliche Werke,* ed. Dmitri Mereschkowski (Munich: R. Piper Verlag, 1917).

180. Walter Benjamin, "'Der Idiot' von Dostojewskij," in *W.B., GS,* II:1, 240. For a general discussion of pre-1914 German attitudes toward Dostoyevsky, see Leo Löwenthal, "Die Auffassung Dostojewskis im Vorkriegsdeutschland," *Zeitschrift für Sozialforschung* 3 (1934): 343–382.

181. Benjamin, "'Der Idiot' von Dostojewskij" II:1, 240, 241.

182. Löwy, Interview with Ernst Bloch, 44.

183. Bloch and Lukács's relationship to Dostoyevsky is treated in detail in Ferenc Féher, "Am Scheideweg des romantischen Antikapitalismus," unpublished ms. (1976), 111–174.

184. Löwy, Interview with Ernst Bloch, 44. On the Lukács-Dostoyevsky problem, also see György Márkus, "Life and the Soul: The Young Lukács and the Problem of Culture," in *Lukács Reappraised,* ed. Agnes Heller (New York: Columbia University Press, 1983), 1–27.

185. Scholem, *The Story of a Friendship,* 81.

186. Bloch, *Geist der Utopie,* 410. Also see Löwy, Interview with Ernst Bloch, 41, 42; Féher, "Am Scheideweg."

187. Benjamin, "'Der Idiot' von Dostojewskij," II:1, 240, 241.

188. Baeck, *The Essence of Judaism,* 232.

189. Bloch, "Über einige politische Programme," 162.

190. See Walter Benjamin, *Moskauer Tagebuch* (Frankfurt am Main: Suhrkamp Verlag, 1980).

191. Theodor W. Adorno, *Prisms,* trans. Samuel Weber and Shierry Weber (London: Spearman, 1967), 236.

192. See my "Unclaimed Heritage: Ernst Bloch's *Heritage of Our Times* and the Theory of Fascism," *New German Critique* 11 (Spring 1977): 5–21.

193. On this theme, see Eugene Lunn, *Marxism and Modernism: A Historical Study of Lukács, Brecht, Benjamin and Adorno* (Berkeley and Los Angeles: University of California Press, 1982).

194. Walter Benjamin, "Zentralpark," in *Charles Baudelaire* (Frankfurt am Main: Suhrkamp Verlag, 1974), 177.

195. Ferenc Féher, "Arato-Breines and Löwy on Lukács," *New German Critique* 23 (Spring/Summer 1981): 134.

196. As Leo Bersani argues in *The Culture of Redemption* (Cambridge, Mass.: Harvard University Press, 1990).

197. T. W. Adorno, *Minima Moralia: Reflections from a Damaged Life,* trans. E. F. N. Jephcott (London: Verso Books, 1978), 247.

198. Nadezhda Mandelstam, *Hope against Hope: A Memoir,* trans. Max Hayward (New York: Athenaeum, 1978), 42.

CHAPTER 2

1. See, for example, Heimo Schwilk and Ulrich Schacht, eds., *Die Selbstbewusste Naton: "Anschwellender Bockgesang" und weitere Beiträge zu einer deutschen Debatte* (Frankfurt am Main: Ullstein, 1994).

2. The lack of attention to Ball's anti-Semitism can to no small degree be attributed to the strange publication history of the *Critique* in the Federal Republic of Germany during the 1970s and 1980s. The second edition of *Zur Kritik der deutschen Intelligenz,* published by Rogner and Bernhard in Munich in 1970, was heavily censored, apparently by the editor, Gerd-Klaus Kaltenbrunner. Although neither the deletions nor the reasons for removing the offensive material are acknowledged in Kaltenbrunner's lengthy introduction, twenty-four passages, including sections several pages in length, were removed. The majority of the excised passages consist of those that reveal Ball's anti-

Semitism, for example, allusions to the "conspiracy of Protestant and Jewish theology" or to "Jewish-Junker world domination." Several others soften his anti-Catholicism and antitheism. Without mentioning the deletions in his introduction, Kaltenbrunner explicitly denied that the *Critique* is anti-Semitic: "That Ball was no anti-Semite is demonstrated by his repeated polemic against Treitschke, H. St. Chamberlain, and other anti-Jewish ideologues, as well as his sympathy for Heine or Karl Kraus, those Jewish spirits who most relentlessly criticized the German misery." Gerd-Klaus Kaltenbrunner, "Introduction," in *Zur Kritik der deutschen Intelligenz* (Munich: Rogner & Bernhard, 1970), 25. Kaltenbrunner's comments are all the more duplicitous, since if the *Critique* is not anti-Semitic, then why was it necessary to excise the relevant passages and offer no explanation or indication? Nor do Ball's negative references to anti-Semitic ideologues who are never criticized for their anti-Jewish writings, or positive ones to "Jewish" opponents of German patriotism, add up to a convincing argument for the claim that Ball is not an anti-Semite. The point, however, is that the practice of "editing" a historical work in order to make its author more publicly acceptable is scandalous no matter how noble the motives. Even more scandalous in this case is the deceptive commentary that neglects to mention that many egregious passages had been removed while Ball is defended against a hypothetical charge of anti-Semitism. In the (third) German edition published by Suhrkamp Verlag in Frankfurt in 1980, the offensive introduction no longer appears, though—perhaps unwittingly—the expurgated version reappears with only the misleading notation that "the first edition appeared in 1919 in *Der Freie Verlag*, Berne." At best the sad publication history of the *Critique* reveals the disingenuous side of the public taboo against anti-Semitism in the German Federal Republic. It is regrettable that such duplicitous practices might have been thought justified by the fear that Ball could be accused of anti-Semitism and that his posthumous reputation had to be managed accordingly. Brian Harris, who first uncovered this editorial practice in his 1979 dissertation, was right to note that "nothing is to be gained by editing the *Critique* to soften its original anti-Semitism." See Brian L. Harris, "Hugo Ball's Critique of the German Mind: Notes to Hugo Ball's *Zur Kritik der deutschen Intelligenz*" (Ph.D dissertation, University of Texas at Austin, 1979), 151–152.

3. No critical edition of the *Critique* yet exists in German. All quotations are from Hugo Ball, *Critique of the German Intelligentsia*, trans. Brian Harris (New York: Columbia University Press, 1993).

4. The most important studies of Ball are Gerhardt Edward Steinke, *The Life and Work of Hugo Ball: Founder of Dadaism* (The Hague: Mouton, 1967); Peter Uwe Hohendahl, "Hugo Ball," in *Expressionismus als Literatur: Gesammelte Studien*, ed. Wolfgang Rothe (Bern: Francke, 1969); Harris, "Hugo Ball's Critique of the German Mind"; Philip Mann, *Hugo Ball: An Intellectual Biography* (London: Institute of Germanic Studies, University of London, 1987); Seth Taylor, *Left-Wing Nietzscheans: The Politics of German Expressionism 1910–1920* (Berlin: Walter de Gruyter, 1990).

5. Emmy Ball-Hennings, *Ruf und Echo: Mein Leben mit Hugo Ball* (Frankfurt am Main: Suhrkamp Verlag, 1990), 15.

6. Hugo Ball, "Nietzsche in Basel: Eine Streitschrift," in *Hugo Ball: Der*

Künstler und die Zeitkrankheit: Ausgewählte Schriften, ed. Burkhard Schlichting (Frankfurt am Main: Suhrkamp Verlag, 1988), 61–102.

7. Ibid., 79.

8. See Steven E. Aschheim, *The Nietzsche Legacy in Germany, 1890–1990* (Berkeley and Los Angeles: University of California Press, 1992), 70.

9. Hohendahl, "Hugo Ball," 740.

10. Ball-Hennings, *Ruf und Echo,* 33.

11. Ball, "Nietzsche in Basel," 66.

12. Hugo Ball, *Die Flucht aus der Zeit* (Munich: Duncker & Humblot, 1927), November 20, 1915, 71. Translations are my own, though I have profitably consulted the English translation of Ball's diaries, *Flight Out of Time: A Dada Diary,* ed. John Elderfield, trans. Ann Raimes (New York: Viking Press, 1974).

13. Hugo Ball, "Kandinsky," in *Der Künstler und die Zeitkrankheit,* 45.

14. Letter of August 7, 1914, in *Hugo Ball: Briefe 1911–1927,* ed. Annemarie Schütt-Hennings (Zurich: Benziger, 1957). Cited in Jindrich Toman, "Im Krieg regt sich das Urgewässer: Hugo Ball und der Kriegsausbruch 1914," *Hugo Ball Almanach* 5 (1981): 8.

15. Ball, *Flucht aus der Zeit,* November 1914, 16. See also Taylor, *Left-Wing Nietzscheans,* 173.

16. Mann, *Hugo Ball,* 53.

17. Ball, *Flucht aus der Zeit,* November 1914, 16.

18. See John Elderfield, Introduction to *Flight Out of Time,* xix; and Taylor, *Left-Wing Nietzscheans,* 174.

19. Mann, *Hugo Ball,* 61; Taylor, *Left-Wing Nietzscheans,* 174.

20. Ball, *Flucht aus der Zeit,* August 7, 1919, 235.

21. Mann, *Hugo Ball,* 79.

22. Ball, *Flucht aus der Zeit,* December 13, 1915, 49.

23. Ibid., March 30, 1916, 86.

24. Mann, *Hugo Ball,* 85–94; Hohendahl, "Hugo Ball," 746.

25. Ball, *Flucht aus der Zeit,* April 11, 1917, 158.

26. Ibid., June 13, 1916, 99.

27. Hugo Ball, *Flametti oder vom Dandysmus der Armen* (Berlin, 1918), 161. See Mann, *Hugo Ball,* 62–66.

28. Ball, "Kandinsky," 47.

29. Ball, *Flucht aus der Zeit,* June 7, 1917, 172; Mann, *Hugo Ball,* 109.

30. See Martin Korol, "Einleitung," in Ernst Bloch, *Kampf, nicht Krieg: Politische Schriften 1917–1919* (Frankfurt am Main: Suhrkamp Verlag, 1985).

31. Bloch, who also repeated the charge, exempted Ball from culpability. See Martin Korol, "Hugo Ball: Korrespondenz mit Johann Wilhelm Muehlon," *Hugo Ball Almanach* 4 (1980): 59. The evidence for this charge remains inconclusive. Ball-Hennings, *Ruf und Echo,* 115; Mann, *Hugo Ball,* 111, 112. See, for example, Hugo Ball, "Propaganda hier und dort (31 August 1918)," in *Der Künstler und die Zeitkrankheit,* 226.

32. Hohendahl, "Hugo Ball," 750.

33. Ball, *Flucht aus der Zeit,* October 6, 1917, 205.

34. Ball, *Critique,* 5.

35. Ernst Bloch, "Über einige politische Programme und Utopien in der Schweiz," *Archiv für Sozialwissenschaft und Sozialpolitik* 46, no. 1 (1918): 161.

36. Ball, *Flucht aus der Zeit*, September 7, 1917, 198.

37. Ibid., September 26, 1917, 203.

38. Mann, *Hugo Ball*, 81.

39. Bloch, "Über einige politische Programme und Utopien," 161.

40. Ball, *Flucht aus der Zeit*, November 11, 1917, 213.

41. Mann, *Hugo Ball*, 114–115.

42. Hugo Ball, "Bakunin Brevier, Part I, 40," unpublished ms. Cited in Manfred Steinbrenner, "Theoretischer Anarchismus und 'Imitatio Christi': Zur Bedeutung der Einflussnahme Michail Bakunin's auf das Werk Hugo Balls," *Hugo Ball Almanach* 7 (1983): 75.

43. Ball, *Flucht aus der Zeit*, November 14, 1917, 212.

44. Ball-Hennings, *Ruf und Echo*, 121.

45. Ball, *Flucht aus der Zeit*, November 14, 1917, 213.

46. Mann, *Hugo Ball*, 116.

47. Ball, *Flucht aus der Zeit*, November 18, 1917, 213.

48. Ball-Hennings, *Ruf und Echo*, 124.

49. The citation stems from Bakunin's preface to his translation of Hegel's "Gymnasialrede." Ball, "Bakunin Brevier," pt. 1; cited in Steinbrenner, "Theoretischer Anarchismus," 73.

50. See chapter 1 and Michael Löwy, "Jewish Messianism and Libertarian Utopia in Central Europe (1900–1933)," *New German Critique* 20 (Spring/Summer 1980): 105–115.

51. On Bloch's wartime anticommunism, see Peter Zudeick, *Der Hintern des Teufels: Ernst Bloch—Leben und Werk* (Moos: Elster Verlag, 1985), 76.

52. Ball, *Flucht aus der Zeit*, December 5, 1917, 217; May 5, 1918, 231.

53. Ibid., April 28, 1918, 228.

54. Ball, *Critique*, 7.

55. Ball, *Flucht aus der Zeit*, April 15, 1918, 222.

56. Ibid., August 11, 1917, 184.

57. Ball-Hennings, *Ruf und Echo*, 120.

58. Ball, *Critique*, 124.

59. Hohendahl, "Hugo Ball," 750.

60. Hugo Ball, "Die deutsche "Demokratie" und Russland," in *Der Künstler und die Zeitkrankheit*, 205.

61. Ball, *Flucht aus der Zeit*, April 19, 1918, 223.

62. Ball-Hennings, *Ruf und Echo*, 124.

63. Ball, *Flucht aus der Zeit*, October 29, 1917, 211.

64. Ibid., July 17, 1918, 233.

65. Mann, *Hugo Ball*, 109, 110.

66. Hugo Ball, "Abbruch und Wiederaufbau," in *Der Künstler und die Zeitkrankheit*, 273.

67. Ball, *Critique*, 11.

68. Ball-Hennings, *Ruf und Echo*, 114.

69. Ibid., 153, 154.

70. Ball, *Flucht aus der Zeit,* August 11, 1917, 184, 185.

71. Ball-Hennings, *Ruf und Echo,* 158.

72. Hugo Ball, "Carl Schmitts Politische Theologie," in *Der Künstler und die Zeitkrankheit,* 303–335. Also see Joachim Schickel, *Gespräche mit Carl Schmitt* (Berlin: Merve Verlag, 1993), 31–59.

73. Review of the *Critique,* Paul von Mathies [PM], *Die Freie Zeitung* 3, no. 15 (February 19, 1919): 59.

74. Ball, *Flucht aus der Zeit,* February 17, 1919, 238.

75. Review of the *Critique,* Ernst Bloch, *Die Weltbühne* 15, no. 29 (1919): 53.

76. Ernst Bloch, "Über einige politische Programme und Utopien in der Schweiz," 162.

77. Gershom Scholem, *Walter Benjamin: The Story of a Friendship,* trans. Harry Zohn (Philadelphia: Jewish Publication Society of America, 1981), 79.

78. Ball, *Flucht aus der Zeit,* June 5, 1919, 247.

79. Ibid., July 31, 1918, 234.

80. Ball, *Critique,* 142–144.

81. Cited in Ball, *Critique,* 145.

82. Ball, *Critique,* 144.

83. Hugo Ball, "Die Umgehung der Instanzen" (November 16, 1918), in *Der Künstler und die Zeitkrankheit,* 233.

84. Ernst Bloch, *Briefe 1903–1975* (Frankfurt am Main: Suhrkamp Verlag, 1985), 1:232–233. The affair is discussed in Korol, "Einleitung," 51, 52. For an apologetic account that attributes Ball's anti-Semitism to Bloch's plagiarism of his ideas, see Volker Knüfermann, "Hugo Ball und Ernst Bloch als Beiträger der 'Freien Zeitung' Berne 1917–1919," *Hugo Ball Almanach* 12 (1988): 31–33.

85. Korol notes that no documentary evidence for a rupture exists in Ball's published writings. However, Knüfermann points out that Ball's letters indicate that tensions existed as early as 1918, when Ball charged that Bloch had used his "ideas without attribution." Knüfermann "risks the hypothesis that Ball, irritated by the earlier history of Bloch's plagiarism, saw in this publication [of Bloch's *Schadet Oder Nützt Deutschland eine Niederlage seines Militärs?* (Berne, 1918)] a new and heavier burden on their friendship, and that from this perspective the sharp utterance about 'anational Israelites' of 16 November 1918, might be explained." Knüfermann, "Hugo Ball und Ernst Bloch," 38; See also Korol, *Kampf nicht Krieg,* 52, and *Hugo Ball Briefe 1911–1927,* 119. Hennings mentions that an attempted visit to the Blochs in Thun that did not take place since the Blochs had already returned to Germany was "a great disappointment for Ball." Ball-Hennings, *Ruf und Echo,* 133.

86. Bloch, *Briefe,* I, 232, 233.

87. Ibid.

88. H. Herrigel, "Kritik der deutschen Intelligenz," *Frankfurter Zeitung* 752 (October 9, 1925). Cited in *Hugo Ball (1886–1986): Leben und Werk.* February 23 to March 31, 1986, Primasens (Berlin, 1986), 269.

89. Ball-Hennings, *Ruf und Echo,* 121.

90. Ibid., 128.

91. Ball, *Flucht aus der Zeit,* October 4, 1915, 46.
92. Hermann Bahr, "Zur Kritik der deutschen Intelligenz," *1919* (Leipzig, Vienna, and Zurich, 1920): 73–76.
93. Ball, "Abbruch und Wiederaufbau," in *Der Künstler und die Zeitkrankheit,* 293.
94. See, for example, Kuno Fischer, *Immanuel Kant* (Mannheim, 1860). See Hauke Brunkhorst, *Die Intellektuelle im Land der Mandarine* (Frankfurt am Main: Suhrkamp Verlag, 1987), 88.
95. Reinhart Koselleck, *Critique and Crisis: Enlightenment and the Pathogenesis of Modern Society* (Cambridge, Mass.: MIT Press, 1988), 11.
96. Ernst Bloch, "Anfragen," *Politische Messungen, Pestzeit, Vormärz, Ernst Bloch Gesamtausgabe* 11: 383.
97. Fritz Stern, *The Failure of Illiberalism: Essays on the Political Culture of Modern Germany* (Chicago: University of Chicago Press, 1971), 18, 19.
98. Primo Levi, "The Memory of Offense," in *Bitburg in Moral and Political Perspective,* ed. Geoffrey Hartman (Bloomington: Indiana University Press, 1986), 131.
99. Andreas Huyssen, "After the Wall: The Failure of German Intellectuals," *New German Critique* 52 (Winter 1991): 109.
100. Dan Diner, *America in the Eyes of the Germans: An Essay on Anti-Americanism,* trans. Allison Brown (Princeton: Markus Wiener, 1996), 108.
101. Günter Grass, *Deutscher Lastenausgleich: Wider das dumpfe Einheitsgebot. Reden und Gespräche* (Frankfurt am Main: Luchterhand, 1990), 11.
102. Peter Schneider, *The German Comedy: Scenes of Life after the Wall,* trans. Philip Boehm and Leigh Hafrey (New York: Farrar, Straus, Giroux, 1991), 76.
103. See, for example, Brigitte Seebacher-Brandt, *Die Linke und die Einheit* (Berlin: Corso bei Siedler, 1991), 22.

CHAPTER 3

1. The letter from Beaufret was brought to Heidegger by Jean-Michel Palmier in September or October 1945. Heidegger responded in a letter dated November 23, 1945, and Beaufret's first visit to Heidegger took place in September 1946. Heidegger's "Brief über den Humanismus" was sent to Beaufret in December, and he subsequently published a partial translation of the "Letter" by Joseph Rovain in the journal *Fontaine* 63 in November 1947.
2. Hannah Arendt, *Willing* (New York: Harcourt Brace Jovanovich, 1978), 188.
3. Theodor W. Adorno, *Jargon der Eigentlichkeit: Zur deutschen Ideologie* (Frankfurt am Main: Suhrkamp Verlag, 1964), 10.
4. Karl Löwith, *Martin Heidegger and European Nihilism,* ed. Richard Wolin, trans. Gary Steiner (New York: Columbia University Press, 1995), 39.
5. Martin Heidegger, *Gesamtausgabe* 9, *Wegmarken* (1919–1961) (Frankfurt am Main: Vittorio Klostermann, 1976), 313. (This standard edition will henceforth be referred to as *GA.*)

6. Hugo Ott, *Martin Heidegger: Unterwegs zu Seiner Biographie* (Frankfurt am Main: Campus, 1988), 293.

7. Letter from Louis Sauzin to René le Senne, Baden Baden, 17 December 1945, *La regle du jeu* 2, no. 4 (May 1991): 165.

8. "Letter to the Freiburg University Denazification Commission, December 22, 1945," in Richard Wolin, ed., *The Heidegger Controversy: A Critical Reader* (New York: Columbia University Press, 1991), 144–153; and Ott, *Martin Heidegger,* 315–317.

9. Letter from Louis Sauzin to René le Senne, 17 December 1945, *Le jeu de regle,* 166.

10. Ott, *Martin Heidegger,* 324.

11. Heidegger's collapse is described in Rüdiger Safranski, *Ein Meister aus Deutschland: Heidegger und seine Zeit* (Munich: Carl Hanser Verlag, 1994), 405.

12. For a comprehensive analysis of the relationship, see Herman Rapaport, *Heidegger and Derrida: Reflections on Time and Language* (Lincoln: University of Nebraska Press, 1989).

13. Martin Heidegger, "Letter on Humanism," in *Basic Writings,* ed. David Farrell Krell (San Francisco: Harper & Row, 1976), 199. (All subsequent references to this English translation appear in the text as LH.)

14. See Wolin, ed., *The Heidegger Controversy,* 29–40.

15. Richard J. Bernstein, *The New Constellation: The Ethical-Political Horizons of Modernity/Postmodernity* (Cambridge, Mass.: MIT Press, 1991), 79; Jürgen Habermas, "Work and *Weltanschauung:* The Heidegger Controversy from a German Perspective," in *The New Conservatism: Cultural Criticism and the Historians' Debate,* ed. and trans. Shierry Weber Nicholsen (Cambridge, Mass.: MIT Press, 1989), 142.

16. Victor Farias, *Heidegger and Nazism,* trans. Gabriel R. Ricci (Philadelphia: Temple University Press, 1989); Ott, *Martin Heidegger;* Richard Wolin, *The Politics of Being: The Political Thought of Martin Heidegger* (New York: Columbia University Press, 1990); Tom Rockmore, *On Heidegger's Nazism and Philosophy* (Berkeley and Los Angeles: University of California Press, 1992).

17. Hannah Arendt, "Martin Heidegger at Eighty," in *Heidegger and Modern Philosophy,* ed. Michael Murray (New Haven: Yale University Press, 1978), 301–302; Richard Rorty, "Taking Philosophy Seriously," *The New Republic* (April 11, 1988): 32–33.

18. Ernst Nolte, *Heidegger: Politik und Geschichte im Leben und Denken* (Frankfurt: Propyläen, 1992). For the most comprehensive survey of approaches to the relationship between politics and philosophy in the case of Heidegger, see Dieter Tomä, *Die Zeit des Selbst und die Zeit danach: Zur Kritik der Textgeschichte Martin Heideggers 1910-1976* (Frankfurt am Main: Suhrkamp Verlag, 1990), 469–474.

19. Philippe Lacoue-Labarthe, *Heidegger, Art, and Politics,* trans. Chris Turner (Oxford: Basil Blackwell, 1990), 86.

20. Gianni Vattimo, *The Adventure of Difference: Philosophy after Nietzsche and Heidegger* (Baltimore: Johns Hopkins University Press, 1993), 53.

21. Wolin, *The Politics of Being,* 16–66.

22. Luc Ferry and Alain Renault, *Heidegger and Modernity*, trans. Franklin Philip (Chicago: University of Chicago Press, 1990), 31–54.

23. Löwith, *Martin Heidegger*, 76; and Wolin, *The Politics of Being*, 144–146.

24. Habermas, "Work and *Weltanschauung*," 159.

25. See Rockmore, *On Heidegger's Nazism*; Otto Pöggeler, "Heidegger's Political Self-Understanding," in Wolin, *The Heidegger Controversy*, 198–244; Thomas Sheehan, "Heidegger and the Nazis," *New York Review of Books* (June 16, 1988): 38–47.

26. Otto Pöggeler, *Martin Heidegger's Path of Thinking*. With an Afterword to the Second Edition. Trans. David Magurshak and Sigmund Barber (Atlantic Highlands, N.J.: Humanities Press, 1987), 278. Cited in Wolin, *Politics of Being*, 192.

27. The proprietary and exclusionary policies of the Heidegger Archive in Freiburg are discussed in Josef Chytry, "The Timelessness of Martin Heidegger's National Socialism," *New German Critique* 58 (Winter 1993): 90, 91. Also see Jeffrey Andrew Barash, "Martin Heidegger in the Perspective of the Twentieth Century: Reflections on the Heidegger *Gesamtausgabe*," *Journal of Modern History* 64, no. 1 (March 1992): 52–69.

28. Martin Heidegger, *An Introduction to Metaphysics*, trans. Ralph Mannheim (New York: Anchor Books, 1961; German edition, 1953), 30.

29. Ibid., 31.

30. Ibid., 31, 32.

31. "Only a God Can Save Us": *Der Spiegel's* Interview with Martin Heidegger" (1966), in Wolin, *The Heidegger Controversy*, 113.

32. Heidegger, *Introduction to Metaphysics*, 31.

33. In his *Total Mobilization* (1930), Jünger argued that this task cannot be accomplished without a ruthless embrace of nihilism and technology as the only path to removing the obstacles to renewal—a view that Heidegger endorsed. On Heidegger's relationship to Jünger, see Wolin, *Politics of Being*, 88–92; Michael E. Zimmerman, *Heidegger's Confrontation with Modernity: Technology, Politics, Art* (Bloomington: Indiana University Press, 1990), 35–36.

34. *GA*, 40, 41. Also see Nicolas Tertulian, "Seinsgeschichte als Legitimation der Politik," in *Martin Heidegger—Faszination und Erschrecken: Die politische Dimension einer Philosophie*, ed. Peter Kemper (Frankfurt am Main: Campus, 1990), 51–71.

35. Heidegger, *Introduction to Metaphysics*, 31.

36. On Heidegger's "ideal Nazism," see Rockmore, *On Heidegger's Nazism*, 109–111 passim.

37. Heidegger's lecture is cited in Silvio Vietta, *Heideggers Kritik am Nationalsozialismus und an der Technik* (Tübingen: Max Niemayer, 1989), 19–47. The subsequent 1950 version published in *Holzwege* as "The Age of the World Picture" differs substantially from the original, substituting a general critique of technology for more specific references to historical examples derived from the Nazi movement, e.g., "der Wesensgestalt des Arbeiters u. des Soldaten." See Vietta, *Heideggers Kritik*, 36. Vietta's effort to depict Heidegger as an opponent of National Socialism is vastly exaggerated and not substantiated by the other-

wise interesting material that he, having had privileged access to the documentary material, brings to light. Heidegger's criticisms of the technology cult of National Socialism are at best indices of the failure of his own conception of Nazism, not of any overt rejection.

38. Rockmore, *On Heidegger's Nazism,* 204–205; Pöggeler, "Heidegger's Political Self-Understanding"; Wolin, *The Heidegger Controversy,* 223–229; Vietta, *Heideggers Kritik.*

39. *GA,* 65; *Beiträge zur Philosophie,* 19.

40. Pöggeler, "Heidegger's Self-Understanding," 205.

41. The story of Bottai's career and his relations with Grassi are documented in Farias, *Heidegger and Nazism,* 259–267. On Bottai, see G. B. Guerri, *Giuseppe Bottai, un fascista critico* (Milan: Rizzoli Editore, 1976).

42. Wilhelm Schäfer, *Wider die Humanisten: Eine Rede* (Munich: Albert Langen–Georg Müller Verlag, 1943), 7.

43. See Dietrich Strothmann, *Nationalsozialistische Literaturpolitik: Ein Beitrag zur Publizistik im Dritten Reich* (Bonn: H. Bouvier, 1960), 233.

44. Domenico Losurdo, "Heidegger and Hitler's War," in *The Heidegger Case,* ed. Tom Rockmore and Joseph Margolis (Philadelphia: Temple University Press, 1992), 145.

45. Losurdo, "Heidegger and Hitler's War," 146.

46. For example, in the lectures of the summer of 1941: "Geschichte bedeutet hier, dem Anschein nach zunächst wiederum willkürlich, *das Ereignis einer Entscheidung über das Wesen der Wahrheit.*" *GA,* 51:21.

47. Cited in Losurdo, "Heidegger and Hitler's War," 147, 151.

48. Ernst Krieck, "Die Geburt der Philosophie," *Volk im Werden* 10/11, no. 18 (1940): 229.

49. Ott, *Martin Heidegger,* 241.

50. Krieck, "Die Geburt der Philosophie," 230.

51. Ernesto Grassi, ed., *Geistige Überlieferung: Ein Jahrbuch* (Berlin: Verlag Helmut Küpper, 1940). Grassi began his studies in the neo-Hegelian tradition of Croce and Gentile in Milan, working subsequently with Husserl, Hartmann, Jaspers, and Heidegger in the early 1930s, when he became a fervent disciple. In 1938, under the auspices of Eugenio Castelli, director of the Istituto degli Studi Storici de Rome, Grassi founded an institute dedicated to the "Studia humanitatis," along with two German collaborators, Karl Reinach and Walter Otto. Presumably, *Geistige Überlieferung,* in which both Reinach and Otto published articles, was the product of this undertaking. Eventually Grassi's institute was closed because it was suspected of "resistance to Nazi pan-Germanism," though information about the precise circumstances is unavailable. After the war Grassi continued his efforts to refute Heidegger's philogermanic view that only German romanticism was capable of contacting the authentic core of Greek thought and that Italian humanism was only a "superficial aestheticism." On this theme, see Luce Fontaine-De Visscher, "Un débat sur l'humanisme Heidegger et E. Grassi," *Revue Philosophique de Louvain* 3 (August 1995): 285–330.

52. Ott, *Martin Heidegger,* 269.

53. Farias, *Heidegger and Nazism,* 262, 267, 268.

54. Wilhelm Brachmann, "Gegenwärtiger Humanismus," *Nationalsozialistischer Monatshefte,* Heft 140 (November 1941): 926–932. Also see Ott, *Martin Heidegger,* 268–273.

55. Brachmann, "Gegenwärtiger Humanismus," 932; Ott, *Martin Heidegger,* 270.

56. " . . . der Geist der griechischen Philosophie seit Nietzsche vernehmlicher als je zu uns spricht." E. Grassi and W. F. Otto, "Die Frage der geistigen Überlieferung, Zwei Briefe zur Bestimmung der Ausgabe," *Geistige Überlieferung,* 28.

57. Farias, *Heidegger and Nazism,* 262.

58. Ibid.; Ott, *Martin Heidegger,* 271.

59. Farias, *Heidegger and Nazism,* 263.

60. Wilhelm Brachmann, "Der gegenwärtige Humanismus: Ein Beitrag zur Geistes- und Glaubensgeschichte der Gegenwart," *Kant-Studien,* n.s., 44 (1944): 15.

61. Martin Heidegger, *Platon's Lehre von der Wahrheit* (Bern: Francke Verlag, 1947), 49.

62. Ibid.

63. Hans Drexler, *Der dritte Humanismus: Ein kritischer Epilog,* 2d ed. (Frankfurt am Main, 1942), 86.

64. Heidegger was not alone in this "Hellocentric" view, even if he considered himself its most profound thinker. It also characterizes the "higher" National Socialism of the neoclassical sculptor Arno Breker, the classicist Walter F. Otto, and Hitler's architect Albert Speer, all of whom were put off by the "vulgar" racism of the Nordic ideologues. These distinctions are important because they help locate Heidegger more clearly in the ideological matrix of National Socialism; they also begin to dissolve the monolithic view of National Socialist ideology that both Heidegger's defenders and critics often adopt. On antiquity and the Nietzsche cult in National Socialism, see Rockmore, *On Heidegger's Nazism,* 63.

65. "The consummation of Germany's defeat stimulated a new phase in Heidegger's reflection: now the war and the will to power themselves became expressions in their own right of the technical "massification" of the modern world." Losurdo, "Heidegger and Hitler's War," 156; Pöggeler, "Heidegger, Nietzsche, and Politics," in *The Heidegger Controversy,* 136, 137.

66. Martin Heidegger, *Was heisst Denken?* (Tübingen: Niemeyer, 1954), cited in Pöggeler, "Heidegger's Political Self-Understanding," 207.

67. Georg Lukács, "Heidegger Redivivus," *Sinn und Form* 1, no. 3 (Berlin, 1949): 37–62.

68. See the discussion of this point in Zimmerman, *Heidegger's Confrontation with Modernity,* 90–91.

69. *Martin Heidegger—Elisabeth Blochmann, Briefwechsel 1918–1969,* ed. Joachim W. Storck (Marbach am Neckar: Marbacher Schriften, 1990), 92.

70. Cited in Wolfgang Schirmacher, *Technik und Gelassenheit* (Freiburg: Alber, 1983), 37.

71. The exchange is translated in Wolin, *The Heidegger Controversy,* 152–164.

72. Heidegger's notorious silence has been the subject of many commentaries, including Jean-François Lyotard's *Heidegger and "the Jews,"* trans. Andreas

Michel and Mark Roberts (Minneapolis: University of Minnesota Press, 1990), which focuses on Heidegger's "forgetting" not merely the murder of the Jews but the entire history of the "Jewish" "West" as well. His interpretation ignores the fact that Heidegger was not merely silent about the fate of the Jews, but often defiant in his rage against the German catastrophe. For a more subtle account, see Berel Lang, *Heidegger's Silence* (Ithaca: Cornell University Press, 1996).

73. On this aspect of Heidegger's thought, see Wolin, *The Politics of Being,* 137–147.

74. Habermas, "Work and *Weltanschauung,*" 160.

75. This insight is John D. Caputo's, in *Demythologizing Heidegger* (Bloomington: Indiana University Press, 1993), 145.

76. Letter from Louis Sauzin to René le Senne, December 17, 1945, 165.

77. Arendt referred to these interviews as "inane lies with what I think is a clearly pathological streak." See Hannah Arendt to Karl Jaspers, July 9, 1946, *Correspondence of Hannah Arendt and Karl Jaspers 1926–1969,* ed. Lotte Kohler and Hans Saner, trans. Robert and Rita Kimber (New York: Harcourt Brace Jovanovich, 1992), 48. On Heidegger's first contacts with French intellectuals, see Jürg Altwegg, *Die Republik des Geistes: Frankreich's Intellektuelle zwischen Revolution und Reaktion* (Munich: R. Piper Verlag, 1989), 90–92; Jean-Michel Palmier, "Wege und Wirken Heideggers in Frankreich," in *Die Heidegger Kontroverse,* ed. Jürg Altwegg (Frankfurt am Main: Athenäum, 1988). On the French reception of Heidegger in the 1930s, see Pierre Aubenque, "Heidegger's Wirkungsgeschichte in Frankreich," in Kemper, ed., *Martin Heidegger—Faszination und Erschrecken,* 114–120.

78. Max Müller, *Existenzphilosophie im geistigen Leben der Gegenwart,* 3d ed. (Heidelberg: F. H. Kerle Verlag, 1964), 17.

79. See Otto Friedrich Bollnow, "Heidegger's neue Kehre," *Zeitschrift für Religions- und Geistesgeschichte* 2 (1949–1950): 113–128; Egon Vietta, "Being, World and Understanding: A Commentary on Heidegger" (trans. Susanne Jung-Bauer), *Review of Metaphysics* 5 (1951–1952): 157–172.

80. Adorno, *Jargon der Eigentlichkeit,* 16.

81. Beda Allemann, *Hölderlin und Heidegger,* 2d ed. (Zürich: Atlantis Verlag, 1956), 164; Bollnow, "Heidegger's neue Kehre," 113–128.

82. Quoted in Annie Cohen-Solal, *Sartre: A Life,* trans. Anna Cancogni (New York: Pantheon, 1987), 153.

83. The letter is published in Hugo Ott, "In der kleinen Skihütte zusammen philosphieren," *Frankfurter Allgemeine Zeitung,* January 19, 1994, 27. *Being and Time* was not translated into French until 1964. Even today there are two translations and a heated dispute over their legitimacy and adequacy. Heidegger's work began to appear in French translation in the 1930s with Henri Corbin's translation of "What Is Metaphysics?" and several other essays in 1937. For discussion of the reception of Heidegger in France and the semantic problems raised by Corbin's translation, see Michel Palmier, "Wege und Wirken Heideggers in Frankreich," 50, 51. Also see Palmier's *Les écrits politiques de Heidegger* (Paris: L'Herne, 1968).

84. Ott, "In der kleinen Skihütte," 27.

85. Ibid.

86. Alfred de Towarnicki's account and that of Maurice de Gandillac were the first partially false, and certainly apologetic, versions of Heidegger's involvement to appear in France. Those that challenged them, apart from Löwith, were among the most dogmatic and orthodox communists, such as Henri Lefebvre and Armand Cuvillier.

87. In the February 1946 issue of *Les Temps Modernes* Sartre introduced the debate with this comment: "The French press speaks of Heidegger as a Nazi; it is a fact that he was a member of the Nazi party. But if it were only a matter of judging a philosophy by the political courage and lucidity of the philosopher, Hegel's would not be worth much. One might conclude that a philosopher would be disloyal to his greatest thoughts if they resulted in political decisions." *Les Temps Modernes* 1, no. 4 (January 1946): 713. De Waehlens challenged Karl Löwith's account of the close connection between Heidegger's notion of historicity and the resolute decision for National Socialism by claiming that the notion of "authenticity" in *Being and Time* implied no political choices, apart from those that "reject Nazism and in its ideals" of nation, state, and war. Even those like the philosopher Eric Weill, who demurred, focused more on Heidegger's behavior after the war than on the connections between his philosophy and politics. On the debate in *Les Temps Modernes*, see Rockmore, *On Heidegger's Nazism*, 252–256; Jean Pierre Faye, "Heidegger und seine französischen Interpreten," in *Vermittler: Deutsch-französisches Jahrbuch 1*, ed. Jürgen Siess (Frankfurt am Main: Syndikat, 1981), 161–178.

88. Jean Beaufret, "A propos de l'existentialisme," *Confluences* 3 (April 1945): 307. In these articles Beaufret anticipated the argument of the "Letter" when he emphasized the distinction between Heidegger's notion of Dasein as a being-in-the-world that transcends subjectivity, conscience, or *ego* and Sartre's version of "L'etre," which is pure subjectivity redefined as radical liberty.

89. Jean Beaufret, *Entretiens avec Fréderic de Towarnicki* (Paris: PUF, 1984), 4.

90. See Michel Kajman, "Heidegger et le fil invisible," *Le Monde* (January 22, 1988), 1.

91. Jean Beaufret, "Qu'est-ce que l'existentialisme?" Interview par Henri Magnan, *Le Monde* 306 (December 11, 1945): 3; 310 (December 15, 1945): 3.

92. After the war, Sartre argued that this lapse of character was irrelevant to his philosophy. See *Les Temps Modernes* 1, no. 4 (January 1946): 713.

93. The remark is cited in Beaufret, "A propos de l'existentialisme," 314.

94. Jean Beaufret, "Martin Heidegger et le Problème de la Vérité," *Fontaine* 63 (November 1947): 758–785; Beaufret, *Entretiens*, 7.

95. He concentrated particularly on Armand Cuvillier (Percivax), author of an anti-Heideggerian pamphlet, *Les infiltrations germaniques dans la pensée française* (Paris: Éditions Universelles, 1945), and perhaps the first to portray Heidegger as "the metaphysician of Nazism." According to Cuvillier, the popularity of existentialism (Heidegger and Jaspers) in Germany during the 1920s and 1930s could only be explained by the totally desperate and hopeless situation of German youth, a state of mind that also explained the postwar Heidegger "craze" in France. Beaufret in turn accused Cuvillier of, among other

things, a profound ignorance of German thought, existentialism, and Marxism, as well as of an extreme chauvinism. (In response, Cuvillier cited the egregious lines of the Rectorial Address and pointed to Beaufret's tendentious coupling of Heidegger with anti-Nazism.) Jean Beaufret, "Vers une critique marxiste de l'existentialisme," *Revue Socialiste,* n.s., 2 (July 1946): 149–152; and the response by Cuvillier, in *Revue Socialiste* 4: 450–460.

96. Jean Beaufret, "Questions du Communisme, Entretiens-Réponse à la enquete de Roger Stéphane," *Confluences* 18–20 (1947): 43.

97. On this point see Tony Judt, *Past Imperfect: French Intellectuals, 1944–1956* (Berkeley and Los Angeles: University of California Press, 1992), 124. Also Maurice Merleau-Ponty, *Humanism and Terror: An Essay on the Communist Problem,* trans. John O'Neill (Boston: Beacon Press, 1971).

98. Herbert Marcuse, *Hegels Ontologie und der Grundlegung einer Theorie der Geschichtlichkeit* (Frankfurt am Main: Vittorio Klostermann Verlag, 1932); Kostas Axelos, *Marx, penseur de la technique: De l'aliénation de l'homme a la conquete du monde* (Paris: Editions de Minuit, 1969). Also see Karel Kosik, *Die Dialektik des Konkreten* (Frankfurt am Main: Lüchterhand, 1967); Enzo Paci, "Towards a New Phenomenology," *Telos* 5 (Spring 1970): 58–81; and the discussion in Martin Jay, *Marxism and Totality: The Adventures of a Concept from Lukács to Habermas* (Berkeley: University of California Press, 1984).

99. Jacques Derrida, "The Ends of Man," in *Margins of Philosophy,* trans. Alan Bass (Chicago: University of Chicago Press, 1982), 108–136. All subsequent references appear in the text as EM.

100. Jacques Derrida, "Violence and Metaphysics: An Essay on the Thought of Emannuel Levinas," in *Writing and Difference,* trans. Alan Bass (Chicago: University of Chicago Press, 1978), 89. All subsequent references appear in the text as VM.

101. Tzvetan Todorov, *Times Literary Supplement* (June 17–23, 1988): 676.

102. See, for example, Alan D. Schrift, "Foucault and Derrida on Nietzsche and the End(s) of 'Man,' " in *Exceedingly Nietzsche: Aspects of Contemporary Nietzsche Interpretation,* ed. David Farrell Krell and David Wood (London: Routledge, 1988), 146.

103. Habermas, "Work and *Weltanschauung,*" 165.

104. See Bernstein, *The New Constellation,* 79–141.

105. Dominique Janicaud, "Reconstructing the Political," *Heidegger and the Political: The Graduate Faculty Philosophy Journal* 14, no. 2; 15, no. 1 (1991): 139.

106. Jacques Derrida, *Of Spirit: Heidegger and the Question,* trans. Geoffrey Bennington and Rachel Bowlby (Chicago: University of Chicago Press, 1989). Subsequent references appear in the text as OS.

107. Pöggeler, "Heidegger's Self-Understanding," 277.

108. Lacoue-Labarthe, *Heidegger, Art and Politics,* 86.

109. Ibid., 95.

110. Jacques Derrida, "Philosophers' Hell: An Interview," in Wolin, *The Heidegger Controversy,* 269.

111. Ferry and Renaut, *Heidegger and Modernity,* 103.

112. See Robert Hullot-Kentor, "Back to Adorno," *Telos* 81 (Fall 1989): 13.

CHAPTER 4

1. Heidegger's notorious silence has been the subject of many commentaries; see chapter 3, note 72. A rather acrimonious debate was provoked by Jacques Derrida's suggestion that Heidegger's silence was a perhaps not unconscious strategy to force us to read him in light of his political involvement, whereas a confession would have been an invitation to neglect the connection between his politics and philosophy. Jacques Derrida, "Philosophers' Hell: An Interview," in Richard Wolin, *The Heidegger Controversy: A Critical Reader* (New York: Columbia University Press, 1991), 269. For a discussion of this interview and the controversy, see Wolin's introduction to the second edition published by MIT Press.

2. An exception is Alan M. Olson, ed., *Heidegger and Jaspers* (Philadelphia: Temple University Press, 1994).

3. Hans Saner, *Karl Jaspers: Mit Selbstzeugnissen und Bilddokumenten* (Hamburg: Rowholt, 1970), 147.

4. Hannah Arendt, "Karl Jaspers: A Laudatio," in *Men in Dark Times* (New York: Harcourt, Brace & World, 1955), 74.

5. Karl Jaspers, "Nachwort 1962, Über meine 'Schuldfrage,' in *Die Schuldfrage* (Munich: Piper Verlag, 1965), 84.

6. Moses Moskowitz, "The Germans and the Jews: Postwar Report," *Commentary*, no. 1–2 (1946): 8. Cited in Frank Stern, *Im Anfang war Auschwitz: Antisemitismus und Philosemitismus im deutschen Nachkrieg* (Tel Aviv: Bleicher Verlag, 1991), 11.

7. Carl Schmitt, *Ex Captivitate Salus: Erfahrungen der Zeit 1945/47* (Cologne, 1950), 70. Cited in Helmut Lethen, *Verhaltenslehren der Kälte: Lebensversuche zwischen den Kriegen* (Frankfurt am Main: Suhrkamp Verlag, 1994), 219. Schmitt composed this little ditty about Jaspers:

> Wie hat sein Bußgerede mich empört
> Wie ekelt mir vor seinen faulen Fischen
> Jetzt ist er endlich, wo er hingehört:
> Im Spiegel und der Deutschen Telewischen.

> [How he outraged me with his talk of atoning
> How he disgusted me by his lazy fishin'
> Now he is finally where he belongs:
> In *Der Spiegel* and on German television.]

8. On Jaspers in the press of the German Democratic Republic, see Wolfgang Schneider, *Tanz der Derwische: Von Umgang mit der Vergangeheit im widervereinigten Deutschland* (Lüneberg: Zu Klampen, 1992), 94.

9. T. W. Adorno, *Jargon der Eigentlichkeit* (Frankfurt am Main: Suhrkamp Verlag, 1964). According to Adorno, the excessively theological vocabulary of the text, with its emphasis on words like "covenant," "calling," "encounter," and "authentic conversation," was not merely imprecise and evasive; the words used were the very same euphemisms that the Nazi terror itself hid behind. It

was a vocabulary so banal and so elevated, so removed from events, that even the ubiquitous demand for authentic communication prevented it from taking place at all.

10. See Klaus von Beyme, "Karl Jaspers—Vom Philosphischen Aussenseiter zum Praeceptor Germaniae," in *Heidelberg 1945*, ed. Jürgen C. Hess, Hartmut Lehmann, and Volker Sollin (Stuttgart: Franz Steiner Verlag, 1996), 130–148.

11. Karl Jaspers, "A Reply to My Critics," in *The Philosophy of Karl Jaspers*, ed. Paul Arthur Schlipp (LaSalle, Ill.: Open Court, 1981), 753.

12. Karl Jaspers, "Heidegger" (1981), in *The Philosophy of Karl Jaspers*, 75/12.

13. See Hugo Ott, *Martin Heidegger: Unterwegs zu seine Biographie* (Frankfurt: Campus, 1988), 339; and Hugo Ott, "Martin Heidegger und der Nationalsozialismus," in *Heidegger und die praktische Philosophie*, ed. Annemarie Gethmann-Siefert and Otto Pöggeler (Frankfurt am Main: Suhrkamp Verlag, 1988), 66.

14. Hannah Arendt, *The Life of the Mind*. Vol. 2. *Willing* (New York: Harcourt Brace Jovanovich, 1978), 200.

15. Saner, *Karl Jaspers*, 48. Initially, Jaspers did attempt to emigrate to Basel where he repeatedly was offered a teaching post.

16. See Seyla Benhabib, "Kritik des 'postmodernen Wissens': Eine Auseinandersetzung mit Jean-François Lyotard, *Postmoderne: Zeichen eines kulturellen Wandels*," ed. Andreas Huyssen and Klaus Scherpe (Hamburg: RoRoRo, 1986), 103–127.

17. Jürgen Habermas, "On the Public Use of History," in *The New Conservatism: Cultural Criticism and the Historians' Debate*, ed. and trans. Shierry Weber Nicholsen (Cambridge, Mass.: MIT Press, 1989), 233.

18. The Lambert Schneider Verlag was licensed in Heidelberg by the U.S. Military Information Control Division shortly after the publisher Lambert Schneider emerged from hiding in a Hessian village. Schneider also published *Die Wandlung*, which Dolf Sternberger edited, and Alexander Mitscherlich's report on the Nuremberg Doctor's Trial, *Das Diktat der Menschenverachtung*. Apart from the preface, I rely throughout on the later edition: Karl Jaspers, *Die Schuldfrage: Von der politischen Haftung Deutschlands* (Munich: R. Piper Verlag, 1987). All references in parentheses refer to this edition.

19. Karl Jaspers, *Die Schuldfrage*, 1st ed. (Heidelberg: Verlag Lambert Schneider, 1946), 12.

20. Daniel Penham, "Report to 307th Counter Intelligence Corps Detachment Headquarters Seventh United States Army," February 23, 1946, 7. Crum Papers, Marshall Research Library, Lexington, Va. A copy of the report was kindly provided to the author by Professor Daniel Penham.

21. Karl Jaspers to Hannah Arendt, September 18, 1946, in *Correspondence of Hannah Arendt and Karl Jaspers, 1926–1969*, ed. Lotte Kohler and Hans Saner, trans. Robert Kimber and Rita Kimber (New York: Harcourt Brace Jovanovich, 1992), 58. All subsequent references to the English-language edition of the Correspondence are noted as *Correspondence* unless otherwise indicated.

22. This conflict is described in Renato de Rosa, ed., *Karl Jaspers Erneuer-*

ung der Universität: Rede und Schriften 1945/6 (Heidelberg: Verlag Lambert Schneider, 1986), 402, 403. However, de Rosa's account is partial to Bauer and does not do justice to the situation produced by Penham's arrival, uncritically adopting the faculty's opinion of Penham's character as "pathological." In fact, both Penham and the Harvard sociologist Captain Edward Y. Hartshorne were equally mistrustful of Bauer and were overruled by Major Earl L. Crum, who wanted to dispense with elaborate denazification procedures. The story is best told by Uta Gerhardt, "Die Amerikanischen Militäroffiziere und der Konflikt um die Wiederöffnung der Universität Heidelberg," in *Heidelberg 1945*, 30–54, and James F. Tent, "Edward Yarnall Hartshorne and the Reopening of the Ruprecht-Karls-Universität in Heidelberg, 1945: His Personal Account," in *Heidelberg 1945*, 55–81.

23. As Prof. Dr. Eike Wolgast points out, Bauer was sympathetic to the 1934 eugenic laws to "protect against hereditary illnesses" but was not himself a Nazi. See Eike Wolgast, "Karl Heinrich Bauer—der erste Heidelberger Nachkriegsrektor: Weltbild und Handeln 1945–1946," in *Heidelberg 1945*, 107–129.

24. Conversation with Daniel Penham, Heidelberg, Germany, May 1992.

25. This version is repeated without comment by de Rosa, who also writes that Penham's judgment was clouded by resentment and that he obsessively pursued matters that were long since resolved. See de Rosa, *Karl Jaspers*, 400.

26. On Jaspers's admiration for Bauer, see Wolgast, "Karl Heinrich Bauer."

27. See the letter from Karl Jaspers to Fritz Ernst, cited in de Rosa, *Karl Jaspers*, 412. According to Jaspers, when Penham confronted him demanding to know who had drafted the Senate document, Jaspers assumed responsibility, though it was apparently Ernst who had drafted it.

28. Karl Jaspers, "Philosophical Autobiography," in *The Philosophy of Karl Jaspers*, 69.

29. For Jaspers's views on the university, see de Rosa, *Karl Jaspers*, 400–422.

30. See Klaus von Beyme, "Karl Jaspers: Vom Philosphischen Aussenseiter zum Praeceptor Germaniae," in *Heidelberg 1945*, 130–148.

31. For a useful, if partisan, account of the conditions under which the Stuttgart declaration came about, see Walter Bodenstein, *Ist der Besiegte Schuldig? Kritischer Rückblick auf das Stuttgarter Schuldbekenntnis* (Asendorf: Mut Verlag, 1985).

32. Nachlass Karl Jaspers, Basel. Cited in de Rosa, *Karl Jaspers*, 374.

33. Dolf Sternberger, "Jaspers und der Staat," in *Karl Jaspers Werk und Wirkung: Zum 80 Geburtstag Karl Jaspers* (Munich: R. Piper Verlag, 1963), 133.

34. Ibid., 134.

35. See Ralf Dahrendorf, "Kulturpessemismus vs. Forschrittshoffnung: Eine Notwendige Abgrenzung," in *Stichworte zur 'Geistigen Situation der Zeit,'* Bd. 1: Nation und Republik, ed. Jürgen Habermas (Frankfurt am Main: Suhrkamp Verlag, 1979), 223.

36. Karl Jaspers, *Die geistige Situation der Zeit* (Berlin: Sammlung Göschen, 1932), 142 f.

37. Sternberger, "Jaspers und der Staat," 135.

38. Max Weber, *Ancient Judaism*, ed. and trans. Hans H. Gerth and Don Martindale (New York: Free Press, 1952), 327. For a comprehensive discussion of Weber and Judaism, see Gary A. Abraham, *Max Weber and the Jewish Question* (Urbana: University of Illinois Press, 1992).

39. Hannah Arendt, "The Jew as Pariah: A Hidden Tradition" (April 1944), in *The Jew as Pariah: Jewish Identity and Politics in the Modern Age*, ed. Ron H. Feldman (New York: Grove Press, 1978), 67–91.

40. Jaspers to Arendt, May 16, 1947, *Correspondence*, 87.

41. Karl Jaspers, "Philosophical Autobiography," 64.

42. Weber, *Ancient Judaism*, 327.

43. Karl Jaspers, "Philosophical Autobiography," 64.

44. Karl Jaspers, "Geleitwort für die Zeitschrift 'Die Wandlung,' 1945" in de Rosa, ed., *Karl Jaspers*, 111.

45. Hannah Arendt, "Jaspers as Citizen of the World," in *The Philosophy of Karl Jaspers*, 541.

46. Ibid.

47. Ibid., 543.

48. Habermas's contribution to the change of paradigm in critical theory is specifically centered on an intersubjective understanding of communication that substitutes a more encompassing theory of communicative rationality for the philosophy of consciousness. For a detailed discussion, see Jürgen Habermas, *The Theory of Communicative Action*, vol. 1, trans. Thomas McCarthy (Boston: Beacon Press, 1984), 389, 390.

49. Cited in Sternberger, "Jaspers und der Staat," 137.

50. See, for example, Karl Jaspers, "Erneuerung der Universität," in de Rosa, ed., *Karl Jaspers*, 93–105.

51. Jaspers, "Geleitwort für die Zeitschrift 'Die Wandlung' 1945," 109.

52. Ibid.

53. Ibid., 110.

54. Ibid., 109.

55. Karl Jaspers, "Philosophical Autobiography," 68, 69.

56. Ibid.

57. See Martin Löw-Beer, "Verschämter oder missionarischer Völkermord? Eine Analyse des Nürnberger Prozesses," *Babylon: Beiträge zur jüdischen Gegenwart*, Heft 1 (1986): 55–69.

58. For a critical study of the Morgenthau plan and its propagandistic uses in postwar Germany, see Bernd Greiner, "Mit Sigmund Freud im Apfelhain— oder Was Deutsche in 45 Jahren über Henry Morgenthau gelernt haben," *Mittelweg* 35, no. 3 (1992): 44, 45.

59. Karl Jaspers, "Von der biblischen Religion," *Die Wandlung*, Jg. 1, Heft 5 (1945–1946): 408.

60. Jaspers to Arendt, May 3, 1947, *Correspondence*, 84.

61. Jaspers to Arendt, May 16, 1947, *Correspondence*, 88.

62. Arendt, "Jaspers as Citizen of the World," 541.

63. Ibid., 549.

64. Cited in de Rosa, *Karl Jaspers*, 295.

65. Habermas, "Karl Jaspers: The Figures of Truth (1958)," 47.

66. Jaspers to Arendt, October 19, 1946, *Correspondence*, 62, 63.

67. Above all, in 1930 Jaspers rejected her linkage of "Jewish existence" with a particular historical destiny: "You objectify 'Jewish existence' existentially—and in doing so perhaps cut existential thinking off at the roots. The concept of being-thrown-back-on-oneself can no longer be taken altogether seriously if it is *grounded* in terms of the fate of the Jews instead of being rooted in itself." Karl Jaspers to Hannah Arendt, March 30, 1930, *Correspondence*, 10.

68. Jaspers to Arendt, May 16, 1947, *Correspondence*, 87.

69. Hannah Arendt to Karl Jaspers, August 17, 1946, *Correspondence*, 56.

70. Arendt to Jaspers, June 30, 1947, *Correspondence*, 90.

71. Hannah Arendt, "The Moral of History," in *The Jew as Pariah*, 107.

72. Arendt to Jaspers, June 30, 1947, *Correspondence*, 91.

73. Hannah Arendt to Kurt Blumenfeld, October 14, 1952, *Hannah Arendt—Kurt Blumenfeld* " . . . in keimem Besitz verwurzelt." Die Korrespondenz, ed. Ingeborg Nordmann and Iris Pilling (Hamburg: Rotbuch Verlag, 1995), 68.

74. Elisabeth Young-Bruehl, *Hannah Arendt: For Love of the World* (New Haven: Yale University Press, 1982), 216.

75. Arendt was indeed successful in securing a translation published by Dial Press as *The Question of German Guilt*, trans. E. B. Ashton, in 1947.

76. Cited in Young-Bruehl, *Hannah Arendt*, 216.

77. Hannah Arendt to Karl Jaspers, August 17, 1946, *Correspondence*, 53.

78. Ibid., 54.

79. Hannah Arendt, "Organized Guilt and Universal Responsibility," in *The Jew as Pariah*, 230.

80. Arendt to Jaspers, August 17, 1946, *Correspondence*, 54.

81. Hannah Arendt, "The Image of Hell," *Commentary*, no. 2–3 (September 1946): 291–295.

82. Jaspers to Arendt, October 19, 1946, *Correspondence*, 62.

83. Adorno, *Jargon der Eigentlichkeit*, 16.

84. Arendt to Jaspers, August 17, 1946, *Correspondence*, 54.

85. See the discussion of this theme in Agnes Heller and Ferenc Féher, *The Postmodern Political Condition* (New York: Columbia University Press, 1989), 85.

86. Hannah Arendt, "What Is Existential Philosophy?" in *Essays in Understanding 1930–1954*, ed. Jerome Kohn and Hannah Arendt (New York: Harcourt Brace, 1994), 163–187. See also the instructive article by Margaret Canovan, "Socrates or Heidegger? Hannah Arendt's Reflections on Philosophy and Politics," *Social Research* 57, no. 1 (Spring 1990): 137.

87. Arendt, "What Is Existential Philosophy?" 183.

88. Karl Jaspers to Martin Heidegger, March 25, 1950, *Martin Heidegger—Karl Jaspers, Briefwechsel 1920–1963*, ed. Walter Biemel and Hans Saner (Frankfurt am Main: Vittorio Klostermann; Munich: R. Piper Verlag, 1990), 199. Hereafter cited as *Heidegger—Jaspers Briefwechsel*.

89. Heidegger to Jaspers, March 7, 1950, *Heidegger—Jaspers Briefwechsel*, 196, 197.

90. Ibid., 194.

91. Ibid., 195.

92. Karl Jaspers to Hannah Arendt, January 7, 1951, *Correspondence*, 161, 162.

93. Arendt to Jaspers, March 4, 1951, *Correspondence*, 167, 168.

94. Arendt to Jaspers, September 29, 1949, *Correspondence*, 142. Young-Bruehl, *Hannah Arendt*, 246, 247. See also Elzbieta Ettinger, *Hannah Arendt—Martin Heidegger* (New Haven: Yale University Press, 1995), 66–78. Ettinger misattributes Arendt's remark, "You see: I have a bad conscience," to her attitude toward Heidegger's "wartime behavior" (meaning the Rectorate?) and not, as it is clearly intended here, to her having elicited the letter to Jaspers.

95. "Letter to the Freiburg University Denazification Commission, December 22, 1945," in Wolin, *The Heidegger Controversy*, 144–153; and Ott, *Heidegger*, 315–317. It is clear from their correspondence that Heidegger was aware of the letter and its contents.

96. Karl Jaspers, *Notizen zu Martin Heidegger*, ed. Hans Saner (Munich: R. Piper Verlag, 1989), 104. Hereafter cited in the text within parentheses as *N*.

97. Jaspers, "Philosophical Autobiography," 75/12.

98. Paul Hühnerfeld, "Philosophen prägen das Bild der Zeit: Sartre und Jaspers in neuen Büchern," *Die Zeit*, December 1, 1949, 9. Cited in *Heidegger—Jaspers Briefwechsel*, 285.

99. Ibid., 286. The letter appeared in *Die Zeit*, December 22, 1949, 12.

100. See Jaspers, "Philosophical Autobiography," 75/10.

101. Ibid.

102. Jürgen Habermas, "Work and *Weltanschauung*: The Heidegger Controversy from a German Perspective," in *The New Conservatism*, 142.

103. Hannah Arendt, *The Life of the Mind*. Vol. 2: *Willing* (New York: Harcourt Brace Jovanovich, 1978), 200.

104. Habermas, "Karl Jaspers," 51, 52.

105. Karl Jaspers, *Die geistige Situation der Zeit* (1931). English translation: *Man in the Modern Age*, trans. Eden Paul and Cedar Paul (New York: Doubleday, 1952), 127.

106. Jaspers to Heidegger, September 9, 1922, *Heidegger—Jaspers Briefwechsel*, 32.

107. Heidegger to Jaspers, July 14, 1923, *Heidegger—Jaspers Briefwechsel*, 42.

108. Jaspers to Heidegger, August 23, 1933, *Heidegger—Jaspers Briefwechsel*, 155.

109. Jessica Benjamin, *The Bonds of Love: Psychoanalysis, Feminism, and the Problem of Domination* (New York: Pantheon, 1988), 120.

110. Jaspers to Heidegger, March 19, 1950, *Heidegger—Jaspers Briefwechsel*, 198.

111. Heidegger to Jaspers, April 8, 1950, *Heidegger—Jaspers Briefwechsel*, 200.

112. Ibid., 201.

113. Ibid., 202.

114. Ibid., 210.

115. Ibid., 173.

116. Ibid., 211.

117. Theodor W. Adorno, *Jargon der Eigentlichkeit: Zur deutschen Ideologie* (Frankfurt am Main: Suhrkamp Verlag, 1964), 9.

118. See Anson Rabinbach, "The Jewish Question in the German Question," in *Reworking the Past: Hitler, the Holocaust and the Historians' Debate,* ed. Peter Baldwin (Boston: Beacon Press, 1990), 45–73.

119. Karl Jaspers, *Max Weber* (Munich: R. Piper Verlag, 1988), 126.

120. Karl Jaspers, *Freiheit und Wiederveiningung* (Munich: R. Piper Verlag, 1960), 53. Also cited in Schneider, *Tanz der Derwische,* 99.

121. Jaspers, *Freiheit und Wiedervereinigung,* 53.

122. Günter Grass, *Deutscher Lastenausgleich: Wider das dumpfe Einheitsgebot* (Frankfurt am Main: Luchterhand, 1990), 11.

123. For example, Heimo Schwilk and Ulrich Schacht, eds., *Die Selbst-Bewusste Nation. "Anschwellender Bockgesang" und weitere Beiträge zu einer deutschen Debatte* (Berlin: Ullstein, 1994).

124. Willy Brandt, Foreword to Karl Jaspers, *Freiheit und Wiedervereinigung* (Munich: R. Piper Verlag, 1990), 3.

125. Jürgen Habermas, "Historical Consciousness and Post-Traditional Identity," in *The New Conservatism,* 251, 252.

126. Habermas, "On the Public Use of History," in *The New Conservatism,* 233.

127. Ott, *Martin Heidegger,* 317.

CHAPTER 5

1. For an overview and indispensable guide to the problems of authorship and composition of *Dialectic of Enlightenment,* see Gunzelin Schmid Noerr, "Nachwort des Herausgebers: Die Stellung der 'Dialektik der Aufklärung' in der Entwicklung der Kritischen Theorie. Bemerkungen zu Autorschaft, entstehung, einigen theoretischen Implikationen und späterer Einschätzung durch die Autoren," in *Max Horkheimer Gesammelte Schriften,* Bd. 5, ed. Alfred Schmidt and Gunzelin Schmid Noerr (Frankfurt am Main: Fischer Verlag, 1987), 423–452 (hereafter cited as *GS*5).

2. See especially Rolf Wiggershaus, *Die Frankfurter Schule: Geschichte, Theoretische Entwicklung, Politische Bedeutung* (Munich: Hanser Verlag, 1986), 338–383.

3. Max Horkheimer and Theodor W. Adorno, *Dialectic of Enlightenment,* trans. John Cumming (New York: Seabury Press, 1972), ix (hereafter cited as *DE*); and *GS*5, "Dialektik der Aufklärung und Schriften 1940-1950," 13. For the documentation, see Alfred Schmidt and Gunzelin Schmid Noerr, eds., *Max Horkheimer Gesammelte Schriften,* Bd. 12, "Nachgelassene Schriften 1931–1949" (Frankfurt am Main: Fischer Verlag, 1985) (hereafter cited as *GS*12).

4. *GS*5, 486.

5. *GS*5, 427–429.

6. Robert Hullot-Kentor, "Back to Adorno," *Telos* 81 (Fall 1989): 8.

7. Cited in Gunzelin Schmid Noerr, "Nachwort," *GS*5, 430.

8. See, for example, *GS12*, 19.1.1939; 23.1.1939.

9. Cited in Wiggershaus, *Frankfurter Schule*, 361.

10. Max Horkheimer, "The End of Reason," *Studies in Philosophy and Social Science* IX (1941): 370.

11. Jürgen Habermas, *The Philosophical Discourse of Modernity: Twelve Lectures*, trans. Frederick Lawrence (Cambridge, Mass.: MIT Press, 1987), 120, 121.

12. Jürgen Habermas, "Remarks on the Development of Horkheimer's Work," in *On Max Horkheimer*, ed. Seyla Benhabib, Wolfgang Bonss, and John McCole (Cambridge, Mass.: MIT Press, 1993), 51, 56, 57.

13. Habermas, *Philosophical Discourse*, 117. Richard Wolin also claims that though it was "allegedly jointly dictated by Horkheimer and Adorno, the work's basic theoretical inclinations seem to be overwhelmingly indebted to Adorno's influences and proclivities. In fact, its fundamental argument tended to contradict not only the institute's previous positions on Western philosophy, metaphysics, and so forth, but also its philosophy of history, which had been, in the Marxist tradition, basically progressivist." Richard Wolin, *The Terms of Cultural Criticism: The Frankfurt School, Existentialism, Poststructuralism* (New York: Columbia University Press, 1992), 41.

14. Habermas, "Remarks on the Development of Horkheimer's Work," in *On Max Horkheimer*, 57.

15. Letter, Theodor W. Adorno to Max Horkheimer, February 22, 1937, Max Horkheimer Correspondence. Max Horkheimer-Archiv, Stadt und Universitätsbibliothek, Frankfurt am Main (hereafter cited as MHA). Also in *Max Horkheimer Gesammelte Schriften*, Bd. 16, *Briefswechsel 1937–1940*, 50 (hereafter cited as *GS16*).

16. This remark obviously alludes to Adorno's now famous 1933 review attempting to accommodate to the Nazi regime in the hope that it would soon collapse. Theodor W. Adorno to Max Horkheimer, May 9, 1945, *Max Horkheimer Gesammelte Schriften*, Bd. 17, *Briefwechsel 1941–1948* (Frankfurt am Main: Fischer Verlag, 1996), 634. For a discussion of the 1933 incident, see Wiggershaus, *Frankfurter Schule*, 180.

17. Alfred Schmidt, "Max Horkheimer's Intellectual Physiognomy," in *On Max Horkheimer*, 32.

18. See Herbert Schädelbach, "Max Horkheimer and the Moral Philosophy of German Idealism," in *On Max Horkheimer*, 290.

19. Hullot-Kentor, "Back to Adorno," 13.

20. Theodor W. Adorno, "Zur Philosophie der neuen Musik," cited in Wiggershaus, *Frankfurter Schule*, 340.

21. MHA, Horkheimer to Adorno, November 11, 1941.

22. See Anson Rabinbach, Review of Seyla Benhabib, Wolfgang Bonss, and John McCole, eds., *On Max Horkheimer: New Perspectives*, in *German Politics and Society* 33 (Fall 1994): 157–162.

23. Max Horkheimer, "The Present Situation of Social Philosophy," in *Between Philosophy and Social Science: Selected Early Writings*, trans. G. Frederick Unger, Matthew S. Kramer, and John Torpey (Cambridge, Mass.: MIT Press, 1993), 3.

24. *GS*12, 371. For a lucid discussion of Adorno's relationship to Benjamin on this point, see Susan Buck-Morss, *The Origin of Negative Dialectics: Theodor W. Adorno, Walter Benjamin and the Frankfurt Institute* (New York: Free Press, 1977), 85, 86.

25. *GS*12, 371.

26. Ibid., 473.

27. Ibid., 474.

28. Ibid., 472.

29. Ibid., 473.

30. Ibid., 506.

31. Ibid., 508.

32. Ibid., 492.

33. Theodor W. Adorno, *Kierkegaard: Construction of the Aesthetic,* trans. Robert Hullot-Kentor (Minneapolis: University of Minnesota Press, 1989), 114 (hereafter cited in the text as *K*).

34. *GS*12, 509.

35. Ibid.

36. This characterization of their differences is in part indebted to Benjamin Snow [pseud. for Susan Buck-Morss], "Introduction to Adorno's 'The Actuality of Philosophy,'" *Telos* 31 (Spring 1977): 117. Her apt characterization reads: "Adorno, the metaphysician with no faith in metaphysics; Horkheimer, the moralist with no belief in Divine Providence."

37. *GS*12, 507.

38. MHA, Adorno to Horkheimer, June 12, 1941. Also see *GS*17, 60, 61. On Benjamin's letter to Gretel Adorno and Adorno's comment that it represented his testament, see Walter Benjamin, *Gesammelte Schriften* I:3, ed. Rolf Tiedemann and Hermann Schweppenhäuser (Frankfurt am Main: Suhrkamp Verlag, 1980), 1223. Benjamin's letter was unsent but arrived with the manuscript in June 1941.

39. MHA, Adorno to Horkheimer, June 12, 1941. In thesis XVI Benjamin wrote, "Er überläßt es andern, bei der Hure 'Es war einamal' im Bordell des Historismus sich auszubeben." Benjamin, *Gesammelte Schriften,* I:2, 702. The word *whore* appears in typescript, the words *ratio* and *reden* in handwriting. Interestingly, *ratio* is replaced by *degredativ* in the published version of the letter, *GS*17, 61, but the latter does not appear in the manuscript.

40. Theodor Adorno and Max Horkheimer, "Odysseus or Myth and Enlightenment," *New German Critique* 56 (Spring/Summer 1992), 139 (hereafter cited in the text as *O*). Robert Hullott-Kentor's translation is often superior to Cummings's, but both have been consulted.

41. Theodor W. Adorno, *Minima Moralia: Reflections from a Damaged Life,* trans. E. F. N. Jephcott (London: Verso, 1974), 39.

42. Claude Lévi-Strauss, *Totemism,* trans. Rodney Needham (Boston: Beacon Press, 1963), 3.

43. Adorno's use of the category of mimesis is exhaustively treated in Josef Früchtl, *Mimesis: Konstellation eines Zentralbegriffs bei Adorno* (Würzburg, 1986). For a historical survey of the uses of the term from the classical writers through modern anthropology and aesthetics, see Christoph Wulf, "Mimesis,"

in Gunter Gebauer et al., *Historische Anthropologie: Zum Problem der Human-wissenschaften heute oder Versuche einer Neubegründung* (Reinbek bei Hamburg: Rowohlt, 1989), 83–126; and for a contemporary use of the category in the analysis of violence and its taming, see René Girard, *Violence and the Sacred*, trans. Patrick Gregory (Baltimore: Johns Hopkins University Press, 1977), 78, 79, and passim.

44. Theodor W. Adorno, *Negative Dialectics*, trans. E. B. Ashton (New York: Seabury Press, 1973), 44, 45. Cited in Buck-Morss, *Origin of Negative Dialectics*, 90. Also see Hauke Brunkhorst, *Theodor W. Adorno: Dialektik der Moderne* (Munich: R. Piper Verlag, 1990), 293.

45. Martin Jay, "Mimesis und Mimetologie: Adorno und Lacoue-Labarthe," in *Auge und Affekt: Wahrnehmung und Interaktion*, ed. Gertrud Koch (Frankfurt: Fischer Verlag, 1995), 181, 182.

46. Sigmund Freud, *Totem and Taboo*, trans. and ed. James Strachey, *Standard Edition* 13 (London: Hogarth Press, 1955), 145.

47. Ibid., 67.

48. Ibid., 105, 149.

49. Ibid., 73.

50. See *DE* 23, 24. I have altered the translation slightly to conform to the original. See *GS*5, 46. For an interpretive essay on this passage, I am indebted to Micha Brumlik, *Schrift, Wort Und Ikone: Wege aus dem Bilderverbot* (Frankfurt am Main: Fischer Taschenbuch Verlag, 1994), 27–60.

51. Brumlik, *Schrift, Wort, und Ikone*, 29.

52. Gertrud Koch, "Mimesis und Bildverbot in Adornos Ästhetik," in *Die Einstellung ist die Einstellung* (Frankfurt am Main: Suhrkamp Verlag, 1992), 20.

53. Andrew Hewitt, "A Feminine Dialectic of Enlightenment? Horkheimer and Adorno Revisited," *New German Critique* 56 (Spring/Summer 1992): 162.

54. Adorno, *Minima Moralia*, 152. However, the possibility that Enlightenment could contribute to reenchantment and not merely to disenchantment is suggested by Horkheimer in a compilation of notes and drafts, retrospectively entitled "New York Notes." True Enlightenment does not drown out mythology. Rather, its power is appeased: "In refusing the blind domination of nature the dialectical spirit withdraws from domination through nature, without, however, cutting off from things the possibility of enchanting them."

55. Miriam Hansen, "Mass Culture as Hieroglyphic Writing: Adorno, Derrida, Kracauer," *New German Critique* 56 (Spring/Summer 1992): 47.

56. Ibid., 53.

57. Adorno, *Minima Moralia*, 152.

58. Ibid., 154.

59. Ibid.

60. *GS*12, 454.

61. Ibid., 457.

62. Ibid., 456.

63. Ibid., 440. For an important discussion of the paradoxical attitude of Freud and *Dialectic of Enlightenment* toward paternal authority, see Jessica Benjamin, *The Bonds of Love: Psychoanalysis, Feminism, and the Problem of*

Domination (New York: Pantheon, 1988), 145, 146. Benjamin also emphasizes Freud's avoidance of the theme of Oedipus' "efforts to evade the prophecy" of the oracle.

64. Friedrich Nietzsche, *Beyond Good and Evil*, trans. Walter Kaufmann (New York: Random House, 1966), 161.

65. GS12, 461.

66. GS12, 459.

67. For an introduction to Caillois's theory of mimesis, see Denis Hollier, "Mimesis and Castration 1937," *October* 31 (Winter 1984): 4–15; the two articles are "La mante religieuse" and "Mimétisme et psychasthénie légendaire," both published in the journal *Minotaure* (1934–1935).

68. T. W. Adorno, Review of Roger Caillois, *La mante religieuse: Recherches sur la nature et la signification du mythe,* in *Zeitschrift für Sozialforschung* 7 (1938): 411.

69. Hollier, "Mimesis and Castration," 13.

70. *Briefwechsel Adorno-Benjamin,* Adorno to Benjamin, September 22, 1937 (Frankfurt am Main: Suhrkamp Verlag, 1994), 277. As if to underscore the "mantis" as the emblem of fascist regression to undifferentiated and captivating feminine destructiveness, Adorno added that myths first emerge when "a conflict comes into existence between the self-identical human essence [*Menschenwesen*] and the husband-eating woman." For Adorno, myths explained the fact that human beings were once animal and now have become something else, while, as he remarked, Caillois basically took pleasure in the fact that they are still animals.

71. Horkheimer to Pollock, June 17, 1943, in Wiggershaus, *Frankfurter Schule,* 362.

72. Ibid., 363.

73. Ibid., 357, 358.

74. MHA, Franz Neumann to Adorno, August 14, 1940.

75. Theodor Adorno to Max Horkheimer, August 5, 1940, GS16, 764.

76. Max Horkheimer to Theodor W. Adorno, September 16, 1940, GS16, 758.

77. Theodor Adorno to Max Horkheimer, September 18, 1940, GS16, 761.

78. MHA, Adorno to Horkheimer, September 18, 1940. The theses comprise 4 typescript pages. They are published in GS16, 761–764.

79. Ibid.

80. Ibid.

81. MHA, Adorno to Horkheimer, September 4, 1940.

82. MHA, Adorno to Horkheimer, October 2, 1941. Cited in Wiggershaus, *Frankfurter Schule,* 346.

83. Wiggershaus, *Frankfurter Schule,* 362.

84. See the argument by Dan Diner, "Reason and the 'Other': Horkheimer's Reflection on Anti-Semitism and Mass Annihilation," in *On Max Horkheimer,* esp. 340–343.

85. Freud, *Moses and Monotheism,* 113.

86. Max Horkheimer, "Zur Psychologie des Antisemitismus," (1943),

GS12, 175. See also Sigmund Freud, *Moses and Monotheism: Three Essays,* *Standard Edition* 23 (London: Hogarth Press, 1964), 91.

87. Freud, *Moses and Monotheism,* 113.

88. The Jews, however, also represent, as chapter 1 notes, the suppression of mimesis in the proscription on images. The emphasis on the Jews as a "nomadic" people, on their permanent condition of exile, and on the exile of Odysseus suggests the double power attributed to them: as rationalizers and as the permanent reminders of their premythic state. The relationship among mimesis, narcissism, and paranoid projection is explored in Andrew Hewitt, "The Frankfurt School and the Political Pathology of Homosexuality," in Hewitt, *Political Inversions* (Stanford: Stanford University Press, 1996), 71.

89. Habermas, *The Philosophical Discourse of Modernity,* 120, 121.

90. Ibid.

91. Theodor W. Adorno, "Wagner, Nietzsche, and Hitler," *Kenyon Review* 9, no. 1 (1947): 160.

92. MHA, Adorno to Horkheimer, July 30, 1941. In GS17, 113.

93. Adorno, *Minima Moralia,* 98.

94. GS12, 565.

95. Ibid., 567.

96. Ibid. See, for example, Friedrich Nietzsche, *On the Genealogy of Morals,* trans. Walter Kaufmann (New York: Random House, 1967), 89.

97. Nancy S. Love has argued that Nietzsche's theory of exchange permitted critical theory to "transcend Marx's complicity in the dialectic of Enlightenment." What "ties us to Nietzsche," Adorno said on the occasion of the institute debate, is that his cultural criticism raised the whole problem of whether socialism was in danger of transforming itself into a "pragmatism that threatened to encompass the globe." Nietzsche had seen that not only democracy but socialism had become an ideology and "had in certain critical things gone further than Marx, insofar as he had a certain sharper thunder against the bourgeois." Whether one agrees with Love that in *Dialectic of Enlightenment* the shift from Marx to Nietzsche ultimately results in a "schizophrenic" failure to choose between contradictory alternatives or, conversely, with Habermas that the "Nietzscheanism" of *Dialectic of Enlightenment* concedes too much to the critique of Enlightenment, both propositions ignore the radically different ways that Nietzsche is deployed throughout. See Nancy S. Love, "Marx, Nietzsche, and Critical Theory," *New German Critique* 41 (Spring/Summer 1987): 81; and GS12, 568.

98. Friedrich Nietzsche, *The Birth of Tragedy,* in *The Philosophy of Nietzsche* (New York: Modern Library, 1954), 1047. For this reference I am indebted to the article by Peter Pütz, "Nietzsche and Critical Theory," *Telos* 50 (Winter 1981–1982): 109.

99. Max Horkheimer, "The End of Reason," *Studies in Philosophy and Social Science* 9 (1941): 384.

100. Theodor W. Adorno to Max Horkheimer, November 3, 1944, GS17, 601.

101. Max Horkheimer to Theodor W. Adorno, November 13, 1944, GS17, 603.

102. Max Horkheimer to Isaac Rosengarten, September 12, 1944, GS17, 599.

103. Max Horkheimer, "The End of Reason," 384.

104. MHA, Theodor W. Adorno to Max Horkheimer, October 30, 1944.

105. Ibid.

106. MHA, Horkheimer to Adorno, November 2, 1944.

107. Cited in Hullot-Kentor, "Back to Adorno," 11.

108. Theodor W. Adorno to Max Horkheimer, July 30, 1941, GS17, 114.

109. Walter Benjamin, "On Language as Such and on the Language of Man," in Walter Benjamin, *Reflections,* ed. Peter Demetz, trans. Edmund Jephcott (New York: Harcourt Brace Jovanovich, 1978), 329.

110. David Roberts has argued that Adorno's utopia of reconciliation "may be seen as the rational veneer for a profoundly arational *mysticism* of redemptive mimesis beyond and behind all civilization." *Art and Enlightenment: Aesthetic Theory After Adorno* (Lincoln: University of Nebraska Press, 1991), 70. In his later work Adorno attempted to further elucidate the connection between mimesis in the primordial and aesthetic domains: "As the mimetic struggle against taboo, art attempts to give the answer and gives it as an answer free of judgment—but then again not; thereby the answer becomes enigmatic, like the dread of the primordial world which changes, but does not disappear." Peter Uwe Hohendahl regards this enigmatic character not as "mystical" but as an imperative to interpretation. Cited in Peter Uwe Hohendahl, *Prismatic Thought: Theodor W. Adorno* (Lincoln: University of Nebraska Press, 1995), 237.

111. GS12, 118.

112. Ibid., 595.

113. Ibid.

114. Ibid.

115. Ibid., 599, 603.

116. Adorno, *Minima Moralia,* 151.

117. Ibid.

CONCLUSION

1. George Konrad, *Antipolitics: An Essay,* trans. Richard E. Allen (San Diego: Harcourt Brace Jovanovich, 1984), 14.

2. Hugo Ball, *Flight Out of Time: A Dada Diary,* ed. John Elderfield, trans. Ann Raimes (New York: Viking, 1974), 145.

3. Ernst Bloch, *Tagträume,* 110. Cited in Peter Zudeick, *Der Hintern des Teufels: Ernst Bloch—Leben und Werk* (Moos: Elster Verlag, 1985), 71.

4. Rüdiger Safranski, *Ein Meister aus Deutschland: Heidegger und seine Zeit* (Munich: Carl Hanser Verlag, 1994), 124.

5. Martin Heidegger to Karl Jaspers, June 27, 1922, *Martin Heidegger Karl Jaspers Briefwechsel,* 29.

6. Theodor W. Adorno, "Erinnerungen," in *Über Walter Benjamin* (Frankfurt am Main: Suhrkamp Verlag, 1968), 10.

7. See, for example, Susan Buck-Morss, *The Origin of Negative Dialectics:*

Theodor W. Adorno, Walter Benjamin, and the Frankfurt Institute (New York: Free Press, 1977). For a memoir of their early relationship, see *Theodor W. Adorno—Walter Benjamin Briefwechsel 1928–1940,* ed. Henri Lonitz (Frankfurt am Main: Suhrkamp Verlag, 1994).

8. Theodor W. Adorno, *Negative Dialectics,* trans. E. B. Ashton (New York: Seabury, 1973), 118.

9. Ibid.

10. Theodor W. Adorno, Letter to *Diskus,* January 1963, *Gesammelte Schriften* 19, 637.

11. Arthur Koestler, *Darkness at Noon,* trans. Daphne Hardy (New York: Macmillan, 1941), 98.

12. For a discussion of his influence, see Luc Ferry and Alain Renaut, *Heidegger and Modernity,* trans. Franklin Philip (Chicago: University of Chicago Press, 1990).

13. See Joseph Margolis, "On the Responsibility of Intellectuals: Reflections on Heidegger and Jaspers," in *Heidegger and Jaspers,* ed. Alan M. Olson (Philadelphia: Temple University Press, 1994), 77.

14. Andreas Huyssen, "After the Wall: The Failure of German Intellectuals," in Huyssen, *Twilight Memories: Marking Time in a Culture of Amnesia* (New York: Routledge, 1995), 38.

15. Martin Heidegger, "German Students," November 3, 1933, in *The Heidegger Controversy: A Critical Reader,* ed. Richard Wolin (New York: Columbia University Press, 1991), 46.

16. Max Horkheimer to Isaac Rosengarten, September 12, 1944, GS17, 599.

17. On this point, see the discussion by Saul Friedländer, *Probing the Limits of Representation: Nazism and the "Final Solution,"* ed. Saul Friedländer (Cambridge, Mass.: Harvard University Press, 1992), 5.

18. See Leo Bersani, *The Culture of Redemption* (Cambridge, Mass.: Harvard University Press, 1990). In Jürgen Habermas, "Modernity versus Postmodernity," *New German Critique* 22 (Winter 1981): 14, Habermas indicts postmodernism for its suppression of utopia but does not address its assimilation of the apocalypse.

Index

Designer:	U.C. Press Staff
Compositor:	J. Jarrett Engineering, Inc.
Text:	10/13 Sabon
Display:	Sabon
Printer & Binder:	Thomson-Shore